How to
Master Skills for the

Second Edition

TOEFL® iBT
SPEAKING   Basic

 DARAKWON

How to
Master Skills for the

Second Edition

TOEFL® iBT

SPEAKING Basic

Publisher Kyudo Chung
Editor Sangik Cho
Authors Arthur H. Milch, Jasmine C. Swaney, Denise McCormack, E2K
Proofreader Michael A. Putlack
Designers Minji Kim, Yeji Kim

First Published in August 2007 By Darakwon, Inc.
Second edition first published in March 2025 by Darakwon, Inc.
Darakwon Bldg., 211, Munbal-ro, Paju-si, Gyeonggi-do 10881
Republic of Korea
Tel: 02-736-2031 (Ext. 250)
Fax: 02-732-2037

ISBN 978-89-277-8087-8 14740
     978-89-277-8084-7 14740 (set)

www.darakwon.co.kr

Photo Credits
Shutterstock.com

Components Main Book / Answer Key / Free MP3 Downloads
7 6 5 4 3 2 1   25 26 27 28 29

Table of **Contents**

INTRODUCTION

1 Information on the TOEFL® iBT

A The Format of the TOEFL® iBT

Section	Number of Questions or Tasks	Timing	Score

Reading	**20 Questions**
	
	• 2 reading passages
	  – with 10 questions per passage
	  – approximately 700 words long each
		35 Minutes	30 Points

Listening	**28 Questions**
	
	• 2 conversations
	  – 5 questions per conversation
	  – 3 minutes each
	
	• 3 lectures
	  – 6 questions per lecture
	  – 3-5 minutes each
		36 Minutes	30 Points

Speaking	**4 Tasks**
	
	• 1 independent speaking task
	  – 1 personal choice/opinion/experience
	  – preparation: 15 sec. / response: 45 sec.
	
	• 2 integrated speaking tasks: Read-Listen-Speak
	  – 1 campus situation topic
	    reading: 75-100 words (45 sec.)
	    conversation: 150-180 words (60-80 sec.)
	  – 1 academic course topic
	    reading: 75-100 words (50 sec.)
	    lecture: 150-220 words (60-120 sec.)
	  – preparation: 30 sec. / response: 60 sec.
	
	• 1 integrated speaking task: Listen-Speak
	  – 1 academic course topic
	    lecture: 230-280 words (90-120 sec.)
	  – preparation: 20 sec. / response: 60 sec.
		17 Minutes	30 Points

Writing	**2 Tasks**
	
	• 1 integrated writing task: Read-Listen-Write
	  – reading: 230-300 words (3 min.)
	  – lecture: 230-300 words (2 min.)
	  – a summary of 150-225 words (20 min.)
	
	• 1 academic discussion task
	  – a minimum 100-word essay (10 min.)
		30 Minutes	30 Points

B What Is New about the TOEFL® iBT?

- The TOEFL® iBT is delivered through the Internet in secure test centers around the world at the same time.
- It tests all four language skills and is taken in the order of Reading, Listening, Speaking, and Writing.
- The test is about 2 hours long, and all of the four test sections will be completed in one day.
- Note taking is allowed throughout the entire test, including the Reading section. At the end of the test, all notes are collected and destroyed at the test center.
- In the Listening section, one lecture may be spoken with a British or Australian accent.
- There are integrated tasks requiring test takers to combine more than one language skill in the Speaking and Writing sections.
- In the Speaking section, test takers wear headphones and speak into a microphone when they respond. The responses are recorded and transmitted to ETS's Online Scoring Network.
- In the Writing section, test takers must type their responses. Handwriting is not possible.
- Test scores will be reported online. Test takers can see their scores online 4-8 business days after the test and can also receive a copy of their score report by mail.

2 Information on the Speaking Section

The Speaking section of the TOEFL® iBT measures test takers' English speaking proficiency. This section takes approximately 17 minutes and has four questions. The first question is called Independent Speaking Task, and you will be asked to speak about a familiar topic based on your personal preference. The remaining three questions are Integrated Speaking Tasks, and you will be required to integrate different language skills—listening and speaking or listening, reading, and speaking.

A Types of Speaking Tasks

- **Task 1** Independent Speaking Task: Personal Preference
  - This task will ask you to make and defend a personal choice between two possible opinions, actions, or situations. You should justify your choice with reasons and details.
  - You will be given 15 seconds to prepare your answer and 45 seconds to say which of the two options you think is preferable.

- **Task 2** Integrated Speaking Task: Reading & Conversation
  - This task will ask you to respond to a question based on what you have read and heard. You will first read a short passage presenting a campus-related issue and will then listen to a dialogue on the same topic. Then, you will be asked to summarize one speaker's opinion within the context of the reading passage.
  - You will be given 30 seconds to prepare your answer and 60 seconds to speak on the question. You should be careful not to express your own opinion in your response.

- **Task 3** Integrated Speaking Task: Reading & Lecture
  - This task also asks you to respond to a question based on what you have read and heard. You will first read a short passage about an academic subject and will then listen to an excerpt from a lecture

on that subject. Then, you will be asked to combine and convey important information from both the reading passage and the lecture.

– You will be given 30 seconds to prepare your answer and 60 seconds to speak on the question.

• **Task 4** Integrated Speaking Task: Lecture

– In this task, you will first listen to an excerpt from a lecture that explains a term or concept and gives some examples to illustrate it. Then, you will be asked to summarize the lecture and explain how the examples are connected with the overall topic.

– You will be given 20 seconds to prepare your answer and 60 seconds to respond to the question.

B Types of Speaking Topics

• Personal Experience and Preference

– The question in Task 1 will be about everyday issues of general interest to test takers. For example, a question may ask about a preference between studying at home and at the library, a preference between living in a dormitory and an off-campus apartment, or a preference between a class with a lot of discussion and one without discussion.

• Campus Situations

– The question in Task 2 will be about campus-related issues. For example, a question may ask about a university policy, rule, or procedure, future university plans, campus facilities, or the quality of life on campus.

• Academic Course Content

– The question in Task 3 will be about academic subjects. For example, a question may ask about a life science, a social science, a physical science, or a topic in the humanities like animal domestication or economics.

– The question in Task 4 will also be about academic-related topics. For example, a question may ask about a process, a method, a theory, an idea, or a phenomenon of any type in fields like natural science, social science, or psychology.

C Important Features of Evaluation

• Delivery

Delivery means how clear your speech is. In order to get good grades on the speaking tasks, you should speak smoothly and clearly, have good pronunciation, pace yourself naturally, and have natural-sounding intonation patterns.

• Language Use

Language use is about the effectiveness of your use of grammar and vocabulary to express your ideas. In order to get good grades on the speaking tasks, you should be able to use both basic and more complex language structures and choose the appropriate words.

• Topic Development

Topic development is related to how fully you respond to the question and how coherently you give your ideas. In order to get good grades on the speaking test, you should make sure that the relationship between your ideas and your progression from one idea to the next is clear and easy to follow.

HOW TO USE THIS BOOK

How to Master Skills for the TOEFL® iBT Speaking Basic is designed to be used either as a textbook for a TOEFL® iBT speaking preparation course or as a tool for individual learners who are preparing for the TOEFL® test on their own. With a total of twenty-four units, this book is organized to prepare you for the test by providing you with a comprehensive understanding of the test and a thorough analysis of every question type. Each unit provides a step-by-step program that helps develop your test-taking abilities. At the back of the book are two actual tests of the Speaking section of the TOEFL® iBT.

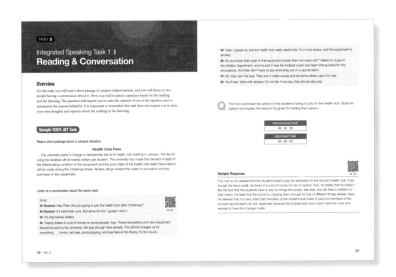

❶ Overview

This section is designed to prepare you for the type of task the part covers. You will be given a full sample question and a model answer in an illustrative structure. You will also be given information on time allotments.

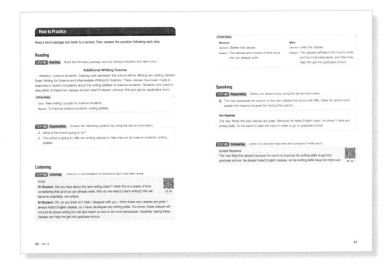

❷ How to Practice

This section will show you how to do the exercises in each unit step by step. With directions and model answers, you will have a comprehensive understanding of the ways to practice in each unit.

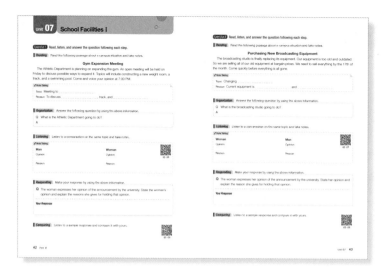

❸ Exercise

In this part of the unit, you will actually do a lot of exercises that the unit covers. The topics in the questions will be various and will reflect actual TOEFL® questions. You will be given an example to refer to and a sample response to compare with yours at the end.

❹ Actual Test

This part will give you a chance to experience an actual TOEFL® iBT test. You will be given two sets of tests that are modeled on the Speaking section of the TOEFL® iBT. The topics are similar to those on the real test, as are the questions. This similarity will allow you to develop a sense of your test-taking ability.

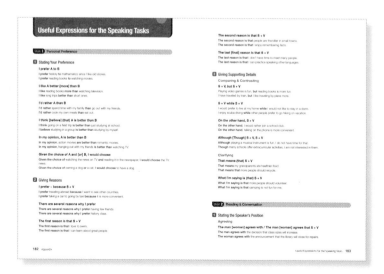

❺ Useful Expressions for the Speaking Tasks

There are a number of expressions and collocations that are typically used in every task and topic. This supplementary part will provide you with a chance to review the expressions and collocations you need to remember while working on each unit.

PART I

Independent Speaking Task
Personal Preference

....

The independent speaking section consists of one task. You will be
presented with a question or a situation. Then, you will provide a
response based upon your own ideas, opinions, and experiences. In this
section, you will not read or listen to any other material. You will be
given 15 seconds to prepare your answer after the question is presented,
and you will have 45 seconds to respond to the question.

Independent Speaking Task I
Personal Preference

Overview

This task is about a personal choice. It asks you to make and defend a choice from a given pair of options: two possible opinions, actions, or situations. In this task, the questions mostly ask you to take a position and defend it. When responding to this task, you are to give some details and examples as well as reasons to justify your answer.

Sample TOEFL iBT Task

Q Some students study for an exam up to the exact moment that it starts. Others stop studying an hour or more before it begins. Which method do you prefer and why? Please include specific examples and details to support your explanation.

PREPARATION TIME
00 : 15 : 00

RESPONSE TIME
00 : 45 : 00

01-01

Sample Response

When I study for an exam, I like to study right up until the last minute. I feel that stopping an hour or so before the test is a waste of a good hour of study time. As far as I am concerned, it is important to cram as much information into my head as possible, so I should use every last minute before the test. There have been many times when something I studied right before an exam appeared on the test. I was repaid for being diligent in my studies.

Read and answer the question following each step.

Q Some people like to travel alone. Others like to travel with different people. Which option do you prefer and why? Please include specific examples and details to support your explanation.

STEP 01 Opinion State your opinion.

I prefer traveling with others to traveling alone.

STEP 02 Reasons Give your reasons.

1   *It is safer to travel with others than to travel alone.*
2   *You can save money on places like hotels if you travel with others.*

STEP 03 Responding Make your response by using the above information.

I prefer traveling with others to traveling alone. The reason is that it is safer to travel with others. I can also save money on places like hotels if I travel with others. So I like traveling with others.

STEP 04 Comparing Listen to a sample response, and compare it with yours.

Sample Response
I prefer traveling with others to traveling alone. I feel this way for the following reasons. First, it is safer to travel with others than to travel alone. Some places can be dangerous, so it is safer to travel with a group of people. Second, you can save money on places like hotels if you travel with others. Hotels are cheaper if you split the cost with someone else.

01-02

Exercise 1A Read and answer the question following each step.

Q Some students like to study alone while others like to study in groups. Which do you think is better and why? Please include specific examples and details to support your explanation.

Opinion State your opinion.

Study alone

Example I like studying in groups better than studying alone.

Your Opinion

Reasons Give your reasons.

Example

1 We can correct one another.

2 We can explain the things that we know well to others.

Your Reasons

1

2

Responding Make your response by using the above information.

Example

I like studying in groups better than studying alone. First, when I am in a group, everyone can correct one another when we make mistakes. Second, we can explain the things that we know well to others. So if I am good at something but some other members are not, I can explain it to them to help them understand.

- -

Your Response

Comparing Listen to a sample response and compare it with yours.

01-03

Exercise 1B Read and answer the question following each step.

Q Some students like to study alone while others like to study in groups. Which do you think is better and why? Please include specific examples and details to support your explanation.

▌**Opinion** State your opinion.

With others

Example For me, studying alone is much better than studying in groups.

Your Opinion

▌**Reasons** Give your reasons.

Example

1 I can study the things that I want to study.

2 I feel that I can improve much more quickly.

Your Reasons

1

2

▌**Responding** Make your response by using the above information.

Example

For me, studying alone is much better than studying in groups. To begin with, I can study the things that I want to study when I am alone. In a group, I may not get to study the topics that I need to focus on. In addition, I feel that I can improve much more quickly by studying alone. I don't have to study at others' paces, so I can study much faster by myself. This helps me improve at a better rate than I would if I were studying in a group.

- -

Your Response

▌**Comparing** Listen to a sample response and compare it with yours.

01-04

Exercise 2A Read and answer the question following each step.

Q Some people think that they can learn better by themselves than with a teacher while others think that it is always better to learn from a teacher. Which do you think is better and why? Please include specific examples and details to support your explanation.

Opinion State your opinion.

With a teacher

Example In my opinion, it's always better to learn with a teacher.

Your Opinion

Reasons Give your reasons.

Example

1 Books can't teach us everything.

2 Teachers can reduce the number of mistakes we make.

Your Reasons

1

2

Responding Make your response by using the above information.

Example

In my opinion, it's always better to learn with a teacher. For one thing, teachers can provide me with the information I need in order to understand the textbooks. After all, books can't teach us everything. For another thing, learning with teachers can reduce the number of mistakes we make. They can guide us in our studies and keep us from making too many errors.

- -

Your Response

Comparing Listen to a sample response and compare it with yours.

01-05

Exercise 2B Read and answer the question following each step.

 Some people think that they can learn better by themselves than with a teacher while others think that it is always better to learn from a teacher. Which do you think is better and why? Please include specific examples and details to support your explanation.

Opinion   State your opinion.

By oneself

Example   As for me, I prefer studying by myself to studying with a teacher.

Your Opinion

Reasons   Give your reasons.

Example

1 I can decide on the study method that suits me the best.

2 I can develop my creativity as well as increase my knowledge.

Your Reasons

1

2

Responding   Make your response by using the above information.

Example

As for me, I prefer studying by myself to studying with a teacher. There are two reasons I feel this way. First, by studying alone, I can choose the study method that suits me the best. I know much better than a teacher the way that I prefer to study. Second of all, when I study by myself, I can develop my creativity as well as increase my knowledge. When I study with a teacher, I have to follow the teacher's methods. That isn't creative. By myself, however, I can improve my creative ability.

Your Response

Comparing   Listen to a sample response and compare it with yours.

01-06

Exercise 1A Read and answer the question following each step.

Q If you had some extra money, would you spend it right away or save it? Which choice do you prefer and why? Please include specific examples and details to support your explanation.

Opinion State your opinion.

Save the money

Example I think that I would save the money.

Your Opinion

Reasons Give your reasons.

Example

1 Saving for a rainy day is always important.

2 If I save now, I can have more money in the future.

Your Reasons

1

2

Responding Make your response by using the above information.

Example

I think that I would save the money. For one, saving for a rainy day is always important. I want to be prepared in case something bad happens in the future. If I spend the money now, I won't be prepared for the future. In addition, if I save now, I can have more money in the future. By putting the money in the bank or investing it in some other way, I can make my money grow. That way, I'll have more money in the future.

Your Response

Comparing Listen to a sample response and compare it with yours.

01-07

Exercise 1B Read and answer the question following each step.

Q If you had some extra money, would you spend it right away or save it? Which choice do you prefer and why? Please include specific examples and details to support your explanation.

Opinion State your opinion.

Spend the money

Example I think I would prefer to spend all of the money right away.

Your Opinion

Reasons Give your reasons.

Example

1 The value of money decreases as time passes.
2 Spending money can help the economy grow.

Your Reasons

1
2

Responding Make your response by using the above information.

Example

I think I would prefer to spend all of the money right away. First, because of inflation, the value of money decreases as time passes. So the best way to get full value for my money is to spend it immediately. Second, spending money can help the economy grow. If people don't buy anything, then companies have no need to manufacture more products. It's therefore important for people like me to spend money.

Your Response

Comparing Listen to a sample response and compare it with yours.

01-08

Exercise 2A Read and answer the question following each step.

Q Some people like to spend their free time doing indoor activities while others like to spend their free time doing outdoor activities. Which do you prefer and why? Please include specific examples and details to support your explanation.

Opinion State your opinion.

Outdoors

Example As for me, I've always liked to spend my free time outdoors.

Your Opinion

Reasons Give your reasons.

Example

1 Generally, outdoor activities are healthier than indoor ones.

2 It is important to spend time outside.

Your Reasons

1

2

Responding Make your response by using the above information.

Example

As for me, I've always liked to spend my free time outdoors. The reasons are simple. First, outdoor activities are generally healthier than indoor ones. I can play sports, jog, or do many other healthy activities. Second, since I stay indoors most of the time, it is important to spend time outside. It's good for the body to spend some time outside in the sun.

Your Response

Comparing Listen to a sample response and compare it with yours.

01-09

Exercise 2B Read and answer the question following each step.

 Some people like to spend their free time doing indoor activities while others like to spend their free time doing outdoor activities. Which do you prefer and why? Please include specific examples and details to support your explanation.

Opinion State your opinion.

Indoors

Example When I have free time, I prefer to spend it indoors.

Your Opinion

Reasons Give your reasons.

Example

1 There is no need to worry about the weather.

2 Indoor activities are typically safer than outdoor ones.

Your Reasons

1

2

Responding Make your response by using the above information.

Example

When I have free time, I prefer to spend it indoors. The reasons are as follows. First, if I spend my free time indoors, I don't need to worry about the weather. That way, if it rains or snows, it won't interrupt my plans. Next, indoor activities are typically safer than outdoor ones. Therefore, I don't have to worry that much when I am inside doing something. If I were outside, I would often have to consider my safety.

- -

Your Response

Comparing Listen to a sample response and compare it with yours.

01 - 10

Exercise 1A Read and answer the question following each step.

Q Some high schools require all of their students to wear school uniforms. Other high schools permit their students to decide what to wear to school. Which of these two school policies do you think is better and why? Please include specific examples and details to support your explanation.

Opinion State your opinion.

Uniforms

Example When it comes to school uniforms, I believe that they are a good idea.

Your Opinion

Reasons Give your reasons.

Example

1 Uniforms give students a feeling of togetherness.
2 Uniforms can increase school spirit.

Your Reasons

1
2

Responding Make your response by using the above information.

Example

When it comes to school uniforms, I believe that they are a good idea. First of all, uniforms give students a feeling of togetherness. Students wearing the same uniform will feel closer to their classmates because of their uniforms. Additionally, uniforms can increase school spirit. Many students are proud of their uniforms, and this, in turn, makes them proud of their schools.

Your Response

Comparing Listen to a sample response and compare it with yours.

01 - 11

Exercise 1B Read and answer the question following each step.

 Some high schools require all of their students to wear school uniforms. Other high schools permit their students to decide what to wear to school. Which of these two school policies do you think is better and why? Please include specific examples and details to support your explanation.

Opinion State your opinion.

No uniforms

Example In my opinion, students should be able to wear whatever they want.

Your Opinion

Reasons Give your reasons.

Example

1 Wearing their own clothes allows students to express themselves.

2 Uniforms take away from students' individuality.

Your Reasons

1

2

Responding Make your response by using the above information.

Example

In my opinion, students should be able to wear whatever they want. For one, wearing their own clothes allows students to express themselves. Students prefer wearing all kinds of different clothes and colors. Schools should allow the students to express themselves as individuals. Furthermore, uniforms take away from students' individuality. Students don't want to wear the same clothes others are wearing. Instead, they prefer the kinds of clothes they like, not the ones that the principal tells them to wear.

Your Response

Comparing Listen to a sample response and compare it with yours.

01-12

Exercise 2A Read and answer the question following each step.

 Q Some people believe that students should have one long vacation each year. Others believe that students should have several short vacations throughout the year. Which viewpoint do you agree with and why? Please include specific examples and details to support your explanation.

Opinion State your opinion.

Short vacations

Example I think that it's better for students to have many short vacations as opposed to one long one.

Your Opinion

Reasons Give your reasons.

Example

1 A long vacation interrupts the flow of studying.

2 Frequent short vacations help students keep their stress down.

Your Reasons

1

2

Responding Make your response by using the above information.

Example

I think that it's better for students to have many short vacations as opposed to one long one. I feel this way for a couple of reasons. First, a long vacation interrupts the flow of studying. Once students return to school after a long vacation, it takes them a couple of weeks to get used to studying again. Second of all, frequent short vacations help students keep their stress down. School can be very stressful, so giving students one or two weeks to recover every couple of months is a good way to reduce students' stress.

Your Response

Comparing Listen to a sample response and compare it with yours.

01-13

Exercise 2B Read and answer the question following each step.

 Q Some people believe that students should have one long vacation each year. Others believe that students should have several short vacations throughout the year. Which viewpoint do you agree with and why? Please include specific examples and details to support your explanation.

Opinion   State your opinion.

A long vacation

Example As far as I'm concerned, a long vacation is more preferable to a short one.

Your Opinion

Reasons   Give your reasons.

Example

1 Students can take long trips during these vacations.

2 It is possible to get a part-time job during a long vacation.

Your Reasons

1

2

Responding   Make your response by using the above information.

Example

As far as I'm concerned, a long vacation is more preferable to several short ones. Since the vacation lasts a long time, students can benefit in many ways. First, students can take long trips during these vacations. These trips are not only fun but are also sometimes educational. Indeed, students can learn things on these trips that they cannot learn at school. In addition, it is possible to get a part-time job during a long vacation. This will provide students with invaluable job experience for the future.

- -

Your Response

Comparing   Listen to a sample response and compare it with yours.

01-14

Unit 04 Multimedia

○

Exercise 1A Read and answer the question following each step.

Q Some people like to use the Internet while others like to use books in the library when they look for information. Which option do you prefer and why? Please include specific examples and details to support your explanation.

Opinion State your opinion.

Internet

Example In my experience, it's better to use the Internet than books in a library.

Your Opinion

Reasons Give your reasons.

Example

1 The Internet is more convenient.

2 The Internet has more information.

Your Reasons

1

2

Responding Make your response by using the above information.

Example

In my experience, it's better to use the Internet than books in a library. First of all, the Internet is more convenient. I can get all of the information that I want by using the computer in my home. In addition, the Internet has more information. I can get information from places all over the world off the Internet. That is impossible to do in a library.

Your Response

Comparing Listen to a sample response and compare it with yours.

01 - 15

Exercise 1B Read and answer the question following each step.

 Q Some people like to use the Internet while others like to use books in the library when they look for information. Which option do you prefer and why? Please include specific examples and details to support your explanation.

Opinion State your opinion.

Books

Example As for me, I am partial to using books in the library when I need information.

Your Opinion

Reasons Give your reasons.

Example

1 Books have more reliable information.

2 Books are easier to read.

Your Reasons

1

2

Responding Make your response by using the above information.

Example

As for me, I am partial to using books in the library when I need information. First, books have more reliable information. All books have editors to check over them for mistakes. But anyone can put information on the Internet. You can't always trust everything you read on the Internet. In addition, books are easier to read. I like to pick up a book when I read it. Reading from a computer screen is sometimes inconvenient.

Your Response

Comparing Listen to a sample response and compare it with yours.

01-16

Exercise 2A Read and answer the question following each step.

Q Some people think that governments should spend as much money as possible on developing technology. Other people think that money should be spent on more basic needs. Which opinion do you agree with and why? Please include specific examples and details to support your explanation.

Opinion State your opinion.

Basic needs

Example In my opinion, governments should spend more money on satisfying people's basic needs.

Your Opinion

Reasons Give your reasons.

Example

1 People's needs are more important than improving existing technology.

2 Private organizations, not the government, can develop technology on their own.

Your Reasons

1

2

Responding Make your response by using the above information.

Example

In my opinion, governments should spend more money on satisfying people's basic needs. First, people's needs are more important than improving existing technology. A government's first obligation is to take care of its people. Next, private organizations, not the government, can develop technology on their own. In fact, these organizations are often much more efficient than governments at developing new technology.

Your Response

Comparing Listen to a sample response and compare it with yours.

01-17

Exercise 2B Read and answer the question following each step.

 Q Some people think that governments should spend as much money as possible on developing technology. Other people think that money should be spent on more basic needs. Which opinion do you agree with and why? Please include specific examples and details to support your explanation.

Opinion State your opinion.

Technology

Example I believe the government should spend as much money as possible on developing technology.

Your Opinion

Reasons Give your reasons.

Example

1 People should be able to take care of themselves without relying on the government.

2 Advanced technology can help improve everyone's quality of life.

Your Reasons

1

2

Responding Make your response by using the above information.

Example

I believe the government should spend as much money as possible on developing technology. First, people should be able to take care of themselves without relying on the government. If people work hard, they can take care of their own needs. The government shouldn't get involved in people's private lives. In addition, advanced technology can help improve everyone's quality of life. For example, if people create better farming methods, food can become cheaper and more plentiful. That will improve people's lives, so they don't need to depend upon the government.

- -

Your Response

Comparing Listen to a sample response and compare it with yours.

01-18

Exercise 1A Read and answer the question following each step.

Q Do you agree or disagree with the following statement?
It is desirable for friends to have different opinions from each other.
Please include specific examples and details to support your explanation.

Opinion   State your opinion.

Agree

Example Friends can have different opinions from each other.

Your Opinion

Reasons   Give your reasons.

Example

1 I can learn new ideas and beliefs from my friends.

2 I like knowing people who think differently than me.

Your Reasons

1

2

Responding   Make your response by using the above information.

Example

I agree with the statement. In my opinion, it's desirable for friends to have different opinions from each other. First of all, I can learn new ideas and beliefs from my friends. This helps me increase my knowledge. Second, I like knowing people who think differently than me. I love defending my beliefs when my friends challenge them.

Your Response

Comparing   Listen to a sample response and compare it with yours.

01-19

Exercise 1B Read and answer the question following each step.

 Do you agree or disagree with the following statement?
It is desirable for friends to have different opinions from each other.
Please include specific examples and details to support your explanation.

Opinion   State your opinion.

Disagree

Example I don't believe it's desirable for friends to have different opinions from each other.

Your Opinion

Reasons   Give your reasons.

Example

1 I can't be friends with people if we have nothing in common.

2 It's hard to be friendly to people I often disagree with.

Your Reasons

1

2

Responding   Make your response by using the above information.

Example

I don't believe it's desirable for friends to have different opinions from each other. So I disagree with the statement. One reason is that I can't be friends with people if we have nothing in common. We would have nothing to do together because of our different opinions. Another reason is that it's hard to be friendly to people I often disagree with. I should be nice to my friends, but I can't be nice to people I disagree with.

Your Response

Comparing   Listen to a sample response and compare it with yours.

01-20

Exercise 2A Read and answer the question following each step.

Q Do you agree or disagree with the following statement?

It is better to work for a year after high school than to go straight to college.

Please include specific examples and details to support your explanation.

Opinion State your opinion.

Agree

Example I agree that it's better to work for a year after high school than to go straight to college.

Your Opinion

Reasons Give your reasons.

Example

1 A person can make money before going to college.

2 It is possible to get some experience by working.

Your Reasons

1

2

Responding Make your response by using the above information.

Example

I agree that it's better to work for a year after high school than to go straight to college. To begin with, a person can make money before going to college. By saving money, the person will not have to work part time while attending college later. In addition, it is possible to get some experience by working. That will help a person find a job more easily after graduating from college.

Your Response

Comparing Listen to a sample response and compare it with yours.

01 - 21

Exercise 2B Read and answer the question following each step.

Q Do you agree or disagree with the following statement?

It is better to work for a year after high school than to go straight to college.

Please include specific examples and details to support your explanation.

Opinion State your opinion.

Disagree

Example It's much better to go straight to college after high school, so I disagree with the statement.

Your Opinion

Reasons Give your reasons.

Example

1 I might forget what I learned in high school if I take a break.

2 The sooner I finish college, the faster I can find a job.

Your Reasons

1

2

Responding Make your response by using the above information.

Example

It's much better to go straight to college after high school, so I disagree with the statement. I have two reasons for thinking this way. Firstly, I might forget what I learned in high school if I take a break. So returning to college after a year off might be too hard for me. Secondly, the sooner I finish college, the faster I can find a job. I want to begin my career as soon as possible. So I would prefer to go straight to college.

- -

Your Response

Comparing Listen to a sample response and compare it with yours.

01-22

Exercise 1A Read and answer the question following each step.

Q Do you agree or disagree with the following statement?
Students should only take classes in their majors and related fields.
Please include specific examples and details to support your explanation.

Opinion State your opinion.

Agree

Example I agree that students should only take classes in their majors and related fields.

Your Opinion

Reasons Give your reasons.

Example

1 Students need to learn their majors as well as possible.

2 Students can get good jobs by focusing on their majors.

Your Reasons

1

2

Responding Make your response by using the above information.

Example

I agree that students should only take classes in their majors and related fields. For one thing, students need to learn their majors as well as possible. By only taking classes in their majors and related fields, they can learn those subjects very well. In addition, students can get good jobs by focusing on their majors. This will help them become successful and earn money in the future.

- -

Your Response

Comparing Listen to a sample response and compare it with yours.

01-23

Exercise 1B Read and answer the question following each step.

Q Do you agree or disagree with the following statement?

Students should only take classes in their majors and related fields.

Please include specific examples and details to support your explanation.

Opinion State your opinion.

Disagree

Example I disagree that students should only take classes in their majors and related fields.

Your Opinion

Reasons Give your reasons.

Example

1 Students can become well-rounded individuals by taking many kinds of classes.

2 Students might need the knowledge they learn in other classes in the future.

Your Reasons

1

2

Responding Make your response by using the above information.

Example

I disagree that students should only take classes in their majors and related fields. First, students can become well-rounded individuals by taking many kinds of classes. This will help them gain knowledge in many different fields, not just in one or two. In addition, students might need the knowledge they learn in other classes in the future. For instance, they might get jobs in other fields. In that case, they will need to have knowledge outside their majors.

- -

Your Response

Comparing Listen to a sample response and compare it with yours.

01-24

Do you agree or disagree with the following statement?
University tuition is too expensive nowadays.
Please include specific examples and details to support your explanation.

Opinion State your opinion.

Agree

Example   I agree that university tuition is too expensive nowadays.

Your Opinion

Reasons Give your reasons.

Example

1 The price keeps going up and up every year.
2 More students have to take out loans to pay for school.

Your Reasons

1

2

Responding Make your response by using the above information.

Example

I agree that university tuition is too expensive nowadays. To begin with, the price keeps going up and up every year. Yet the value of a degree remains the same. This means that the price of tuition is too high. In addition, more students have to take out loans to pay for school. Even parents with good jobs simply do not have enough money to pay their tuition. It is clear to me that the price of university tuition is too high.

Your Response

Comparing Listen to a sample response and compare it with yours.

01-25

Exercise 2B Read and answer the question following each step.

Q Do you agree or disagree with the following statement?
University tuition is too expensive nowadays.
Please include specific examples and details to support your explanation.

Opinion State your opinion.

Disagree

Example   I don't believe that university tuition is too expensive nowadays.

Your Opinion

Reasons Give your reasons.

Example

1 Many good universities have affordable tuition.

2 There are many scholarships available to students.

Your Reasons

1

2

Responding Make your response by using the above information.

Example

I don't believe that university tuition is too expensive nowadays. So I disagree with the statement. Here is one reason. Many good universities have affordable tuition. My cousin went to a good university in his hometown. He said that the tuition there was actually low. Another reason is that there are many scholarships available to students. My older brother earned a scholarship to his university. So he didn't have to pay anything to go to school.

- -

Your Response

Comparing Listen to a sample response and compare it with yours.

01 - 26

PART II

Integrated Speaking Task 1
Reading & Conversation

The integrated speaking section consists of three tasks. These tasks will present you with a reading passage and a listening conversation or lecture or merely a listening lecture. Topics will come from a variety of fields, but they are normally based on campus situations or are academic topics.

In this task, you will be presented with a short reading passage about a campus situation topic. Next, you will listen to a short conversation between two students about the same topic. Then, you will provide a response based upon what you read and heard. You will be asked to describe one student's opinion about the topic in the reading passage. You will be given 30 seconds to prepare your answer after the question is presented, and you will have 60 seconds to respond to the question.

Integrated Speaking Task 1 ▌
Reading & Conversation

Overview

For this task, you will read a short passage of campus-related interest, and you will listen to two people having a conversation about it. Then, you will be asked a question based on the reading and the listening. The question will require you to state the opinion of one of the speakers and to summarize the reasons behind it. It is important to remember this task does not require you to state your own thoughts and opinion about the reading or the listening.

Sample TOEFL iBT Task

Read a short passage about a campus situation.

Health Club Fees

The university plans to charge a membership fee at its health club starting in January. The fee for using the facilities will be twenty dollars per student. The university has made this decision in light of the deteriorating condition of the equipment and the poor state of the health club itself. Renovations will be made during the Christmas break. All fees will go toward the costs of renovation and the purchase of new equipment.

Listen to a conversation about the same topic.

Script

W Student: Hey, Pete. Are you going to join the health club after Christmas?

M Student: If it were free, sure. But since it's not, I guess I won't.

W: It's only twenty dollars.

M: Twenty dollars is a lot of money to some people, Sue. These renovations and new equipment should be paid by the university. We pay enough here already. The school charges us for everything . . . books, lab fees, photocopying, and late fees at the library. It's too much.

02-01

W: Yeah, I guess so, but the health club really needs this. It's in bad shape, and the equipment is ancient.

M: Do you know that most of that equipment is less than two years old? I talked to a guy in the Athletic Department, and he said it was the football coach and team that pushed for the renovations. And they don't have to pay since they are on a sports team.

W: No, that can't be true. They won't make us pay and let some others use it for free.

M: You'll see. Wait until January. It's not fair. If we pay, they should also pay.

 Q The man expresses his opinion of the students having to pay for the health club. State his opinion and explain the reasons he gives for holding that opinion.

PREPARATION TIME
00 : 30 : 00

RESPONSE TIME
00 : 60 : 00

Sample Response

02-02

The man is not pleased that the students have to pay for admission to the school's health club. Even though the fee is small, he thinks it is a lot of money for him to spend. Plus, he states that he doesn't like the fact that the students have to pay for things like books, late fees, and lab fees in addition to their tuition. He feels that the school is charging them enough for lots of different things already. Next, he believes that it is very unfair that members of the student body have to pay but members of the school's sports teams do not, especially because the football team and coach were the ones who wanted to have the changes made.

Read a short passage and listen to a lecture. Then, answer the question following each step.

Reading

STEP 01 **Reading**   Read the following passage about a campus situation and take notes.

Additional Writing Course

Attention, science students. Starting next semester, the school will be offering two writing classes: Basic Writing for Science and Intermediate Writing for Science. These classes have been made in response to recent complaints about the writing abilities of science students. Students who want to take either of these two classes should meet Professor Johnson first and get an application form.

✎ Note Taking

Topic *New writing courses* for science students

Reason To improve science students' *writing abilities*

STEP 02 **Organization**   Answer the following question by using the above information.

Q   What is the school going to do?

A   *The school is going to offer two writing classes to help improve its science students' writing abilities.*

Listening

STEP 03 **Listening**   Listen to a conversation on the same topic and take notes.

Script

02-03

W Student: Did you hear about the new writing class? I think this is a waste of time considering that all of us can already write. Why do we need to learn writing? We will become scientists, not writers.

M Student: Oh, do you think so? Well, I disagree with you. I think these new classes are great. I always hated English classes, so I never developed any writing skills. You know, these classes will not just be about writing but will also teach us how to be more persuasive. Hopefully, taking these classes can help me get into graduate school.

✎ Note Taking

Woman	**Man**
Opinion *Dislikes the classes*	Opinion *Likes the classes*
Reason *The classes are a waste of time since she can already write.*	Reason *The classes will teach him how to write and be more persuasive, and they may help him get into graduate school.*

Speaking

STEP 04 Responding   Make your response by using the above information.

Q The man expresses his opinion of the new classes the school will offer. State his opinion and explain the reasons he gives for having that opinion.

Your Response

The man thinks the new classes are great. Because he hated English class, he doesn't have any writing skills. So he wants to take the class in order to go to graduate school.

STEP 05 Comparing   Listen to a sample response and compare it with yours.

Sample Response

The man likes the classes because he wants to improve his writing skills to get into graduate school. He always hated English classes, so his writing skills have not improved.

02-04

Exercise 1 Read, listen, and answer the question following each step.

Reading   Read the following passage about a campus situation and take notes.

Gym Expansion Meeting

The Athletic Department is planning on expanding the gym. An open meeting will be held on Friday to discuss possible ways to expand it. Topics will include constructing a new weight room, a track, and a swimming pool. Come and voice your opinion at 7:00 PM.

✎ Note Taking

Topic Meeting to _____

Reason To discuss _____, track, and _____

Organization   Answer the following question by using the above information.

Q   What is the Athletic Department going to do?

A

Listening   Listen to a conversation on the same topic and take notes.

✎ Note Taking

Man   **Woman**

Opinion   Opinion

02-05

Reason   Reason

Responding   Make your response by using the above information.

Q   The woman expresses her opinion of the announcement by the university. State the woman's opinion and explain the reasons she gives for holding that opinion.

Your Response

Comparing   Listen to a sample response and compare it with yours.

02-06

Read, listen, and answer the question following each step.

Reading Read the following passage about a campus situation and take notes.

Purchasing New Broadcasting Equipment

The broadcasting studio is finally replacing its equipment. Our equipment is too old and outdated. So we are selling all of our old equipment at bargain prices. We need to sell everything by the 17th of the month. Come quickly before everything is all gone.

✎ Note Taking

Topic Changing ....

Reason Current equipment is .... and ....

Organization Answer the following question by using the above information.

Q What is the broadcasting studio going to do?

A

Listening Listen to a conversation on the same topic and take notes.

✎ Note Taking

Woman	**Man**
Opinion	Opinion
Reason	Reason

02-07

Responding Make your response by using the above information.

Q The woman expresses her opinion of the announcement by the university. State her opinion and explain the reason she gives for holding that opinion.

- -

Your Response

Comparing Listen to a sample response and compare it with yours.

02-08

Reading Read the following passage about a campus situation and take notes.

Renovating the Art Building

The university administration has decided to renovate the art building. Because the school takes pride in providing students with a quality education, the art building will be equipped with the best and most up-to-date facilities. This project will ensure that our school remains competitive and continues to provide our students with a solid education at a reasonable cost.

✎ Note Taking

Topic Renovating ....

Reason To enable the school to remain .... with ....

Organization Answer the following question by using the above information.

Q What is the school going to do to the art building?

A

Listening Listen to a conversation on the same topic and take notes.

✎ Note Taking

02-09

Woman	**Man**
Opinion	Opinion
Reason	Reason

Responding Make your response by using the above information.

Q The man expresses his opinion of the announcement by the university. State his opinion and explain the reasons he gives for holding that opinion.

Your Response

Comparing Listen to a sample response and compare it with yours.

02-10

Exercise 4 Read, listen, and answer the question following each step.

Reading Read the following passage about a campus situation and take notes.

Placing Students in Dormitories According to Majors

The Residential Life Office has decided to place students in dormitories according to their majors. The Residential Life Office feels this will help improve the academic environment of the school and cut down on inappropriate behavior. Double majors will be able to pick which dorm they will live in.

🖊 Note Taking

Topic Placing students in dormitories according to ....

Reason To improve the .... and to decrease ....

Organization Answer the following question by using the above information.

Q What is going to happen to the dormitories?

A

Listening Listen to a conversation on the same topic and take notes.

🖊 Note Taking

Woman	**Man**
Opinion	Opinion
Reason	Reason

02-11

Responding Make your response by using the above information.

Q The woman expresses her opinion of the announcement by the university. State her opinion and explain the reasons she gives for holding that opinion.

Your Response

Comparing Listen to a sample response and compare it with yours.

02-12

Exercise 5 Read, listen, and answer the question following each step.

▌Reading Read the following passage about a campus situation and take notes.

Closure of the School Art Gallery

Due to an increase in enrollment, the administration has decided to make a number of changes to the campus. The first of these will be the closure and conversion of the school art gallery into additional administrative offices. Student artwork now on display in the gallery must be collected by the artists within two weeks, or other arrangements will be made for its removal.

✎ Note Taking

Topic The closing of ....

Reason School needs ....

▌Organization Answer the following question by using the above information.

Q What has the administration decided to do?

A

▌Listening Listen to a conversation on the same topic and take notes.

✎ Note Taking

Man

Opinion

Reason

Woman

Opinion

Reason

02-13

▌Responding Make your response by using the above information.

Q The man expresses his opinion of the announcement by the university. State his opinion and explain the reason he gives for holding that opinion.

- -

Your Response

▌Comparing Listen to a sample response and compare it with yours.

02-14

Exercise 6 Read, listen, and answer the question following each step.

Reading Read the following passage about a campus situation and take notes.

No More Bright Lights

On account of complaints from the Astronomy Department, there will be no more bright lights on campus from 9:00 PM to 5:00 AM. The Astronomy Department needs a darker campus to allow its students properly to observe the stars. This new regulation goes into effect this Friday.

🖉 Note Taking

Topic No more _____ on campus at _____

Reason To allow _____ to observe _____

Organization Answer the following question by using the above information.

Q Why can there be no more bright lights at night?

A

Listening Listen to a conversation on the same topic and take notes.

🖉 Note Taking

Man

Opinion

Reason

Woman

Opinion

Reason

02-15

Responding Make your response by using the above information.

Q The man expresses his opinion of the announcement by the university. State his opinion and explain the reasons he gives for holding that opinion.

Your Response

Comparing Listen to a sample response and compare it with yours.

02-16

Exercise 1 Read, listen, and answer the question following each step.

Reading Read the following passage about a campus situation and take notes.

Improvements to the School Cafeteria

Due to numerous complaints about the low quality of the cafeteria's food, the university is going to change the style of the cafeteria. Starting next semester, students will be able to eat hot meals, make their own sandwiches, eat from a salad bar, and enjoy pasta and pizza. This should give students many more choices for food every day.

✏ Note Taking

Topic Making improvements to ....

Reason Complaints about ....

Organization Answer the following question by using the above information.

Q Why is the school going to improve the cafeteria?

A

Listening Listen to a conversation on the same topic and take notes.

✏ Note Taking

Woman	Man
Opinion	Opinion
Reason	Reason

02-17

Responding Make your response by using the above information.

Q The woman expresses her opinion of the announcement by the university. State her opinion and the reasons for her opinion.

Your Response

Comparing Listen to a sample response and compare it with yours.

02-18

Exercise 2 Read, listen, and answer the question following each step.

Reading Read the following passage about a campus situation and take notes.

Relocation of Food Vendors

Students and staff, please be advised that construction on the extension of the new cafeteria to accommodate our growing student body will begin early next week. For your convenience, during construction, several food vendors will be relocated to the student center. The administration feels that this will make getting food more convenient for everyone at the university.

✎ Note Taking

Topic Relocation of _____ to _____

Reason To _____

Organization Answer the following question by using the above information.

Q Why will the school relocate several food vendors to the student center?

A

Listening Listen to a conversation on the same topic and take notes.

✎ Note Taking

Man	**Woman**
Opinion	Opinion
Reason	Reason

02-19

Responding Make your response by using the above information.

Q The man expresses his opinion of the university's announcement. State his opinion and his reasons for having that opinion.

Your Response

Comparing Listen to a sample response and compare it with yours.

02-20

Exercise 3 Read, listen, and answer the question following each step.

▎**Reading**   Read the following passage about a campus situation and take notes.

Job Opening for Computer Majors

The new computer laboratory is looking to hire several students as part-time employees. These jobs are available only to students majoring in Computer Science or Computer Engineering. Since the lab is open twenty-four hours a day and has just opened, students can work at just about any time. Student employees will be expected to advise student users on how to operate the computers and to fix any problems that arise.

✎ Note Taking

Topic Part-time employees to ....

Reason Lab .... and needs ....

▎**Organization**   Answer the following question by using the above information.

Q   What are student employees expected to do?

A

▎**Listening**   Listen to a conversation on the same topic and take notes.

✎ Note Taking

Woman	**Man**
Opinion	Opinion
Reason	Reason

02-21

▎**Responding**   Make your response by using the above information.

Q   The woman expresses her opinion of the announcement made by the university. State her opinion and the reasons for her opinion.

- -

Your Response

▎**Comparing**   Listen to a sample response and compare it with yours.

02-22

Exercise 4 Read, listen, and answer the question following each step.

Reading Read the following passage about a campus situation and take notes.

Computer Center Hours

So many students have been using the computer center that not everyone is getting enough time on the machines. Starting next Monday, October 12, students must make reservations to use the computers. Students may only use the computers for two hours at a time. There will be no exceptions to this rule.

✏ Note Taking

Topic Making reservations to ....

Reason Too many .... and not enough ....

Organization Answer the following question by using the above information.

Q Why must students make reservations to use the computers at the computer center?

A

Listening Listen to a conversation on the same topic and take notes.

✏ Note Taking

Woman

Opinion

Reason

Man

Opinion

Reason

02-23

Responding Make your response by using the above information.

Q The woman expresses her opinion of the school's announcement. State her opinion and the reasons she gives for her opinion.

Your Response

Comparing Listen to a sample response and compare it with yours.

02-24

Exercise 5 Read, listen, and answer the question following each step.

Reading   Read the following passage about a campus situation and take notes.

New Computer Class

The university is going to open a new computer class that will focus on designing and creating homepages. The objective of the class is to give students an opportunity to learn about basic computer programming. The class will be open to students of all majors, and no previous experience with computers is required.

🖉 Note Taking

Topic Opening of ....

Reason To give students .... to learn ....

Organization   Answer the following question by using the above information.

Q   What is the purpose of the new class?

A

Listening   Listen to a conversation on the same topic and take notes.

🖉 Note Taking

Man	**Woman**
Opinion	Opinion
Reason	Reason

02-25

Responding   Make your response by using the above information.

Q   The woman expresses her opinion of the school announcement. State her opinion and the reasons she gives for her opinion.

- -

Your Response

Comparing   Listen to a sample response and compare it with yours.

02-26

Exercise 6 Read, listen, and answer the question following each step.

Reading   Read the following passage about a campus situation and take notes.

No More IDs at the Cafeteria

At the discretion of the campus police and in accordance with standard security policies, students will no longer be required to show their school ID cards in the school cafeteria. We hope that this change will make your dining experience more pleasant.

✎ Note Taking

Topic Showing ID card is ....

Reason A change in ....

Organization   Answer the following question by using the above information.

Q Why did the school cancel its policy of having students show their IDs at lunch?

A

Listening   Listen to a conversation on the same topic and take notes.

✎ Note Taking

Woman	Man
Opinion	Opinion
Reason	Reason

02- 27

Responding   Make your response by using the above information.

Q The woman expresses her opinion of the school's decision. State the woman's opinion and her reasons for having that opinion.

Your Response

Comparing   Listen to a sample response and compare it with yours.

02- 28

Exercise 1 Read, listen, and answer the question following each step.

Reading Read the following passage about a campus situation and take notes.

Showing Movies on Campus

The university is going to begin showing movies in the gymnasium. On weekdays, the movies will begin at 9:00 PM. On weekends, the movies will begin at 11:00 PM. All are welcome to attend. Admission is free since the school would like its students to have access to quality entertainment.

✎ Note Taking

Topic Showing _____ in _____

Reason University wants students to _____

Organization Answer the following question by using the above information.

Q What is the school planning to do?

A

Listening Listen to a conversation on the same topic and take notes.

✎ Note Taking

Man	Woman
Opinion	Opinion
Reason	Reason

02-29

Responding Make your response by using the above information.

Q The man expresses his opinion of the school announcement. State his opinion and his reasons for his opinion.

- -

Your Response

Comparing Listen to a sample response and compare it with yours.

02-30

Exercise 2 Read, listen, and answer the question following each step.

Reading Read the following passage about a campus situation and take notes.

Tutoring Program to Be Abolished

Regretfully, the student tutoring program has been canceled. We are sorry for the students that this will inconvenience. The program is being canceled due to a lack of student volunteers. The school would, however, like to encourage the tutors currently working to continue assisting their students.

✏ Note Taking

Topic The abolishing of ....

Reason Are not enough ....

Organization Answer the following question by using the above information.

Q Why is the program being canceled?

A

Listening Listen to a conversation on the same topic and take notes.

✏ Note Taking

Woman	Man
Opinion	Opinion
Reason	Reason

02-31

Responding Make your response by using the above information.

Q The woman expresses her opinion of the school's announcement. State her opinion and then give her reasons for her opinion.

Your Response

Comparing Listen to a sample response and compare it with yours.

02-32

Exercise 3 Read, listen, and answer the question following each step.

Reading Read the following passage about a campus situation and take notes.

New Changes in the School Broadcasting Program

The school is expanding its broadcasting program. Guests from off campus will be invited to strengthen the program. In addition, there will now be more programs being aired. These programs will start earlier and end later. This will help attract more advertisers to the program, which should let the broadcasting program raise more funds.

> ✎ Note Taking
>
> Topic Expanding ....
>
> Reason To attract .... and to help ....

Organization Answer the following question by using the above information.

Q What is going to happen to the broadcasting program?

A

Listening Listen to a conversation on the same topic and take notes.

> ✎ Note Taking
>
> **Woman**   **Man**
>
> Opinion   Opinion
>
> Reason   Reason
>
> 02-33

Responding Make your response by using the above information.

Q The woman expresses her opinion of the school's announcement. State her opinion and then give her reasons for her opinion.

Your Response

Comparing Listen to a sample response and compare it with yours.

02-34

Exercise 4 Read, listen, and answer the question following each step.

Reading Read the following passage about a campus situation and take notes.

Medical Center Opening

The school is opening an on-campus medical center. Students can get free checkups and use the center's services at no cost. This center should be of great assistance to students who are unable to afford medical care or who do not have health insurance.

✎ Note Taking

Topic The opening of ....

Reason To provide .... at no cost

Organization Answer the following question by using the above information.

Q Why is the school opening the medical center?

A

Listening Listen to a conversation on the same topic and take notes.

✎ Note Taking

Man

Opinion

Reason

Woman

Opinion

Reason

02-35

Responding Make your response by using the above information.

Q The man expresses his opinion of the school's announcement. State his opinion and explain the reasons he gives for holding that opinion.

Your Response

Comparing Listen to a sample response and compare it with yours.

02-36

Exercise 5 Read, listen, and answer the question following each step.

Reading Read the following passage about a campus situation and take notes.

Volunteer Activity

All students are now required to perform community service before they graduate. We have initiated this policy to help get our students more involved in the local community. Students should contact the volunteer center for details and to make the necessary arrangements. The staff members on duty will be pleased to answer all of your questions.

✎ Note Taking

Topic Students are required to .... before graduating

Reason To get students ....

Organization Answer the following question by using the above information.

Q What must students do before they graduate?

A

Listening Listen to a conversation on the same topic and take notes.

✎ Note Taking

Woman	Man
Opinion	Opinion
Reason	Reason

02-37

Responding Make your response by using the above information.

Q The woman expresses her opinion of the announcement by the university. State her opinion and give the reasons for her opinion.

Your Response

Comparing Listen to a sample response and compare it with yours.

02-38

Exercise 6 Read, listen, and answer the question following each step.

Reading Read the following passage about a campus situation and take notes.

Change in Heating Policy

As of next Monday, the heat in all of the university's classrooms will be turned off promptly at 5:00 PM in order to save electricity and to reduce costs. Professors who hold classes after 5:00 PM can request that Buildings & Grounds not turn the heat off in their classrooms until after their classes are complete.

✎ Note Taking

Topic _____ in classrooms

Reason To save _____ and to reduce _____

Organization Answer the following question by using the above information.

Q   Why is the university going to turn off the heat at 5:00 PM?

A

Listening Listen to a conversation on the same topic and take notes.

✎ Note Taking

Woman

Opinion

Reason

Man

Opinion

Reason

02-39

Responding Make your response by using the above information.

Q   The woman expresses her opinion of the announcement by the school. State her opinion and the reasons she gives for her opinion.

- -

Your Response

Comparing Listen to a sample response and compare it with yours.

02-40

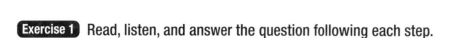

Unit 10 School Systems

Exercise 1 Read, listen, and answer the question following each step.

Reading   Read the following passage about a campus situation and take notes.

New Facility Opens

   The university finally opened the doors of its newest facility last night. It will facilitate research in the area of sleep disorders and the effects of sleep loss on memory. It will also house a new student health center. Students will have to pay normal hospital rates to receive service at the health center.

> ✎ Note Taking
>
> Topic Opening of ....
>
> Reason To conduct .... and to house ....

Organization   Answer the following question by using the above information.

> Q   What did the university do?
>
> A

Listening   Listen to a conversation on the same topic and take notes.

> ✎ Note Taking
>
> | **Man** | **Woman** |
> |---|---|
> | Opinion | Opinion |
> | Reason | Reason |
>
> 02-41

Responding   Make your response by using the above information.

> Q   The man expresses his opinion of the school's announcement. State his opinion and his reasons for having that opinion.
>
> -
>
> **Your Response**

Comparing   Listen to a sample response and compare it with yours.

02-42

Exercise 2 Read, listen, and answer the question following each step.

Reading Read the following passage about a campus situation and take notes.

Cancelation of Recycling Program

After two years, the university is canceling its recycling program. While many students talk about the importance of recycling, almost none of the recycling bins is ever used. From now on, students should simply throw away their garbage in the trashcans that can be found all over campus.

🖊 Note Taking

Topic .... of the university's recycling program

Reason Is not .... by most students

Organization Answer the following question by using the above information.

Q   Why is the recycling program being canceled?

A

Listening Listen to a conversation on the same topic and take notes.

🖊 Note Taking

Man	Woman
Opinion	Opinion
Reason	Reason

02-43

Responding Make your response by using the above information.

Q   The man expresses his opinion of the recycling program. State his opinion and his reasons for having that opinion.

Your Response

Comparing Listen to a sample response and compare it with yours.

02-44

Exercise 3 Read, listen, and answer the question following each step.

Reading   Read the following passage about a campus situation and take notes.

New Bus Route

A new bus route that will greatly benefit the school's students has been added. Bus number 93 will now take students from the school all the way to the New Horizons Shopping Mall so that they can take care of their shopping needs. The bus will run every thirty minutes, and students only have to pay a dollar so long as they show their college ID cards.

✏ Note Taking

Topic Introduction of ....

Reason Enable students to get to ....

Organization   Answer the following question by using the above information.

Q   Where is the new bus going to go?

A

Listening   Listen to a conversation on the same topic and take notes.

✏ Note Taking

Woman

Opinion

Reason

Man

Opinion

Reason

02-45

Responding   Make your response by using the above information.

Q   The woman expresses her opinion of the school's announcement. State her opinion and then give her reasons for her opinion.

Your Response

Comparing   Listen to a sample response and compare it with yours.

02-46

Exercise 4 Read, listen, and answer the question following each step.

Reading Read the following passage about a campus situation and take notes.

Changes to Dormitory Lounge

All the residents of Weston Hall are invited to attend a meeting to discuss the removal of the community television from the lounge. Many students feel the big-screen TV in the lounge is loud and makes it difficult to relax. Students who are both for and against removing the TV can give their opinions this Thursday night at 7:00 PM.

✎ Note Taking

Topic Removal of _____

Reason Is too _____

Organization Answer the following question by using the above information.

Q Why do some students want to remove the TV from the lounge?

A

Listening Listen to a conversation on the same topic and take notes.

✎ Note Taking

Man	**Woman**
Opinion	Opinion
Reason	Reason

02-47

Responding Make your response by using the above information.

Q The man expresses his opinion of the announcement. State his opinion and then give his reasons for his opinion.

Your Response

Comparing Listen to a sample response and compare it with yours.

02-48

Read, listen, and answer the question following each step.

Reading Read the following passage about a campus situation and take notes.

Changes in the Tutoring Program

As of next month, the student tutoring program will offer online tutoring programs to make tutoring more convenient for students. Students can log on and ask questions to a tutor, who will then immediately respond. In addition, students with cameras will be able to be tutored by a video link. This will allow them to stay in their dormitories and use their own computers while still getting tutored.

🖉 Note Taking

Topic Changes in _____

Reason To make tutoring _____

Organization Answer the following question by using the above information.

Q What changes are going to be made to the tutoring program?

A

Listening Listen to a conversation on the same topic and take notes.

🖉 Note Taking

Woman	**Man**
Opinion	Opinion
Reason	Reason

02-49

Responding Make your response by using the above information.

Q The woman expresses her opinion of the school's announcement. State her opinion and the reasons she gives for her opinion.

Your Response

Comparing Listen to a sample response and compare it with yours.

02-50

Exercise 6 Read, listen, and answer the question following each step.

Reading Read the following passage about a campus situation and take notes.

Library Hours

In order to prepare better during finals, some members of the student body would like to discuss having the library extend its hours. If you agree that the library should remain open twenty-four hours per day during this time, we encourage you to join us this Wednesday at 9:00 PM in the library meeting room. There will be a meeting for students wishing to change the library's hours. Come and let your voice be heard.

✎ Note Taking

Topic Extending of ....

Reason To let students ....

Organization Answer the following question by using the above information.

Q Why do the students want the library to stay open twenty-four hours a day?

A

Listening Listen to a conversation on the same topic and take notes.

✎ Note Taking

Man	**Woman**
Opinion	Opinion
Reason	Reason

02-51

Responding Make your response by using the above information.

Q The man expresses his opinion of the announcement. State his opinion and the reasons he gives for his opinion.

Your Response

Comparing Listen to a sample response and compare it with yours.

02-52

Exercise 1   Read, listen, and answer the question following each step.

Reading   Read the following passage about a campus situation and take notes.

New Dorm to Be Built

The school will begin construction on a new dormitory this spring. It will be located behind Deacon Hall. The dorm will have 200 rooms. These rooms include singles, doubles, and triples. This will allow more students to live on campus instead of moving off campus.

✎ Note Taking

Topic   Building a _____

Reason   To allow more _____ to live _____

Organization   Answer the following question by using the above information.

Q   What is the school going to do?

A

Listening   Listen to a conversation on the same topic and take notes.

✎ Note Taking

Woman	**Man**
Opinion	Opinion
Reason	Reason

02-53

Responding   Make your response by using the above information.

Q   The man expresses his opinion of the announcement by the university. State the man's opinion and explain the reasons he gives for holding that opinion.

- -

Your Response

Comparing   Listen to a sample response and compare it with yours.

02-54

Exercise 2 Read, listen, and answer the question following each step.

Reading   Read the following passage about a campus situation and take notes.

Library to Expand

Jefferson Library will be expanding soon. The library will undergo construction to double its current size. It will be able to hold more books, journals, and computers in the future. The library will be closed during the fall semester. Construction will finish in December.

✎ Note Taking

Topic Expanding the size of ....

Reason To .... the size to hold more .... ,

.... , and ....

Organization   Answer the following question by using the above information.

Q   What is going to happen to the library?

A

Listening   Listen to a conversation on the same topic and take notes.

✎ Note Taking

Man   **Woman**

Opinion   Opinion

                                                                        02-55

Reason   Reason

Responding   Make your response by using the above information.

Q   The woman expresses her opinion of the announcement by the university. State her opinion and explain the reasons she gives for holding that opinion.

- -

Your Response

Comparing   Listen to a sample response and compare it with yours.

02-56

Exercise 3 Read, listen, and answer the question following each step.

Reading Read the following passage about a campus situation and take notes.

Chemistry Department to Close

The school has decided to close the Chemistry Department. Few students currently major in chemistry, so there is no need to have the department. Students currently majoring in chemistry must change majors or transfer to another school. For more information, please contact the office of the dean of students.

✎ Note Taking

Topic Closing the _____

Reason There are _____ who are _____ in chemistry now.

Organization Answer the following question by using the above information.

Q Why is the school going to close the Chemistry Department?

A

Listening Listen to a conversation on the same topic and take notes.

✎ Note Taking

Woman	**Man**
Opinion	Opinion
Reason	Reason

02-57

Responding Make your response by using the above information.

Q The man expresses his opinion of the announcement by the university. State his opinion and explain the reasons he gives for holding that opinion.

- -

Your Response

Comparing Listen to a sample response and compare it with yours.

02-58

Exercise 4 Read, listen, and answer the question following each step.

Reading   Read the following passage about a campus situation and take notes.

Art Gallery to Hold Exhibition for Students

     The school's art gallery will be having an exhibition for student artists. The exhibition will last from April 10 to 23. All university students may submit their work for consideration. The work will be viewed by several famous local artists. The top five entries as determined by the judges will receive prizes.

✎ Note Taking

Topic   Holding an _____ for _____

Reason   To let _____ view the work and to have the _____
         receive prizes

Organization   Answer the following question by using the above information.

Q   What is the school art gallery going to do?

A

Listening   Listen to a conversation on the same topic and take notes.

✎ Note Taking

Woman   **Man**

Opinion   Opinion

02-59

Reason   Reason

Responding   Make your response by using the above information.

Q   The woman expresses her opinion of the announcement by the university. State her opinion and explain the reasons she gives for holding that opinion.

- -

Your Response

Comparing   Listen to a sample response and compare it with yours.

02-60

Exercise 5 Read, listen, and answer the question following each step.

Reading   Read the following passage about a campus situation and take notes.

School Newspaper to Be Printed Less Often

Due to the rising costs of paper and ink and the need to save money, the school newspaper will no longer be printed daily. Instead, it will be printed on Monday, Wednesday, and Friday. The paper will still be available online seven days a week. The paper will continue to be provided for free to students, faculty, and staff members.

🖉 Note Taking

Topic   The reduced number of days the _____ is _____

Reason   To _____ due to the rising costs of _____ and

_____

Organization   Answer the following question by using the above information.

Q   What is the school newspaper going to do?

A

Listening   Listen to a conversation on the same topic and take notes.

🖉 Note Taking

Woman

Opinion

Reason

Man

Opinion

Reason

02-61

Responding   Make your response by using the above information.

Q   The man expresses his opinion of the announcement by the university. State his opinion and explain the reasons he gives for holding that opinion.

Your Response

Comparing   Listen to a sample response and compare it with yours.

02-62

Read, listen, and answer the question following each step.

Reading Read the following passage about a campus situation and take notes.

Harper Hall Closed for Renovations

Due to this year's severe winter weather, Harper Hall suffered damage. The building is now closed for repairs. Repairs are expected to last the entire spring semester. All classes in Harper Hall will be moved to other buildings. Please check with the relevant departments for the new classroom listings.

✎ Note Taking

Topic The _____ of Harper Hall for the _____

Reason To _____ the building after it _____ from severe _____

Organization Answer the following question by using the above information.

Q Why is Harper Hall closed?

A

Listening Listen to a conversation on the same topic and take notes.

✎ Note Taking

Woman

Opinion

Reason

Man

Opinion

Reason

02-63

Responding Make your response by using the above information.

Q The man expresses his opinion of the announcement by the university. State his opinion and explain the reasons he gives for holding that opinion.

Your Response

Comparing Listen to a sample response and compare it with yours.

02-64

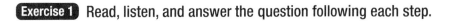

Exercise 1 Read, listen, and answer the question following each step.

Reading Read the following passage about a campus situation and take notes.

No Students in Dorms This Winter Break

This winter break, from December 23 to January 18, no students are permitted to stay in the dormitories. Minor renovations will be conducted in each dorm during this period. All students must check out of their dorm rooms by midnight on December 22. They may return at 1:00 PM on January 18.

✎ Note Taking

Topic No students in _____ during _____

Reason To allow _____ to be conducted

Organization Answer the following question by using the above information.

Q   What will happen this winter break?

A

Listening Listen to a conversation on the same topic and take notes.

✎ Note Taking

Man

Opinion

Reason

Woman

Opinion

Reason

02-65

Responding Make your response by using the above information.

Q   The woman expresses her opinion of the announcement by the university. State the woman's opinion and explain the reasons she gives for holding that opinion.

- -

Your Response

Comparing Listen to a sample response and compare it with yours.

02-66

Read, listen, and answer the question following each step.

Reading   Read the following passage about a campus situation and take notes.

Reducing Noise in Dormitories

Due to many complaints by students, a new noise regulation is now in effect in the school dormitories. From 9:00 PM to 7:00 AM, students in dormitories must be quiet to let students study and sleep. This means no loud music, no yelling, no shouting, and no making noises that can disturb other students. Students who violate this regulation will be fined.

✎ Note Taking

Topic A new _____ in the school _____

Reason To make the _____ quiet for students to _____ and

_____

Organization   Answer the following question by using the above information.

Q   What must students in the dormitories do from now on?

A

Listening   Listen to a conversation on the same topic and take notes.

✎ Note Taking

Man   **Woman**

Opinion   Opinion

Reason   Reason

02-67

Responding   Make your response by using the above information.

Q   The woman expresses her opinion of the announcement by the university. State her opinion and explain the reasons she gives for holding that opinion.

- -

Your Response

Comparing   Listen to a sample response and compare it with yours.

02-68

Exercise 3 Read, listen, and answer the question following each step.

Reading   Read the following passage about a campus situation and take notes.

Fewer Safety Officers on Campus

The university has seen its budget decrease this year. It can therefore no longer employ a large number of safety officers. There will now be ten officers on duty at all times as opposed to the normal twenty. Students are urged to go out around campus with a friend at night.

✎ **Note Taking**

Topic _____ the number of _____ on campus

Reason To compensate for the _____ in the school's _____

Organization   Answer the following question by using the above information.

Q How many safety officers will be on duty now?

A

Listening   Listen to a conversation on the same topic and take notes.

✎ **Note Taking**

Woman	Man
Opinion	Opinion
Reason	Reason

02-69

Responding   Make your response by using the above information.

Q The man expresses his opinion of the announcement by the university. State his opinion and explain the reasons he gives for holding that opinion.

Your Response

Comparing   Listen to a sample response and compare it with yours.

02-70

Exercise 4 Read, listen, and answer the question following each step.

Reading   Read the following passage about a campus situation and take notes.

Have Dinner with the School President

Would you like to have dinner with university president Jason Milo? Starting next week, students may have dinner with the president every Monday and Thursday night. Ten students can dine with him and talk about school and current affairs each night. To apply, visit the office of the president.

✎ Note Taking

Topic   Letting students have .... with the ....

Reason   To let students .... with the president about school and

....

Organization   Answer the following question by using the above information.

Q   What can university students do now?

A

Listening   Listen to a conversation on the same topic and take notes.

✎ Note Taking

Man	Woman
Opinion	Opinion
Reason	Reason

02-71

Responding   Make your response by using the above information.

Q   The woman expresses her opinion of the announcement by the university. State her opinion and explain the reasons she gives for holding that opinion.

- -

Your Response

Comparing   Listen to a sample response and compare it with yours.

02-72

Exercise 5 Read, listen, and answer the question following each step.

Reading Read the following passage about a campus situation and take notes.

Freshman Meal Plans

Beginning in the fall semester, all freshmen must have meal plans of at least fourteen meals a week. This is to ensure that they get enough to eat during the day. This policy is for all students who live in the dorms. Those living at home may apply for a waiver from this program.

> ✎ Note Taking
>
> Topic .... for all ....
> Reason To make sure that .... get enough food ....

Organization Answer the following question by using the above information.

> Q What has the school decided to do?
> A

Listening Listen to a conversation on the same topic and take notes.

> ✎ Note Taking
>
> | **Woman** | **Man** |
> |---|---|
> | Opinion | Opinion |
> | | |
> | Reason | Reason |

02-73

Responding Make your response by using the above information.

> Q The man expresses his opinion of the announcement by the university. State his opinion and explain the reason he gives for holding that opinion.
> ---
> **Your Response**

Comparing Listen to a sample response and compare it with yours.

02-74

Exercise 6 Read, listen, and answer the question following each step.

Reading   Read the following passage about a campus situation and take notes.

New Scholarships Available

Thanks to some generous donors, the school has several new scholarships to offer to students. Each scholarship pays a different amount of money to be used for tuition. These scholarships are based on academic performance, not need. To apply, visit the office of the dean of students.

✎ Note Taking

Topic New _____ for students

Reason To help pay _____ for some _____

Organization   Answer the following question by using the above information.

Q   What is mentioned about the scholarships?

A

Listening   Listen to a conversation on the same topic and take notes.

✎ Note Taking

Man

Opinion

Reason

Woman

Opinion

Reason

02-75

Responding   Make your response by using the above information.

Q   The woman expresses her opinion of the announcement by the university. State her opinion and explain the reasons she gives for holding that opinion.

Your Response

Comparing   Listen to a sample response and compare it with yours.

02-76

PART III

Integrated Speaking Task 2
Reading & Lecture

In this task, you will be presented with a short reading passage about an academic topic. Next, you will listen to a short lecture by a professor about the same topic. Then, you will provide a response based upon what you read and heard. You will be asked to explain how the professor's lecture relates to the reading passage. You will be given 30 seconds to prepare your answer after the question is presented, and you will have 60 seconds to respond to the question.

Integrated Speaking Task 2 ❙
Reading & Lecture

Overview

For this task, you will read a short passage about an academic subject and listen to a professor give a brief excerpt from a lecture on that subject. Then, you will be asked a question based on the passage and lecture. Although the topics are academic in nature, none of the passages or lectures requires you to have prior knowledge of any academic field in particular. You only need to integrate and convey the key information from both sources.

Sample TOEFL iBT Task

Read a short passage about an academic subject.

Crossbreeding

The process by which two plants or animals are bred with one another in order to attain the desired offspring is known as crossbreeding. Typically, crossbreeding is done because it can help the offspring gain important traits, such as resistance to disease, different colors in the cases of flowers, or enhanced productivity or nutritional value. Crossbreeding is also used to created new strains of plants, trees, and flowers. As a general rule, those offspring produced as a result of crossbreeding are stronger and more desirable than both of their parents.

Listen to a lecture about the same topic.

Script

W Professor: Do you know how crucial Gregor Mendel was to the field of genetics? He did simple experiments with peas that led to many important discoveries in the field of heredity.

03-01

By, uh, crossbreeding peas with one another, he managed to get the desired results with regard to various characteristics of peas. It took him several generations of crossbreeding to prove his hypotheses, but in the end, Mendel discovered three basic laws of heredity. The first law said that a plant's sex cells may have two different traits but cannot have both of them. The second law said that offspring inherit their characteristics independent of one another. The third law said that both parent's genes determine what the offspring will be like. This basically explained dominant and recessive genes. Mendel's work was groundbreaking for his time, but it took a while for people to recognize his genius. Nowadays, it is widely acknowledged that without his crossbreeding of peas, the field of genetics would not be as, uh, advanced as it is today.

Q The professor describes the advances in genetics made by Gregor Mendel. Explain how these advances in genetics are related to crossbreeding.

PREPARATION TIME
00 : 30 : 00

RESPONSE TIME
00 : 60 : 00

03-02

Sample Response

The professor discusses Gregor Mendel and his contributions to genetics. Mendel used crossbreeding to make his discoveries. Crossbreeding is the breeding of two separate plants or animals to get a desired result, which is always something positive. Through the crossbreeding of peas, Mendel discovered three basic laws of heredity. These laws helped to explain both dominant and recessive genes, which were two things that people did not know anything about until he conducted his experiments. Thanks to Mendel's crossbreeding, people now know very much about genetics.

How to Practice

Reading

STEP 01 **Reading** Read the following passage about an academic subject and take notes.

Animal Domestication

Animal domestication is done by asserting dominance. In accordance to their natural instincts, wild animals follow the dominant member of their herd. So people domesticate them by assuming the role of the dominant member.

✎ Note Taking

Animal domestication *Done by asserting dominance*

Possible *Because animal's instinct is to follow dominant member*

STEP 02 **Organization** Answer the following question by using the above information.

Q   According to the passage, how is animal domestication done?

A   *People act like the dominant member of the herd. That way, the other animals will follow them.*

Listening

STEP 03 **Listening** Listen to a lecture about the same topic and take notes.

Script

03-03

M Professor: All right . . . Let's take a look at feral horses that live in the wild. Feral horses live in herds and are led by the dominant male horse. In order to domesticate these animals, humans have altered this behavior by eliminating dominant males. This means that no horse is dominant.

✎ Note Taking

Feral horses *Have instinct to follow dominant male*

Domestication *Done by taking dominant status out of male*

Speaking

STEP 04 **Responding** Make your response by using the above information.

> **Q** The professor describes feral horses. Explain how they are related to the principle of domestication.
>
> --
>
> **Your Response**
>
> *People domesticate horses by becoming the dominant member of the herd. This is possible because horses are animals that the principles of animal domestication can apply to.*

STEP 05 **Comparing** Listen to a sample response and compare it with yours.

Sample Response

Feral horses live in herds. And people domesticate the horses by eliminating the dominant males and taking the dominant position. This process is in line with the principles of domestication. According to the principle, animal domestication can be done by assuming the role of the dominant member.

03-04

83

Exercise 1 Read, listen, and answer the question following each step.

Reading Read the following passage about an academic subject and take notes.

Flow

Flow is a mental state of operation that occurs when people concentrate fully on what they are doing. The effects of flow are feelings of focus, involvement, and success. When people are in a state of flow, they feel as if they are filled with creativity. When they are deprived of it, they often feel depressed by the loss of their former mental condition.

> ✎ Note Taking
>
> Flow
>
> Positive effect
>
> Negative effect

Organization Answer the following question by using the above information.

Q According to the passage, what is flow?

A

Listening Listen to a lecture about the same topic and take notes.

> ✎ Note Taking
>
> Ken
>
> Result

03-05

Responding Make your response by using the above information.

Q The professor describes his friend's experience. Explain how this experience is related to flow.

Your Response

Comparing Listen to a sample response and compare it with yours.

03-06

Read, listen, and answer the question following each step.

Reading Read the following passage about an academic subject and take notes.

Behavioral Scripts

Behavioral scripts are actions that are followed when someone encounters a familiar situation. The sequences of actions are acquired through habit and practice. They save a person the time and mental effort it takes to figure out a new situation.

🖉 Note Taking

Behavioral script

Result

Organization Answer the following question by using the above information.

Q According to the passage, what is a behavioral script?

A

Listening Listen to a lecture about the same topic and take notes.

🖉 Note Taking

Problem

Solution

03-07

Responding Make your response by using the above information.

Q The professor describes his experience when he was memorizing a song. Explain how this experience is related to the principle of behavioral script.

Your Response

Comparing Listen to a sample response and compare it with yours.

03-08

Reading   Read the following passage about an academic subject and take notes.

Displacement

Displacement is a psychological effect in which an individual transfers his feelings. The person redirects these feelings from an object that is dangerous or unacceptable to one that is safe or acceptable. An example of this happens when a person punches a pillow when he is angry at a friend.

✎ Note Taking

Displacement

Example

Organization   Answer the following question by using the above information.

Q   According to the passage, what is displacement?

A

Listening   Listen to a lecture about the same topic and take notes.

✎ Note Taking

Problem

Action

Result

03-09

Responding   Make your response by using the above information.

Q   The professor describes one of his birthday experiences. Explain how this experience is related to the concept of displacement.

- -

Your Response

Comparing   Listen to a sample response and compare it with yours.

03-10

Exercise 4 Read, listen, and answer the question following each step.

Reading Read the following passage about an academic subject and take notes.

Impression Management

Impression management is the practice of trying to control what other people think of oneself. It is especially common for first impressions. This type of behavior occurs when an individual presents his dress and manners in the way he would like to be thought of.

✏ Note Taking

Impression management

Example

Organization Answer the following question by using the above information.

Q According to the passage, what is impression management?

A

Listening Listen to a lecture about the same topic and take notes.

✏ Note Taking

Situation

Action

03- 11

Responding Make your response by using the above information.

Q The professor describes one of her experiences at the university. Explain how this experience is related to the concept of impression management.

Your Response

Comparing Listen to a sample response and compare it with yours.

03- 12

Read, listen, and answer the question following each step.

Reading   Read the following passage about an academic subject and take notes.

Group Thinking

Group thinking is the process by which individuals influence each other's decisions as members of a group. This process involves communication between members, both spoken and unspoken, or implied. Group thinking includes the sharing of standards and values that contribute to the advancement of the group as a whole. In a group-thinking situation, some individual ideas or feelings are suppressed in order to serve the needs of the entire group. The results of a group-thinking situation often help the group in the best possible way.

✏ Note Taking

Group thinking

Action

Result

Organization   Answer the following question by using the above information.

Q   According to the passage, what is group thinking?

A

Listening   Listen to a lecture about the same topic and take notes.

✏ Note Taking

Problem

Solution

Result

03-13

Responding   Make your response by using the above information.

Q   The professor describes one of his experiences while working at a company. Explain how this experience is related to the concept of group thinking.

- -

Your Response

Comparing   Listen to a sample response and compare it with yours.

03-14

Read, listen, and answer the question following each step.

Reading Read the following passage about an academic subject and take notes.

The Primacy Effect

The primacy effect happens when people believe their first impression of someone or something even when later impressions contradict it. This effect proves that first impressions are the most lasting ones. It can be clearly seen by the example of someone reading a long list of words. According to the primacy effect, the reader is more likely to remember words from the beginning of the list than from the middle.

> ✎ **Note Taking**
>
> Primacy effect
>
> Example

Organization Answer the following question by using the above information.

Q According to the passage, what is the primary effect?

A

Listening Listen to a lecture about the same topic and take notes.

> ✎ **Note Taking**
>
> Professor's action
>
> Coworker's action

03-15

Responding Make your response by using the above information.

Q The professor describes one of her own experiences at the university. Explain how this experience is related to the primacy effect.

Your Response

Comparing Listen to a sample response and compare it with yours.

03-16

Exercise 1 Read, listen, and answer the question following each step.

Reading   Read the following passage about an academic subject and take notes.

Supply and Demand

The concept of supply and demand is the fundamental model of microeconomics. It describes the interaction between producers and consumers for goods in the marketplace and is based on price and sales. This model is used to look at correlations between the increases and decreases in both the supply and demand of a given item or service.

✎ Note Taking

Supply and demand

Use

Organization   Answer the following question by using the above information.

Q   According to the passage, what is supply and demand?

A

Listening   Listen to a lecture about the same topic and take notes.

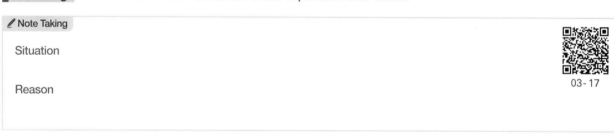

✎ Note Taking

Situation

Reason

03-17

Responding   Make your response by using the above information.

Q   The professor describes an economic situation during Victorian England. Explain how that situation is related to supply and demand.

Your Response

Comparing   Listen to a sample response and compare it with yours.

03-18

Exercise 2 Read, listen, and answer the question following each step.

Reading   Read the following passage about an academic subject and take notes.

Cognitive Dissonance

Cognitive dissonance defines the condition that results from a person holding two incompatible or contradictory thoughts at the same time. If a person feels his father is a good man but sees him do something bad, that person is likely to experience cognitive dissonance.

> ✎ Note Taking
>
> Cognitive dissonance
>
> Example

Organization   Answer the following question by using the above information.

Q   According to the passage, what is cognitive dissonance?

A

Listening   Listen to a lecture about the same topic and take notes.

> ✎ Note Taking
>
> Situation
>
> Problem
>
> Result

03-19

Responding   Make your response by using the above information.

Q   The professor describes a specific event in her life. Explain how this event is related to cognitive dissonance.

- -

Your Response

Comparing   Listen to a sample response and compare it with yours.

03-20

Exercise 3 Read, listen, and answer the question following each step.

Reading   Read the following passage about an academic subject and take notes.

Credibility

Credibility describes the extent to which a person's statements or actions are believed by others. There are three main aspects of credibility. They are competence, trustworthiness, and dynamism. Credibility is considered extremely important in the fields of politics and journalism.

✎ Note Taking

Credibility

Aspects

Organization   Answer the following question by using the above information.

Q According to the passage, what is credibility?

A

Listening   Listen to a lecture about the same topic and take notes.

✎ Note Taking

Situation

Problem

Result

03-21

Responding   Make your response by using the above information.

Q The professor describes Jessica Miller's candidacy for mayor. Explain how her candidacy is related to credibility.

- -

Your Response

Comparing   Listen to a sample response and compare it with yours.

03-22

Read, listen, and answer the question following each step.

Reading   Read the following passage about an academic subject and take notes.

Buyer's Remorse

   Buyer's remorse is an emotional state that occurs when a person feels a sense of regret after purchasing an item. It most often occurs after the purchase of expensive goods like jewelry, cars, and property. However, the feelings it causes can be eased through the justification of the purchase or persuasion.

✎ Note Taking

Buyer's remorse

Easing of feelings

Organization   Answer the following question by using the above information.

Q   According to the passage, what is buyer's remorse?

A

Listening   Listen to a lecture about the same topic and take notes.

✎ Note Taking

Situation

Result

03-23

Responding   Make your response by using the above information.

Q   The professor describes his own experience when buying a new car. Explain how his experience is related to buyer's remorse.

- -

Your Response

Comparing   Listen to a sample response and compare it with yours.

03-24

Exercise 5 Read, listen, and answer the question following each step.

Reading Read the following passage about an academic subject and take notes.

Exaggeration in Advertising

Many advertisements are guilty of exaggerating the effects of the products that their producers want consumers to purchase. Advertisements frequently depict products having qualities or sizes that are greatly exaggerated. People who desire the effects they see in these exaggerated advertisements sometimes purchase products they do not truly want or need. Afterward, they may feel angry at being deceived by an advertisement which made false promises. In some cases, this exaggeration may be considered false advertising, which is often considered a crime.

✎ Note Taking

Exaggeration in advertising

Positive result

Negative result

Organization Answer the following question by using the above information.

Q How does exaggeration in advertising occur?

A

Listening Listen to a lecture about the same topic and take notes.

✎ Note Taking

Situation

Problem

Result

03-25

Responding Make your response by using the above information.

Q The professor describes a time when she purchased a vacuum cleaner. Explain how her experience is related to exaggeration in advertising.

Your Response

Comparing Listen to a sample response and compare it with yours.

03-26

Exercise 6 Read, listen, and answer the question following each step.

Reading Read the following passage about an academic subject and take notes.

Fragrance

The sweet smells of a well-mixed fragrance can affect people's minds in very positive ways. Due to this fact, fragrances are often used in marketing. One fragrance that is used to draw people into food courts in shopping malls is that of baking cinnamon buns. Scientists have discovered that this popular smell makes people hungry. Once they are drawn into the food court, they may spend their money on something other than a cinnamon bun, but it was that smell that brought them there.

✎ Note Taking

Fragrance

Use

Organization Answer the following question by using the above information.

Q   How is fragrance used in marketing?

A

Listening Listen to a lecture about the same topic and take notes.

✎ Note Taking

Use of fragrance

Result

03-27

Responding Make your response by using the above information.

Q   The professor describes an application of perfume in marketing. Explain how this marketing tactic is related to fragrance.

- -

Your Response

Comparing Listen to a sample response and compare it with yours.

03-28

Exercise 1 Read, listen, and answer the question following each step.

▎**Reading**   Read the following passage about an academic subject and take notes.

The Importance of Balance

   Interior decoration is the art of decorating a room so that it serves the lifestyle functions of its users. It focuses on bringing together a balance between the unity and contrasts of the colors that are used on the surrounding walls. Design theory always seeks to find the balance in the decoration of a room so that it is not boring but also not too busy.

> ✎ Note Taking
>
> Importance of balance
>
> Result

▎**Organization**   Answer the following question by using the above information.

Q   According to the passage, why is keeping balance important?

A

▎**Listening**   Listen to a lecture about the same topic and take notes.

> ✎ Note Taking
>
> Unity
>
> Contrast

03-29

▎**Responding**   Make your response by using the above information.

Q   The professor describes the right usage of colors. Explain how this example is related to the importance of balance.

Your Response

▎**Comparing**   Listen to a sample response and compare it with yours.

03-30

Read, listen, and answer the question following each step.

Reading Read the following passage about an academic subject and take notes.

Film Criticism

Film criticism can have a tremendous impact on the financial success of a film. Critics watch a new movie and offer their opinions through various media, such as television, print, the Internet, and the radio. These critics' opinions often help determine whether or not consumers choose to see a new film. Criticism of past films can even determine which films studios and producers choose to make.

> ✎ Note Taking
>
> Film criticism
>
> Result

Organization Answer the following question by using the above information.

Q   According to the passage, how can film criticism affect the movie industry?

A

Listening Listen to a lecture about the same topic and take notes.

> ✎ Note Taking
>
> Prediction
>
> Problem
>
> Result

03-31

Responding Make your response by using the above information.

Q   The professor discusses the movie *Waterworld*. Explain how *Waterworld* is related to film criticism.

- -

Your Response

Comparing Listen to a sample response and compare it with yours.

03-32

Exercise 3 Read, listen, and answer the question following each step.

Reading Read the following passage about an academic subject and take notes.

Hyperbole

Hyperbole is a literary device that is also called exaggeration. By using hyperbole, a writer can emphasize events or characteristics to give them dramatic or comedic effects. Since they are overstatements, people should not take them literally.

✎ **Note Taking**

Hyperbole

Use

Organization Answer the following question by using the above information.

Q According to the passage, what is hyperbole?

A

Listening Listen to a lecture about the same topic and take notes.

✎ **Note Taking**

Situation

Solution

03-33

Responding Make your response by using the above information.

Q The professor explains a statement in a writer's story. Explain how this statement is related to hyperbole.

- -

Your Response

Comparing Listen to a sample response and compare it with yours.

03-34

Exercise 4 Read, listen, and answer the question following each step.

Reading Read the following passage about an academic subject and take notes.

Art Happenings

Art happenings are performances, events, or situations that the creators want other people to regard as art. Art happenings are very different from traditional art. They were created in the 1950s. They were used to describe unusual events that artists held in various places, including abandoned buildings, buses, and parks.

✎ Note Taking

Art happenings

Locations

Organization Answer the following question by using the above information.

Q   According to the passage, what is an art happening?

A

Listening Listen to a lecture about the same topic and take notes.

✎ Note Taking

Situation

Result

03-35

Responding Make your response by using the above information.

Q   The professor describes an art event that occurred in the school cafeteria. Explain how this event is related to art happenings.

Your Response

Comparing Listen to a sample response and compare it with yours.

03-36

Exercise 5 Read, listen, and answer the question following each step.

Reading Read the following passage about an academic subject and take notes.

Bridging Shot

In filmmaking, a bridging shot is one that makes a transition. This is normally the passage of time or a change in locations. Bridging shots can also be used to signify a dramatic change in a character or a state of being. Some of the most popular bridging shots are of spinning clocks, pages tearing away from a calendar, and speeding vehicles, such as trains and cars. Another common kind of bridging shot is that of a line being drawn on a map from one point to another.

> ✎ Note Taking
>
> Bridging shot
>
> Examples
>
> Other example

Organization Answer the following question by using the above information.

Q According to the passage, what is a bridging shot?

A

Listening Listen to a lecture about the same topic and take notes.

> ✎ Note Taking
>
> First movie scene
>
> Second movie scene

03-37

Responding Make your response by using the above information.

Q The professor gives two examples of movie effects. Explain how these examples are related to bridging shots.

- -

Your Response

Comparing Listen to a sample response and compare it with yours.

03-38

Exercise 6 Read, listen, and answer the question following each step.

Reading Read the following passage about an academic subject and take notes.

Outsider Artist

An outsider artist is an individual who creates works of art outside the boundaries of traditional culture. Many of these artists are self-taught and never received any formal training in the techniques of fine art. These artists often work outside the mainstream art world and typically employ unique techniques and materials.

✏ Note Taking

Outsider artist

Definition

Organization Answer the following question by using the above information.

Q According to the passage, what kinds of people are outsider artists?

A

Listening Listen to a lecture about the same topic and take notes.

✏ Note Taking

Henry Roger

Method

03-39

Responding Make your response by using the above information.

Q The professor describes the art of Henry Roger. Explain how Henry Roger is related to outsider artists.

Your Response

Comparing Listen to a sample response and compare it with yours.

03-40

Exercise 1 Read, listen, and answer the question following each step.

Reading Read the following passage about an academic subject and take notes.

Camouflage

Camouflage is a method by which creatures blend in with the environment that surrounds them. Animals do this to fend off predators. Some animals change their colors to camouflage themselves from other animals that are trying to kill and eat them.

✎ Note Taking

Camouflage

Method

Organization Answer the following question by using the above information.

Q According to the passage, what is camouflage?

A

Listening Listen to a lecture about the same topic and take notes.

✎ Note Taking

Cuttlefish

Method

Other fish

03-41

Responding Make your response by using the above information.

Q The professor describes the cuttlefish and its ability to change colors. Explain how the cuttlefish's ability is related to camouflage.

Your Response

Comparing Listen to a sample response and compare it with yours.

03-42

Read, listen, and answer the question following each step.

Reading   Read the following passage about an academic subject and take notes.

The Importance of Sleep

Sleep is a period of rest that most animals need. Sleeping animals have reduced movements and slower reactions to light and sound. Humans experience several stages of sleep. In some of these stages, their subconscious minds are very active. Humans must sleep regularly in order to maintain the cognitive functions of the brain. When humans are deprived of their required amount of sleep, their bodies deteriorate rapidly.

> 🖊 Note Taking
>
> Sleep effects
>
> Importance of sleep

Organization   Answer the following question by using the above information.

Q   Why is sleep important for humans?

A

Listening   Listen to a lecture about the same topic and take notes.

> 🖊 Note Taking
>
> Sleep
>
> Test
>
> Result

03-43

Responding   Make your response by using the above information.

Q   The professor describes an exam that tested cognitive performance. Explain how this test is related to the importance of sleep.

Your Response

Comparing   Listen to a sample response and compare it with yours.

03-44

Reading   Read the following passage about an academic subject and take notes.

Ecosystem

An ecosystem is a group of living creatures and nonliving features that have formed a system of relationships. As certain species in an ecosystem die, newly formed ones replace them. This continual process is called a lifecycle. If the lifecycle within an ecosystem is broken, the ecosystem itself might die. If the lifecycle remains unbroken, then the ecosystem will live and prosper indefinitely.

✎ Note Taking

Ecosystem

Result

Organization   Answer the following question by using the above information.

Q According to the passage, what is an ecosystem?

A

Listening   Listen to a lecture about the same topic and take notes.

✎ Note Taking

Problem

Result

Solution

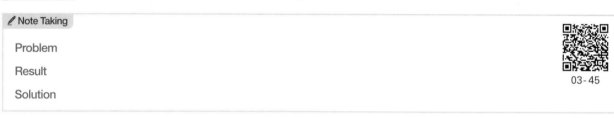

03-45

Responding   Make your response by using the above information.

Q The professor describes an oil spill in the Great Barrier Reef. Explain how this oil spill is related to ecosystems.

Your Response

Comparing   Listen to a sample response and compare it with yours.

03-46

Exercise 4 Read, listen, and answer the question following each step.

Reading   Read the following passage about an academic subject and take notes.

Symbiosis

Symbiosis describes the way in which two different organisms live together as members of a community. A symbiotic relationship must be beneficial to at least one of the organisms involved. There are many symbiotic relationships all throughout nature.

✎ Note Taking

Symbiosis

Result

Organization   Answer the following question by using the above information.

Q   According to the passage, what is symbiosis?

A

Listening   Listen to a lecture about the same topic and take notes.

✎ Note Taking

Example

Relationship

Adaptation

03-47

Responding   Make your response by using the above information.

Q   The professor describes the relationship between the clownfish and the sea anemone. Explain how this relationship is related to symbiosis.

- -

Your Response

Comparing   Listen to a sample response and compare it with yours.

03-48

Exercise 5 Read, listen, and answer the question following each step.

Reading Read the following passage about an academic subject and take notes.

Eusociality

Some animals are capable of specializing within their species through reproduction. This is called eusociality. This process is carried out through the breeding of sterile members, which perform specialized tasks for the reproductive members. Common eusocial species are ants, bees, and wasps.

✎ Note Taking

Eusociality

Method

Species

Organization Answer the following question by using the above information.

Q   According to the passage, what is eusociality?

A

Listening Listen to a lecture about the same topic and take notes.

✎ Note Taking

Termites

Sterile members

Fertile members

03-49

Responding Make your response by using the above information.

Q   The professor describes termites. Explain how termites are related to eusociality.

Your Response

Comparing Listen to a sample response and compare it with yours.

03-50

Exercise 6 Read, listen, and answer the question following each step.

Reading Read the following passage about an academic subject and take notes.

Mimicry

Mimicry is the ability of animals to disguise themselves as another type of organism. They do this to deceive predators into thinking they are not good to eat or to trick prey into thinking that they are not harmful predators.

> ✎ Note Taking
>
> Mimicry
>
> Result

Organization Answer the following question by using the above information.

Q According to the passage, what is mimicry?

A

Listening Listen to a lecture about the same topic and take notes.

> ✎ Note Taking
>
> Stick insect
>
> Leaf insect

03-51

Responding Make your response by using the above information.

Q The professor describes stick and leaf insects. Explain how these insects are related to mimicry.

Your Response

Comparing Listen to a sample response and compare it with yours.

03-52

Exercise 1 Read, listen, and answer the question following each step.

█ **Reading** Read the following passage about an academic subject and take notes.

Ambient Advertising

Ambient advertising is also known as guerilla marketing. It relies on surprise and emotions. Ambient ads are often placed in locations where they are unexpected. This allows them to stand out more. As a result, people tend to notice ambient ads much more than regular advertisements on billboards.

> ✎ Note Taking
>
> Ambient advertising
>
> Action
>
> Result

█ **Organization** Answer the following question by using the above information.

Q According to the passage, what is ambient advertising?

A

█ **Listening** Listen to a lecture about the same topic and take notes.

> ✎ Note Taking
>
> Subway station
>
> Result

03-53

█ **Responding** Make your response by using the above information.

Q The professor describes his experience this morning. Explain how his experience is related to ambient advertising.

Your Response

█ **Comparing** Listen to a sample response and compare it with yours.

03-54

Read, listen, and answer the question following each step.

Reading   Read the following passage about an academic subject and take notes.

Mystery Shoppers

   Some businesses often check on the quality of customer service their employees provide. They hire mystery shoppers to do this. Mystery shoppers visit businesses. Then, they interact with the staff members. They record their interactions and list the positive and negative aspects. This allows managers to know how well their employees are working.

✎ **Note Taking**

Mystery shoppers

Result

Organization   Answer the following question by using the above information.

Q   According to the passage, what are mystery shoppers?

A

Listening   Listen to a lecture about the same topic and take notes.

✎ **Note Taking**

Problem

Solution

03-55

Responding   Make your response by using the above information.

Q   The professor explains her brother's problem at his restaurant. Explain how his experience is related to mystery shoppers.

- -

Your Response

Comparing   Listen to a sample response and compare it with yours.

03-56

Read, listen, and answer the question following each step.

Reading   Read the following passage about an academic subject and take notes.

Credence Goods

It is not possible to judge the quality of some purchases that people make. This is particularly true of vehicle repairs, supplements, and medical treatments. In many cases, people believe that a higher price for one of these purchases means that the quality is greater.

✎ **Note Taking**

Credence goods

Examples

Organization   Answer the following question by using the above information.

Q   According to the passage, what are credence goods?

A

Listening   Listen to a lecture about the same topic and take notes.

✎ **Note Taking**

Purchase

Reason

Result

03-57

Responding   Make your response by using the above information.

Q   The professor describes her experience with multivitamins. Explain how her experience is related to credence goods.

- -

Your Response

Comparing   Listen to a sample response and compare it with yours.

03-58

Reading   Read the following passage about an academic subject and take notes.

Teaser Campaigns

Some businesses use a series of ads to promote their goods or services. The ads are often cryptic and reveal little about the product. These teaser campaigns are meant to create suspense and excitement. This serves to increase publicity and to get people talking about the product.

✎ Note Taking

Teaser campaign

Result

Organization   Answer the following question by using the above information.

Q   According to the passage, what are teaser campaigns?

A

Listening   Listen to a lecture about the same topic and take notes.

✎ Note Taking

Advertisements

Result

03-59

Responding   Make your response by using the above information.

Q   The professor describes an advertisement by a fast-food restaurant. Explain how it is related to teaser campaigns.

Your Response

Comparing   Listen to a sample response and compare it with yours.

03-60

Exercise 5 Read, listen, and answer the question following each step.

Reading Read the following passage about an academic subject and take notes.

Division of Labor

Organizations frequently utilize a work process known as the division of labor. In this process, workers do not all do the same tasks. Instead, each person specializes in one or two tasks. This allows people to become specialists. They can therefore become better, faster, and more efficient at their work. This makes the organization run better.

✎ **Note Taking**

Division of labor

Result

Organization Answer the following question by using the above information.

Q According to the passage, what is division of labor?

A

Listening Listen to a lecture about the same topic and take notes.

✎ **Note Taking**

Problem

03-61

Result

Responding Make your response by using the above information.

Q The professor describes her experience working at a tech company. Explain how it is related to the division of labor.

- -

Your Response

Comparing Listen to a sample response and compare it with yours.

03-62

Read, listen, and answer the question following each step.

Reading Read the following passage about an academic subject and take notes.

Social Responsibility

Social responsibility refers to the actions of businesses that are taken to benefit society, not to make a profit. Companies that are socially responsible make sure that their practices help people and the environment. Companies may not make the most profit possible. However, by being socially responsible, they can help others.

✎ Note Taking

Social responsibility

Result

Organization Answer the following question by using the above information.

Q   According to the passage, what is social responsibility?

A

Listening Listen to a lecture about the same topic and take notes.

✎ Note Taking

Coffee shop's actions

Result

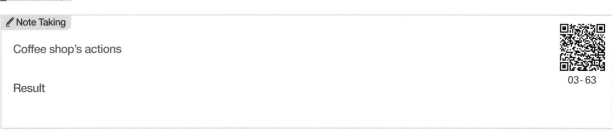

03-63

Responding Make your response by using the above information.

Q   The professor describes an announcement by a coffee shop. Explain how the announcement is related to social responsibility.

Your Response

Comparing Listen to a sample response and compare it with yours.

03-64

Exercise 1 Read, listen, and answer the question following each step.

Reading Read the following passage about an academic subject and take notes.

Invasive Species

Sometimes plants and animals native to one habitat go to another one. In recent years, they have been moving to new habitats because of human actions. In their new environment, these invasive species usually have no natural predators. So these animals may dominate the habitat, thereby causing other animals to die. And these plants may grow too much and cause harm to other plants.

✎ Note Taking

Invasive species

Animals

Plants

Organization Answer the following question by using the above information.

Q According to the passage, what are invasive species?

A

Listening Listen to a lecture about the same topic and take notes.

✎ Note Taking

Burmese pythons

Result

03-65

Responding Make your response by using the above information.

Q The professor discusses the Burmese python in Florida. Explain how it is related to invasive species.

Your Response

Comparing Listen to a sample response and compare it with yours.

03-66

Exercise 2 Read, listen, and answer the question following each step.

| **Reading**　Read the following passage about an academic subject and take notes.

Optimal Foraging Theory

To find food, all animals must expend energy. Sometimes they spend little energy if food is nearby. But other animals must spend large amounts of energy if getting food is hard. All animals try to optimize their foraging. This means that they spend the least amount of energy but get the most amount of food. If they fail to do this, they may become weak and even die.

✎ Note Taking

Optimal foraging theory

Result

| **Organization**　Answer the following question by using the above information.

Q　According to the passage, what is optimal foraging theory?

A

| **Listening**　Listen to a lecture about the same topic and take notes.

✎ Note Taking

First seal

Second seal

03-67

| **Responding**　Make your response by using the above information.

Q　The professor explains his experience watching seals at the beach. Explain how it is related to optimal foraging theory.

Your Response

| **Comparing**　Listen to a sample response and compare it with yours.

03-68

Exercise 3 Read, listen, and answer the question following each step.

Reading   Read the following passage about an academic subject and take notes.

Animal Coloration

Many animals are either brightly colored or have one color on their bodies that really stands out. In many cases, these colors are warnings to other animals. They indicate to predators that they should stay away because the colorful animals are dangerous in some ways. The colorful animals may have poison or venom, or they may have another type of strong defense.

✎ Note Taking

Animal coloration

Result

Organization   Answer the following question by using the above information.

Q   According to the passage, what is animal coloration?

A

Listening   Listen to a lecture about the same topic and take notes.

✎ Note Taking

Skunk

Action

Result

03-69

Responding   Make your response by using the above information.

Q   The professor describes an experience with his dog. Explain how this experience is related to animal coloration.

- -

Your Response

Comparing   Listen to a sample response and compare it with yours.

03-70

Exercise 4 Read, listen, and answer the question following each step.

Reading   Read the following passage about an academic subject and take notes.

Tree Communication

In recent years, scientists have learned that trees of the same species can communicate with one another. They believe that the communication comes through the roots. This communication enables trees to share information regarding pests and droughts with one another. They can also share nutrients through their root systems.

✎ Note Taking

Tree communication

Example

Organization   Answer the following question by using the above information.

Q   According to the passage, what is tree communication?

A

Listening   Listen to a lecture about the same topic and take notes.

✎ Note Taking

Situation

Action

03-71

Responding   Make your response by using the above information.

Q   The professor describes an incident with some of her trees. Explain how this experience is related to tree communication.

- -

Your Response

Comparing   Listen to a sample response and compare it with yours.

03-72

Read, listen, and answer the question following each step.

Reading   Read the following passage about an academic subject and take notes.

Vertical Migration

Migration is a fact of life for many species. Some animals engage in vertical migration. This is particularly true of aquatic animals. Some animals may swim higher or lower in the water at various times of the day. They may do this in order to avoid predators or to feed themselves.

✎ Note Taking

Group migration

Reasons

Organization   Answer the following question by using the above information.

Q   According to the passage, what is vertical migration?

A

Listening   Listen to a lecture about the same topic and take notes.

✎ Note Taking

Fishing boats

Squid actions

Reason

03-73

Responding   Make your response by using the above information.

Q   The professor talks about squid behavior. Explain how it is related to vertical migration.

Your Response

Comparing   Listen to a sample response and compare it with yours.

03-74

Exercise 6 Read, listen, and answer the question following each step.

Reading   Read the following passage about an academic subject and take notes.

Cyclic Population Change

The number of animal species in habitats undergoes almost constant change. In times of plenty, the number of prey animals may increase because they have more food. Then, the number of predators also increases since they have more animals to hunt. As the number of prey animals decreases, there are fewer predators because they have less to eat. This is a constantly repeating cycle.

> ✏ Note Taking
>
> Cyclic population change
>
> Example

Organization   Answer the following question by using the above information.

Q According to the passage, what is cyclic population change?

A

Listening   Listen to a lecture about the same topic and take notes.

> ✏ Note Taking
>
> Coyotes
>
> Rabbits

03-75

Responding   Make your response by using the above information.

Q The professor describes the relationship between coyotes and rabbits in a forest. Explain how it is related to cyclic population change.

Your Response

Comparing   Listen to a sample response and compare it with yours.

03-76

PART IV

Integrated Speaking Task 3
Lecture

....

In this task, you will be presented with a short lecture about an academic topic. Typically, the professor will provide two examples of the topic being discussed. Then, you will provide a response based upon what you heard. You will be asked to discuss the examples provided in the professor's lecture. You will be given 20 seconds to prepare your answer after the question is presented, and you will have 60 seconds to respond to the question.

Integrated Speaking Task 3 ▌
Lecture

Overview

For this task, you will first listen to a professor present a brief lecture on an academic subject, and then you will be asked a question about what you have heard. The topics will vary but not require you to have any prior knowledge of any field in particular. The professor will typically introduce a concept and go on to discuss examples about it. You will be asked to explain the main concept by using the given examples in the lecture.

Sample TOEFL iBT Task

Listen to a lecture about an academic subject.

Script

04-01

M Professor: We all know about the importance of conservation and keeping our environment clean. But how do we convince others to do the same thing? Well, there are many ways. But I want to tell you about two of the most effective ways. The first is by utilizing moral persuasion, and the second is by encouraging people to get involved by volunteering.

By utilizing moral persuasion, we can appeal to people's sense of morality. Does everyone remember Smokey the Bear? His motto was, "Only you can prevent forest fires." You probably remember the TV cartoon character, but did you know Smokey was a real bear? Some firemen saved him from a forest fire. The National Forest Service used the image of a cute bear cub to encourage people to protect their environment and not to start forest fires. They were using a cute animal to convey a moral message.

Now, how about volunteering? Have you ever volunteered to pick up trash on the side of the road? Didn't you feel great afterward? Sure, you did. You probably realized how much trash there was and how important it was to clean it up. If more people started volunteering to do this, they would reach the same conclusion. They'd get out, help clean, and realize they should be more responsible.

Q Using points and examples from the talk, explain two methods that the environmental movement uses to encourage people to care about conservation.

PREPARATION TIME
00 : 20 : 00

RESPONSE TIME
00 : 60 : 00

04-02

Sample Response

The professor mentions that environmentalists often use two ways to convince people that they should care about conservation. The first is to use moral persuasion. The professor mentions Smokey the Bear, who was used to help prevent forest fires. Smokey was a real bear that was saved from a forest fire, so the National Forest Service used his image as a cute bear cub to tell people they should be more concerned about protecting the environment. The other method that environmentalists use is to convince people to volunteer. When people volunteer, first they feel good about helping. In addition, they see for themselves how much work there is to do and how they need to help, so they become more responsible.

Listen to a lecture about an academic subject and answer the question following each step.

Listening

STEP 01 **Listening**   Listen to a lecture and take notes.

Script

W Professor: As the saying goes, necessity is the mother of invention. This means most of the things that have been invented were created because society needed them. For example, people needed to store food for long periods of time, so they invented cans to preserve the food. On the other hand, sometimes things are invented to provide more convenience for people. Bifocals were invented this way. Some people needed two pairs of glasses, one for normal vision and one for reading. So instead of using two different pairs of glasses, someone thought of combining the lenses into one frame.

04-03

✏ **Note Taking**

Subject   *Reasons for inventions*
          Necessity and when society needs them

Solution *Made out of necessity or for convenience*
          Want to store food, invented can; instead of two lenses, created bifocals

---

STEP 02 **Organization**   Make key sentences by using the above notes.

Key Sentences

1   *The saying that "necessity is the mother of invention" reflects the reality that things are created to solve serious problems.*

2   *However, some things are just created to make people's lives more convenient.*

Speaking

STEP 04 **Responding** Make your response by using the above information.

Q Using points and examples from the talk, explain why some things were invented.

Your Response

Things are created when they are necessary. For example, people created cans because they felt the necessity to store foods. Again, people created bifocals because they didn't want to carry two kinds of lenses. People create things they feel are necessities.

STEP 04 **Comparing** Listen to a sample response and compare it with yours.

Sample Response

When people come across problems that they need to find solutions for, they invent them. For instance, people invented cans because they needed to keep food from spoiling. Other inventions came about because people found easier ways of doing things. Bifocals were invented because one pair of glasses was more convenient to carry around than two pairs of glasses.

04-04

Unit 19 Economics

Exercise 1 Listen to a lecture and answer the question following each step.

Listening Listen to a lecture and take notes.

✎ Note Taking

Subject

Detail

04-05

Organization Make key sentences by using the above notes.

Key Sentences

1

2

3

Responding Make your response by using the above information.

Q Using points and examples from the lecture, explain the concept of initial price in economics.

Your Response

Comparing Listen to a sample response and compare it with yours.

04-06

Exercise 2 Listen to a lecture and answer the question following each step.

Listening   Listen to a lecture and take notes.

> ✎ Note Taking
>
> Subject
>
> Detail

04-07

Organization   Make key sentences by using the above notes.

Key Sentences

1

2

Responding   Make your response by using the above information.

Q   Using points and examples from the talk, explain the positive externality effect.

Your Response

Comparing   Listen to a sample response and compare it with yours.

04-08

Exercise 3 Listen to a lecture and answer the question following each step.

Listening Listen to a lecture and take notes.

✎ Note Taking

Subject

Detail

04-09

Organization Make key sentences by using the above notes.

Key Sentences

1

2

Responding Make your response by using the above information.

Q Using points and examples from the talk, explain the importance of store displays.

Your Response

Comparing Listen to a sample response and compare it with yours.

04-10

Exercise 4 Listen to a lecture and answer the question following each step.

Listening   Listen to a lecture and take notes.

✎ Note Taking	
Subject	
Detail	

04-11

Organization   Make key sentences by using the above notes.

Key Sentences

1

2

Responding   Make your response by using the above information.

Q   Using points and examples from the talk, explain how supply and demand affect society.

- -

Your Response

Comparing   Listen to a sample response and compare it with yours.

04-12

Exercise 5 Listen to a lecture and answer the question following each step.

Listening   Listen to a lecture and take notes.

> 🖊 Note Taking
>
> Subject
>
> Detail

04-13

Organization   Make key sentences by using the above notes.

> **Key Sentences**
>
> 1
>
> 2

Responding   Make your response by using the above information.

> **Q** Using points and examples from the talk, explain how recessions affect society.
>
> -
>
> **Your Response**

Comparing   Listen to a sample response and compare it with yours.

04-14

Exercise 6 Listen to a lecture and answer the question following each step.

Listening   Listen to a lecture and take notes.

✎ Note Taking

Subject

Detail

04-15

Organization   Make key sentences by using the above notes.

Key Sentences

1

2

3

Responding   Make your response by using the above information.

Q   Using points and examples from the talk, explain the different types of mentoring relationships.

- -

Your Response

Comparing   Listen to a sample response and compare it with yours.

04-16

Exercise 1 Listen to a lecture and answer the question following each step.

Listening Listen to a lecture and take notes.

✎ Note Taking
Subject
Detail

04-17

Organization Make key sentences by using the above notes.

Key Sentences

1

2

Responding Make your response by using the above information.

Q Using points and examples from the talk, explain how some foods can be altered to last longer.

Your Response

Comparing Listen to a sample response and compare it with yours.

04-18

Exercise 2 Listen to a lecture and answer the question following each step.

Listening   Listen to a lecture and take notes.

✎ Note Taking

Subject

Detail

04-19

Organization   Make key sentences by using the above notes.

Key Sentences

1

2

3

Responding   Make your response by using the above information.

Q Using points and examples from the talk, explain how ants and humans are alike.

Your Response

Comparing   Listen to a sample response and compare it with yours.

04-20

Exercise 3 Listen to a lecture and answer the question following each step.

Listening   Listen to a lecture and take notes.

> ✏ Note Taking
>
> Subject
>
> Detail

04-21

Organization   Make key sentences by using the above notes.

Key Sentences

1

2

Responding   Make your response by using the above information.

Q   Using points and examples from the talk, explain how scientists can figure out where climate changes occurred.

Your Response

Comparing   Listen to a sample response and compare it with yours.

04-22

Exercise 4 Listen to a lecture and answer the question following each step.

Listening Listen to a lecture and take notes.

✏ Note Taking

Subject

Detail

04-23

Organization Make key sentences by using the above notes.

Key Sentences

1

2

3

Responding Make your response by using the above information.

Q Using points and examples from the talk, explain how the asteroid impact theory accounts for the extinction of the dinosaurs.

Your Response

Comparing Listen to a sample response and compare it with yours.

04-24

Exercise 5 Listen to a lecture and answer the question following each step.

Listening Listen to a lecture and take notes.

✎ Note Taking

Subject

Detail

04-25

Organization Make key sentences by using the above notes.

Key Sentences

1

2

3

Responding Make your response by using the above information.

Q Using points and examples from the talk, explain how a foreign species can endanger a native species.

- -

Your Response

Comparing Listen to a sample response and compare it with yours.

04-26

Exercise 6 Listen to a lecture and answer the question following each step.

Listening Listen to a lecture and take notes.

✎ Note Taking

Subject

Detail

04-27

Organization Make key sentences by using the above notes.

Key Sentences

1

2

Responding Make your response by using the above information.

Q Using points and examples from the talk, explain how some animals survive in the desert.

Your Response

Comparing Listen to a sample response and compare it with yours.

04-28

○

Exercise 1 Listen to a lecture and answer the question following each step.

| **Listening** Listen to a lecture and take notes.

✎ Note Taking

Subject

Detail

04-29

| **Organization** Make key sentences by using the above notes.

Key Sentences

1

2

3

| **Responding** Make your response by using the above information.

Q Using points and examples from the talk, explain why children might enjoy doing art.

Your Response

| **Comparing** Listen to a sample response and compare it with yours.

04-30

Listen to a lecture and answer the question following each step.

Listening Listen to a lecture and take notes.

✏ Note Taking

Subject

Detail

04-31

Organization Make key sentences by using the above notes.

Key Sentences

1

2

3

Responding Make your response by using the above information.

Q Using points and examples from the talk, explain why it might be easier for children to learn a language than adults.

Your Response

Comparing Listen to a sample response and compare it with yours.

04-32

Exercise 3 Listen to a lecture and answer the question following each step.

Listening   Listen to a lecture and take notes.

✎ Note Taking

Subject

Detail

04-33

Organization   Make key sentences by using the above notes.

Key Sentences

1

2

Responding   Make your response by using the above information.

Q Using points and examples from the talk, explain how framing has been used to influence people.

Your Response

Comparing   Listen to a sample response and compare it with yours.

04-34

Exercise 4 Listen to a lecture and answer the question following each step.

Listening   Listen to a lecture and take notes.

🖊 Note Taking

Subject

Detail

04-35

Organization   Make key sentences by using the above notes.

Key Sentences

1

2

Responding   Make your response by using the above information.

Q   Using points and examples from the talk, explain the fundamental character judgment flaw.

- -

Your Response

Comparing   Listen to a sample response and compare it with yours.

04-36

Exercise 5 Listen to a lecture and answer the question following each step.

Listening Listen to a lecture and take notes.

✎ Note Taking

Subject

Detail

04-37

Organization Make key sentences by using the above notes.

Key Sentences

1

2

Responding Make your response by using the above information.

Q Using points and examples from the talk, explain how our points of view influence what we see.

Your Response

Comparing Listen to a sample response and compare it with yours.

04-38

Exercise 6 Listen to a lecture and answer the question following each step.

Listening Listen to a lecture and take notes.

✎ Note Taking

Subject

Detail

04-39

Organization Make key sentences by using the above notes.

Key Sentences

1

2

Responding Make your response by using the above information.

Q Using points and examples from the talk, explain two different kinds of memory.

- -

Your Response

Comparing Listen to a sample response and compare it with yours.

04-40

Exercise 1 Listen to a lecture and answer the question following each step.

Listening Listen to a lecture and take notes.

Note Taking

Subject

Detail

04-41

Organization Make key sentences by using the above notes.

Key Sentences

1

2

Responding Make your response by using the above information.

Q Using points and examples from the talk, explain how advertisers use strategies to sell their products.

Your Response

Comparing Listen to a sample response and compare it with yours.

04-42

Exercise 2 Listen to a lecture and answer the question following each step.

Listening Listen to a lecture and take notes.

✏ Note Taking

Subject

Detail

04-43

Organization Make key sentences by using the above notes.

Key Sentences

1

2

3

Responding Make your response by using the above information.

Q Using points and examples from the talk, explain how playing is good for children.

- -

Your Response

Comparing Listen to a sample response and compare it with yours.

04-44

Exercise 3 Listen to a lecture and answer the question following each step.

Listening Listen to a lecture and take notes.

✎ Note Taking

Subject

Detail

04-45

Organization Make key sentences by using the above notes.

Key Sentences

1

2

Responding Make your response by using the above information.

Q Using points and examples from the talk, explain how to be an effective teacher.

- -

Your Response

Comparing Listen to a sample response and compare it with yours.

04-46

Exercise 4 Listen to a lecture and answer the question following each step.

Listening   Listen to a lecture and take notes.

✏ Note Taking

Subject

Detail

04-47

Organization   Make key sentences by using the above notes.

Key Sentences

1

2

Responding   Make your response by using the above information.

Q   Using points and examples from the talk, explain how choosing colors is an important part of interior design.

Your Response

Comparing   Listen to a sample response and compare it with yours.

04-48

Exercise 5 Listen to a lecture and answer the question following each step.

Listening   Listen to a lecture and take notes.

✎ Note Taking

Subject

04-49

Detail

Organization   Make key sentences by using the above notes.

Key Sentences

1

2

3

Responding   Make your response by using the above information.

Q   Using points and examples from the talk, explain how scientists study animal intelligence.

Your Response

Comparing   Listen to a sample response and compare it with yours.

04-50

Listening   Listen to a lecture and take notes.

/ Note Taking

Subject

Detail

04-51

Organization   Make key sentences by using the above notes.

Key Sentences

1

2

3

Responding   Make your response by using the above information.

Q   Using points and examples from the talk, explain how to read a map.

Your Response

Comparing   Listen to a sample response and compare it with yours.

04-52

Exercise 1 Listen to a lecture and answer the question following each step.

▌**Listening** Listen to a lecture and take notes.

✎ Note Taking

Subject

Detail

04- 53

▌**Organization** Make key sentences by using the above notes.

Key Sentences

1

2

3

▌**Responding** Make your response by using the above information.

Q Using points and examples from the lecture, explain two reasons why birds make nests.

- -

Your Response

▌**Comparing** Listen to a sample response and compare it with yours.

04- 54

Exercise 2 Listen to a lecture and answer the question following each step.

Listening Listen to a lecture and take notes.

✎ Note Taking

Subject

Detail

04-55

Organization Make key sentences by using the above notes.

Key Sentences

1

2

3

Responding Make your response by using the above information.

Q Using points and examples from the talk, explain the benefits of young female rhesus monkeys taking care of infants.

Your Response

Comparing Listen to a sample response and compare it with yours.

04-56

Exercise 3 Listen to a lecture and answer the question following each step.

Listening Listen to a lecture and take notes.

✏ Note Taking

Subject

Detail

04-57

Organization Make key sentences by using the above notes.

Key Sentences

1

2

Responding Make your response by using the above information.

Q Using points and examples from the talk, describe the defense methods of porcupines and horned lizards.

Your Response

Comparing Listen to a sample response and compare it with yours.

04-58

Exercise 4 Listen to a lecture and answer the question following each step.

Listening Listen to a lecture and take notes.

✏ Note Taking

Subject

Detail

04-59

Organization Make key sentences by using the above notes.

Key Sentences

1

2

Responding Make your response by using the above information.

Q Using points and examples from the talk, describe two types of whales.

Your Response

Comparing Listen to a sample response and compare it with yours.

04-60

Exercise 5 Listen to a lecture and answer the question following each step.

Listening Listen to a lecture and take notes.

✏ Note Taking

Subject

Detail

04-61

Organization Make key sentences by using the above notes.

Key Sentences

1

2

Responding Make your response by using the above information.

Q Using points and examples from the talk, explain how snakes and bees use venom.

Your Response

Comparing Listen to a sample response and compare it with yours.

04-62

Exercise 6 Listen to a lecture and answer the question following each step.

Listening Listen to a lecture and take notes.

✎ Note Taking

Subject

Detail

04-63

Organization Make key sentences by using the above notes.

Key Sentences

1

2

3

Responding Make your response by using the above information.

Q Using points and examples from the talk, describe two plants that need little sunlight.

Your Response

Comparing Listen to a sample response and compare it with yours.

04-64

Exercise 1 Listen to a lecture and answer the question following each step.

Listening Listen to a lecture and take notes.

✏ Note Taking

Subject

Detail

04-65

Organization Make key sentences by using the above notes.

Key Sentences

1

2

Responding Make your response by using the above information.

Q Using points and examples from the lecture, explain two types of financing.

Your Response

Comparing Listen to a sample response and compare it with yours.

04-66

Listen to a lecture and answer the question following each step.

Listening   Listen to a lecture and take notes.

✎ Note Taking

Subject

Detail

04-67

Organization   Make key sentences by using the above notes.

Key Sentences

1

2

Responding   Make your response by using the above information.

Q   Using points and examples from the talk, explain two disadvantages of advertising.

Your Response

Comparing   Listen to a sample response and compare it with yours.

04-68

Exercise 3 Listen to a lecture and answer the question following each step.

Listening   Listen to a lecture and take notes.

✏ Note Taking

Subject

Detail

04-69

Organization   Make key sentences by using the above notes.

Key Sentences

1

2

Responding   Make your response by using the above information.

Q   Using points and examples from the talk, explain how stores can keep their customers.

- -

Your Response

Comparing   Listen to a sample response and compare it with yours.

04-70

Exercise 4 Listen to a lecture and answer the question following each step.

Listening Listen to a lecture and take notes.

✎ Note Taking

Subject

Detail

04-71

Organization Make key sentences by using the above notes.

Key Sentences

1

2

Responding Make your response by using the above information.

Q Using points and examples from the talk, explain two strategies for making advertisements.

Your Response

Comparing Listen to a sample response and compare it with yours.

04-72

Exercise 5 Listen to a lecture and answer the question following each step.

Listening Listen to a lecture and take notes.

✎ Note Taking

Subject

Detail

04-73

Organization Make key sentences by using the above notes.

Key Sentences

1

2

Responding Make your response by using the above information.

Q Using points and examples from the talk, explain how product packaging can show the value of an item.

- -

Your Response

Comparing Listen to a sample response and compare it with yours.

04-74

Exercise 6 Listen to a lecture and answer the question following each step.

Listening Listen to a lecture and take notes.

✎ Note Taking

Subject

Detail

04-75

Organization Make key sentences by using the above notes.

Key Sentences

1

2

Responding Make your response by using the above information.

Q Using points and examples from the talk, explain two features many ads emphasize.

Your Response

Comparing Listen to a sample response and compare it with yours.

04-76

Actual
Test

Actual Test

01

CONTINUE | VOLUME

05-01

Speaking Section Directions

 Make sure your headset is on.

This section measures your ability to speak about a variety of topics. You will answer four questions by speaking into the microphone. Answer as completely as possible.

In the first question, you will speak about a familiar topic. Your response will be scored on your ability to speak clearly and coherently.

In the next two questions, you will first read a short reading passage. This passage will go away, and you will then listen to a talk on the same topic. You will be asked about the information you have read and heard. You will need to combine information from the reading passage and the talk to provide a complete answer. Your response will be scored on your ability to speak clearly and coherently and how accurately you convey information about what you read and heard.

In the last question, you will listen to part of a lecture. You will be asked about what you have heard. Your response will be scored on your ability to speak clearly and coherently and how accurately you convey information about what you heard.

You may take notes while you read and while you listen to the conversations and lectures. You may use your notes to help prepare your response.

Listen carefully to the directions for each question. The directions will not be written on the screen.

For each question you will be given a short time to prepare your response (15 to 30 seconds, depending on the question). A clock will show how much preparation time is remaining. When the preparation time is up, you will be told to begin your response. A clock will show how much response time is remaining. A message will appear on the screen when the response time has ended.

Task **1**

05-02

Some people like to use a notebook computer. Others prefer to use a desktop computer. Which do you prefer and why? Please include specific examples and details to support your explanation.

PREPARATION TIME
00 : 15 : 00

RESPONSE TIME
00 : 45 : 00

Sample Response ❯

05-03

Task **2**

05-04

No Sports Activities on the Lawn

The lawn in front of the library has become a well-known symbol of our school. Many visitors pass by the lawn, and students like to relax there. The school budgets funds to maintain the lawn and to keep it uncluttered. But students playing games and holding sporting events there have damaged the grass, and students often leave the lawn littered with trash. The school, therefore, has decided to forbid students from using the lawn as a playing field. Let's keep this symbol of our school attractive and well groomed and a place we can all be proud of. This rule is effective immediately.

The woman expresses her opinion of the announcement made by the university. State her opinion and explain the reasons she gives for holding that opinion.

PREPARATION TIME
00 : 30 : 00

RESPONSE TIME
00 : 60 : 00

Sample Response ❯

05-05

VOLUME   HELP   NEXT

Task **3**

05-06

Disciplining Children

Theories on how to discipline a child fall into one of two categories: positive or negative reinforcement. Positive reinforcement involves rewarding a child for good behavior. Once a child learns that good conduct elicits praise, affection, or tangible rewards, the child will continue that behavior in order to receive further rewards. In contrast, negative reinforcement consists of punishing a child for behaving badly. Such penalties might include spanking, sending the child to her room, or forbidding the child to play with his friends.

The professor talks about some effective ways of giving positive reinforcement to children. Explain how the two examples in the lecture are related to disciplining children.

PREPARATION TIME
00 : 30 : 00

RESPONSE TIME
00 : 60 : 00

Sample Response ❯
05-07

Task 4

05-08

Using points and examples from the lecture, explain the processes of direct advertisement and indirect advertisement.

PREPARATION TIME
00 : 20 : 00

RESPONSE TIME
00 : 60 : 00

Sample Response »

05- 09

Actual Test

02

05-10

Speaking Section Directions

 Make sure your headset is on.

This section measures your ability to speak about a variety of topics. You will answer four questions by speaking into the microphone. Answer as completely as possible.

In the first question, you will speak about a familiar topic. Your response will be scored on your ability to speak clearly and coherently.

In the next two questions, you will first read a short reading passage. This passage will go away, and you will then listen to a talk on the same topic. You will be asked about the information you have read and heard. You will need to combine information from the reading passage and the talk to provide a complete answer. Your response will be scored on your ability to speak clearly and coherently and how accurately you convey information about what you read and heard.

In the last question, you will listen to part of a lecture. You will be asked about what you have heard. Your response will be scored on your ability to speak clearly and coherently and how accurately you convey information about what you heard.

You may take notes while you read and while you listen to the conversations and lectures. You may use your notes to help prepare your response.

Listen carefully to the directions for each question. The directions will not be written on the screen.

For each question you will be given a short time to prepare your response (15 to 30 seconds, depending on the question). A clock will show how much preparation time is remaining. When the preparation time is up, you will be told to begin your response. A clock will show how much response time is remaining. A message will appear on the screen when the response time has ended.

Task **1**

05- 11

Some people write letters or send email to keep in touch with their family and friends. Others use the telephone instead. Which do you prefer and why? Please include specific examples and details to support your explanation.

PREPARATION TIME
00 : 15 : 00

RESPONSE TIME
00 : 45 : 00

Sample Response ❯
05- 12

Task **2**

05 - 13

Exchange Student Program

Effective at the start of the fall semester, students will be offered the opportunity to study abroad as exchange students. Tuition and expenses are about the same as they are on campus, and students can choose either a one- or two-semester option. Housing will be provided, usually in a dormitory at the host institution. This program offers an excellent opportunity to learn a new language and to expand your academic horizons. You may also have the chance to work with some of the world's leading scholars. A list of participating universities and other details are available in the Placement Office.

The man expresses his opinion of the announcement made by the university. State his opinion and explain the reasons he gives for holding that opinion.

PREPARATION TIME
00 : 30 : 00

RESPONSE TIME
00 : 60 : 00

Sample Response ❯

05 - 14

Task **3**

05-15

Role Conflict

A role conflict occurs when different aspects of a person's life are incompatible. For example, a mother might feel competing pressures from her parental role and her occupational role. The time demands of caring for her child may make it impossible for her to meet the time demands of her job. The conflict can be resolved only by giving up one role or by making sacrifices in order to succeed in both. Thus, the mother may have to pay for childcare, or she may have to take a less demanding job.

The professor talks about some different roles people have had. Explain how these examples are related to role conflict.

PREPARATION TIME
00 : 30 : 00

RESPONSE TIME
00 : 60 : 00

Sample Response ❯

05-16

Task **4**

05-17

Using points and examples from the talk, explain two theories about how dinosaurs became extinct.

PREPARATION TIME
00 : 20 : 00

RESPONSE TIME
00 : 60 : 00

Sample Response ▶

05- 18

Appendix

Useful Expressions
for the Speaking Tasks

···

This part provides some essential expressions and collocations that
can be used in each unit. They will be given with sample sentences
through which their applications as well as their meanings can be
clarified. Once in your memory, these lexical chunks will help you
give sophisticated responses.

···

Useful Expressions for the Speaking Tasks

TASK 1 **Personal Preference**

1 Stating Your Preference

I prefer A to B
I **prefer** history **to** mathematics since I like old stories.
I **prefer** reading books **to** watching movies.

I like A better [more] than B
I **like** reading books **more than** watching television.
I **like** long trips **better than** short ones.

I'd rather A than B
I'd **rather** spend time with my family **than** go out with my friends.
I'd **rather** cook my own meals **than** eat out.

I think [believe] (that) A is better than B
I **think** going on a field trip **is better than** just studying at school.
I **believe** studying in a group **is better than** studying by myself.

In my opinion, A is better than B
In my opinion, action movies **are better than** romantic movies.
In my opinion, hanging out with my friends **is better than** watching TV.

Given the choice of A and [or] B, I would choose
Given the choice of watching the news on TV **and** reading it in the newspaper, **I would choose** the TV news.
Given the choice of owning a dog **or** a cat, **I would choose** to have a dog.

2 Giving Reasons

I prefer ~ because S + V
I **prefer** traveling abroad **because** I want to see other countries.
I **prefer** taking a car to going by taxi **because** it is more convenient.

There are several reasons why I prefer
There are several reasons why I prefer having few friends.
There are several reasons why I prefer history class.

The first reason is that S + V
The first reason is that I love to swim.
The first reason is that I can learn about great people.

The second reason is that S + V

The second reason is that people are friendlier in small towns.
The second reason is that I enjoy remembering facts.

The last [final] reason is that S + V

The last reason is that I don't have time to meet many people.
The last reason is that I can practice speaking other languages.

3 Giving Supporting Details

Comparing & Contrasting

S + V, but S + V

Playing video games is fun, **but** reading books is more fun.
I have traveled by train, **but** I like traveling by plane more.

S + V while S + V

I would prefer to live at my home **while** I would not like to stay in a dorm.
I enjoy scuba diving **while** other people prefer to go hiking on vacation.

On the other hand, S + V

On the other hand, I would rather join a school club.
On the other hand, talking on the phone is more convenient.

Although [Though] S + V, S + V

Although playing a musical instrument is fun, I do not have time for that.
Though many schools offer extracurricular activities, I am not interested in them.

Clarifying

That means (that) S + V

That means my grandparents ate healthier food.
That means that more people should recycle.

What I'm saying is (that) S + V

What I'm saying is that more people should volunteer.
What I'm saying is that camping is not fun for me.

TASK 2 **Reading & Conversation**

1 Stating the Speaker's Position

Agreeing

The man [woman] agrees with / The man [woman] agrees that S + V

The man agrees with the decision that class sizes will increase.
The woman agrees with the announcement that the library will close for repairs.

The man [woman] approves of

The man approves of the school's decision to change the grading policy.
The woman approves of the History Department's decision to hire some more professors.

The man [woman] supports

The woman supports the establishing of new clubs.
The man supports the decision to make a new dormitory.

The man [woman] thinks [believes] ~ is a good idea

The man thinks lowering the student activities fee is a good idea.
The man thinks requiring everyone to recycle is a good idea.

The man [woman] likes the idea of / The man [woman] likes the idea that S + V

The man likes the idea of requiring students to do extracurricular activities.
The woman likes the idea that students must volunteer in order to graduate.

Disagreeing

The man [woman] disagrees with / The man [woman] disagrees that S + V

The woman disagrees that many students are not playing sports.
The man disagrees with the argument that students should study in their rooms.

The man [woman] is against

The woman is against the university's decision to raise tuition by as much as five percent.
The man is against the announcement by the university that it will close one of the dormitories.

The man [woman] opposes

The woman opposes the increase in the prices of textbooks.
The man opposes making students take five classes a semester.

2 Talking about Reasons

He [She] gives two reasons why he [she]

She gives two reasons why she supports the decision.
He gives two reasons why he likes the news.

The [His, Her] first reason is that S + V

The first reason is that it will help the students.
His first reason is that nobody is interested in that topic.

The [His, Her] other reason is that S + V

The other reason is that it will be too expensive.
Her other reason is that she already has summer plans.

3 Quoting

According to the announcement [letter, article], S + V

According to the announcement, the library will be closing early every day.
According to the letter, students are too noisy at night.

The announcement [letter, article] says (that) S + V

The announcement says that the upcoming school holiday has been canceled.
The letter says that the dormitories are too noisy during exam periods.

According to the student [man, woman], S + V

According to the student, there is too much garbage on campus.
According to the woman, the school should help students try to find jobs.

He [She] mentions (that) S + V

She mentions that the biology labs are dangerous.
He mentions that the food at the cafeteria is not healthy.

He [She] points out (that) S + V

He points out that more night classes are needed.
He points out that there are many talented actors on campus.

He [She] argues (that) S + V

He argues that the school is making a big mistake.
She argues that tuition should not rise any more.

TASK 3 Reading & Lecture

1 Talking about the Topic

The reading defines A as B

The reading defines marsupials as kinds of mammals.
The reading defines pine trees as conifers.

According to the reading, S + V

According to the reading, customers buy more when there are pleasant scents.
According to the reading, animals have limited amounts of resources.

The professor explains

The professor explains what happened to her when she was a student.
The professor explains how advertising works.

The professor talks about

The professor talks about fixed action patterns.
The professor talks about a kind of paradox.

According to the professor, S + V

According to the professor, a variety of animals live in rainforests.

According to the professor, Internet marketing is becoming more popular.

The lecture is about

The lecture is about different marketing techniques.

The lecture is about how elephants communicate.

According to the lecture, S + V

According to the lecture, short-term memories can disappear quickly.

According to the lecture, the Internet has changed society.

2 Explaining the Details

Talking about Subtopics

There are two main A of B

There are two main types of memory.

There are two main kinds of marketing.

One is A, and the other is B

One is long-term memory, and the other is short-term memory.

One is online marketing, and there other is print marketing.

There are two (different) kinds of

There are two different kinds of horses in that area.

There are two different kinds of pandas.

The first (one) is A, and the second (one) is B

The first is hard to obtain, and the second is easy to get.

The first is found in South America, and the second is in Africa.

Talking about Examples

The professor talks about A as an example of B

The professor talks about the bicycle as an example of transportation.

The professor talks about the jaguar as an example of a rainforest animal.

The professor gives an example of A by discussing B

The professor gives an example of an online store by discussing a famous bookseller.

The professor gives an example of the harm of mining by discussing strip mining.

The professor bases his [her] example on

The professor bases his example on an experiment done in the past.

The professor bases her example on studies conducted in a laboratory.

The professor discusses ~ to demonstrate [illustrate]

The professor discusses photosynthesis to illustrate how plants get energy.

The professor discusses Mongolians to demonstrate how they live nomadic lives.

The first example shows how S + V

The first example shows how humans reached the Americas.
The first example shows how early ships were built.

Another example the professor gives is

Another example the professor gives is that of the camel.
Another example the professor gives is a study conducted on that medication.

TASK 4 Lecture

1 Stating the Topic of the Lecture

The lecture is (mainly) about

The lecture is mainly about bird nests.
The lecture is about animal defense methods.

The topic of the lecture is

The topic of the lecture is bioluminescence.
The topic of the lecture is geological formations caused by glaciers.

The professor talks about

The professor talks about animal adaptations to living in salt water.
The professor talks about two types of butterflies.

The professor discusses [explains]

The professor discusses different types of film shots.
The professor explains two famous naval battles.

According to the lecture [professor], S + V

According to the professor, tectonic plates often move.
According to the lecture, the universe is constantly expanding.

According to the lecture [professor], A refers to B

According to the lecture, controlled burns refer to fires that are set on purpose.
According to the professor, erosion refers to the removal of soil from the surface of the planet.

2 Explaining the Details

Talking about Subtopics

The professor says there are two ways (for something) to

The professor says there are two ways for flowers to attract insects.
The professor says there are two ways to mine coal.

The first (one) is A, and the second (one) is B

The first one is by using a shot, and the second one is by taking a pill.
The first is by sailing there, and the second is by walking across a land bridge.

According to the professor, there are two types [kinds] of

According to the professor, there are two types of performers.
According to the professor, there are two kinds of wolves in the forest.

According to the lecture, there are two factors in

According to the lecture, there are two factors in the success of a business.
According to the lecture, there are two factors in remembering something.

One is A, and the other is B

One is dangerous, and the other is relatively safe.
One is possible for anyone, and the other is only something experts can do.

Talking about Examples

The professor gives two examples of

The professor gives two examples of shellfish.
The professor gives two examples of famous photographers.

The professor explains ~ by giving two examples

The professor explains how geysers work by giving two examples.
The professor explains meerkat society by giving two examples.

The professor talks [speaks] about A as an example of B

The professor speaks about oil as an example of a fossil fuel.
The professor talks about the hippo as an example of a land animal comfortable in water.

The professor gives A as an example of B

The professor gives a cereal box design as an example of marketing.
The professor gives Impressionism as an example of an art movement.

The professor gives one more example that shows

The professor gives one more example that shows the different color varieties of the begonia flower.
The professor gives one more example that shows how glaciers can form.

The other example (of something) is

The other example of a dangerous animal is the great white shark.
The other example is the monarch butterfly.

Second Edition

How to
Master Skills for the

TOEFL® iBT
SPEAKING

Answers, Scripts, and Translations

Basic

How to
Master Skills for the

TOEFL® iBT

SPEAKING · Basic

Answers, Scripts,
and Translations

DARAKWON

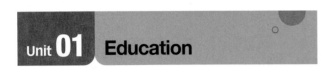

PART I Independent Speaking Task · **Personal Preference**

Unit 01 Education

Exercise 1A ··· p.12

Opinion

To tell the truth, I really prefer studying in groups.

Reasons

1 They help me stay focused on what I am studying.

2 They help me gain a wider perspective on the subject.

Responding

| Example |

해석

나는 혼자서 공부를 하는 것보다 그룹으로 공부하는 것을 더 좋아한다. 첫째, 그룹으로 공부를 하면 잘못된 것이 있는 경우 서로가 고쳐줄 수 있다. 둘째, 자기가 잘 아는 것들을 다른 사람에게 설명해 줄 수 있다. 그래서 나는 잘 알지만 다른 멤버들이 잘 모르는 부분이 있으면 내가 설명을 해서 그들이 잘 이해할 수 있도록 도울 수 있다.

Comparing

Sample Response 🎧 01-03

To tell the truth, I really prefer studying in groups. As a matter of fact, I often have trouble focusing when I study alone. But when I study in a group, I can focus much better. Another thing is that if you study in a group, you can hear more opinions about the subject at hand. So the group helps me gain a wider perspective on the issue I am studying.

해석

사실을 말하자면 나는 그룹으로 공부하는 것을 정말 좋아한다. 실제로 나는 혼자 공부를 하면 종종 집중하는데 어려움을 겪는다. 하지만 그룹으로 공부를 하면 훨씬 더 잘 집중할 수 있다. 다른 이유로는 그룹으로 공부를 하는 경우 주제에 대해 보다 많은 의견을 들을 수 있기 때문이다. 따라서 그룹에서는 내가 공부하는 주제에 관해서 보다 폭넓은 견해를 접할 수 있다.

Exercise 1B ··· p.13

Opinion

I prefer studying alone to studying in groups.

Reasons

1 I don't have to worry about everyone's schedule.

2 I can study by myself anywhere I want to.

Responding

| Example |

해석

내 경우에는 혼자 공부하는 것이 그룹으로 공부하는 것보다 훨씬 더 좋다. 우선 혼자 있으면 내가 공부하고 싶은 부분을 공부할 수 있다. 그룹으로 공부를 하면 내가 집중해야 할 주제를 공부하지 못하는 경우도 있을 수 있다. 게다가 나는 혼자서 공부를 하면 실력이 훨씬 더 빠르게 향상된다고 느껴진다. 다른 사람의 속도에 맞출 필요가 없기 때문에 혼자서 훨씬 더 빠르게 공부할 수 있다. 이로써 그룹으로 공부를 하는 경우보다 실력이 더 빠르게 향상된다.

Comparing

Sample Response 🎧 01-04

The way I see it, I prefer studying alone to studying in groups. Though studying alone may have some disadvantages, I feel that there are more benefits to it. First, when I study alone, I don't have to worry about everyone's schedule. I only need to think about myself and when I want to study. Second of all, I can study by myself anywhere I want to. I don't need a meeting place like study groups do. Instead, I can study anywhere I can find a place to sit down. That's very convenient for me.

해석

내가 생각하기에는 그룹으로 공부를 하는 것보다 혼자 공부하는 것이 더 낫다. 혼자서 공부를 하는 것이 몇 가지 단점이 있을 수도 있지만 내 생각에는 장점이 더 많다. 첫째, 혼자서 공부를 하면 다른 사람들의 일정을 걱정할 필요가 없다. 내 자신과 내가 언제 공부하고 싶은지만 신경을 쓰면 된다. 둘째, 내가 공부를 하고 싶은 곳이면 어느 곳에서나 공부를 할 수가 있다. 스터디 그룹에게 필요한 모임 장소가 필요하지 않다. 대신 앉을 수 있는 곳이면 어디에서나 공부를 할 수 있다. 그러한 점은 내게 매우 편리한 것이다.

Exercise 2A ··· p.14

Opinion

I like learning with teachers better than learning alone.

Reasons

1 They help me increase my knowledge.

2 They encourage me to enjoy learning.

Responding

| Example |

해석

내 생각으로는 선생님에게서 배우는 편이 항상 더 낫다. 우선, 선생님은 교재를 이해하기 위해 필요한 정보를 제공해 줄 수 있다. 어찌되었든 책이 모든 것을 가르쳐 줄 수는 없다. 다음으로, 선생님에게서 배우면 실수를 줄일 수 있다. 선생님은 학습 방향을 제시해 줄 수 있고, 우리가 너무 많은 실수를 하지 않도록 지도해 주실 수 있다.

2

Comparing

Sample Response 🎧 01-05

I like learning with teachers better than learning alone. The reasons for this are very simple. First, teachers help me increase my knowledge. After I read a book, a teacher can explain the important parts of it to me and help me understand it better. This makes me learn more. Teachers also encourage me to enjoy learning. Many of my teachers have made my classes so exciting. Because I enjoyed their classes, this made me like learning, so I learned a lot while also having fun.

해석

나는 독학을 하는 것보다 선생님에게서 배우는 것이 더 좋다. 이유는 매우 간단하다. 우선 선생님은 지식을 향상시켜 준다. 책을 읽은 후 선생님은 책에서 중요한 부분을 내게 설명해 주고 내가 더 잘 이해할 수 있도록 도움을 준다. 이로써 더 많이 배울 수가 있다. 또한 선생님은 내가 즐겁게 배울 수 있도록 만든다. 내가 겪은 많은 선생님들께서 수업을 매우 재미있게 하셨다. 수업이 재미있기 때문에 나는 배우는 것이 좋아졌고, 그래서 즐겁게 많은 것을 배울 수가 있었다.

Exercise 2B p.15

Opinion

As far as I am concerned, I like studying by myself better than studying with a teacher.

Reasons

1 I can be exposed to more sources of information.

2 I can learn how to study by myself.

Responding

| Example |

해석

내 경우에는 선생님에게서 배우는 것보다 독학을 하는 것이 더 좋다. 두 가지 이유 때문에 그렇게 생각한다. 첫째, 혼자 공부를 하면 나한테 가장 잘 맞는 학습법을 선택할 수 있다. 내가 선호하는 학습법은 선생님보다 내가 훨씬 더 잘 안다. 두 번째로, 혼자서 공부를 하면 지식을 쌓을 수 있을 뿐만 아니라 창의성도 기를 수 있다. 선생님에게서 배우면 선생님의 방법을 따라야 한다. 이는 창의적인 것이 아니다. 하지만 혼자서 하면 창의성을 기를 수 있다.

Comparing

Sample Response 🎧 01-06

As far as I am concerned, I like studying by myself better than studying with a teacher. One of the reasons is that if I study by myself, I can be exposed to more sources of information. Teachers usually give us only the material that they want us to read. We don't always get to read opinions or thoughts different from our teachers'. There is also another reason. It is that I can learn how to study by myself much better. Nowadays, more and more students are learning with private tutors, which is expensive. If I learn how to study by myself, I won't need to find a private tutor.

해석

나로서는 선생님에게서 배우는 것보다 혼자서 공부하는 것이 더 좋다. 한 가지 이유는 혼자 공부를 하면 보다 많은 정보를 접할 수 있기 때문이다. 선생님은 보통 우리가 읽기를 바라는 자료만 주신다. 선생님들과 다른 의견이나 사고는 항상 읽어볼 기회가 없다. 또 다른 이유도 있다. 혼자 공부하는 법을 더 잘 익힐 수 있다는 것이다. 요즘에는 점점 더 많은 학생들이 개인 과외 교사에게 배우는데, 이는 비용이 많이 드는 일이다. 혼자서 공부하는 법을 익힐 수 있다면 개인 과외 교사를 구할 필요가 없을 것이다.

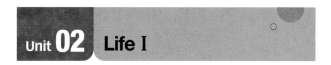

Unit 02 Life I

Exercise 1A p.16

Opinion

I'd rather save my money than spend it right away.

Reasons

1 I'll need a lot more money in the future.

2 By saving, I can build up my money to purchase better things in the future.

Responding

| Example |

해석

나는 돈을 저축하는 쪽을 택할 것이다. 우선 힘든 날을 대비하는 것은 언제나 중요하다. 나는 미래에 좋지 않은 일이 일어나는 경우를 대비하고 싶다. 지금 돈을 쓴다면 미래에 대한 대비를 할 수 없을 것이다. 뿐만 아니라 지금 저축을 하면 나중에 더 많은 돈이 생긴다. 그 돈을 은행에 맡기거나 다른 방식으로 투자를 함으로써 돈을 불릴 수 있다. 그렇게 하면 미래에는 더 많은 돈을 갖게 될 것이다.

Comparing

Sample Response 🎧 01-07

I'd rather save my money than spend it right away. First, I'll need a lot more money in the future. For example, I will have to buy a home and a car in the future and also pay for college. In addition, by saving, I can build up my money to purchase better things in the future. If I save money now, I can have more money in the future to purchase nicer clothes, furniture, or whatever I want to spend my money on.

해석

나는 지금 당장 돈을 쓰기보다 저축을 하고 싶다. 우선 나중에 훨씬 더 많은 돈이 필요할 것이다. 예를 들어 나중에는 집과 차를 사야할 수도 있고, 대학 등록금도

내야 할 수도 있다. 또한 저축을 하면 돈을 모아서 나중에 보다 좋은 것을 살 수도 있다. 지금 돈을 저축하면 나중에는 더 큰 돈을 갖게 되어 더 좋은 옷이나 가구, 혹은 그 돈으로 사고 싶은 어떤 것이던 살 수 있을 것이다.

Exercise 1B p.17

Opinion

As I see it, spending is better than saving.

Reasons

1 Pleasure today is just as important as being secure in the future.
2 You never know what will happen in the future, so you might as well enjoy the present.

Responding

| Example |

해석

나는 지금 당장 모든 돈을 다 쓰는 쪽을 택할 것이다. 첫째, 인플레이션 때문에 시간이 지날수록 화폐 가치는 감소한다. 따라서 내 돈의 가치를 최대한 실현할 수 있는 최선의 방법은 지금 당장 돈을 쓰는 것이다. 두 번째로, 돈을 사용하면 경제 성장에 도움이 될 수 있다. 사람들이 아무것도 사지 않는다면 기업들이 더 이상 제품을 만들 필요가 없다. 따라서 나 같은 사람들이 돈을 쓰는 것이 중요하다.

Comparing

Sample Response 🎧 01-08

As I see it, spending is better than saving. Here are the reasons why I feel that way. First, pleasure today is just as important as being secure in the future. Some people never spend their money. They just save and save and never buy anything. I'd rather enjoy spending my money. You also never know what will happen in the future, so you might as well enjoy the present. Therefore, if I see something that I want, I'm going to buy it now and not worry about saving my money.

해석

내가 보기에는 소비가 저축보다 낫다. 내가 그렇게 생각하는 이유는 다음과 같다. 우선 현재의 만족은 미래의 안전만큼 중요하다. 어떤 사람들은 절대 돈을 쓰지 않는다. 계속해서 모으기만 하고 아무것도 사지 않는다. 나는 오히려 기꺼이 돈을 쓸 것이다. 또한 나중에 어떤 일이 일어날지 결코 알 수도 없으니 현재를 즐기는 편이 더 낫다. 따라서 갖고 싶은 것이 보이면 지금 살 것이며, 저축에 대해서는 걱정을 하지 않을 것이다.

Exercise 2A p.18

Opinion

I prefer to spend my free time doing outdoor activities.

Reasons

1 Being outdoors gives me an opportunity to meet more people.
2 Doing outdoor activities gives me a chance to enjoy nature.

Responding

| Example |

해석

내 경우에는 항상 여가 시간을 야외에서 보내는 것을 좋아한다. 이유는 간단하다. 첫째, 야외 활동은 일반적으로 실내 활동보다 건강에 더 좋다. 스포츠, 조깅, 혹은 기타 건강에 좋은 여러 가지 활동들을 할 수가 있다. 둘째, 나는 주로 실내에서 생활하기 때문에 야외에서 시간을 보내는 것이 중요하다. 햇빛이 비치는 야외에서 시간을 보내는 것은 신체에 도움이 된다.

Comparing

Sample Response 🎧 01-09

I prefer to spend my free time doing outdoor activities. For one thing, being outdoors gives me an opportunity to meet more people. I can meet all kinds of people just by going to the park or walking around my city. Second of all, doing outdoor activities gives me a chance to enjoy nature. There are so many wonderful things outside that I should always take the time to enjoy them.

해석

나는 야외 활동을 하면서 여가 시간을 보내는 것을 좋아한다. 우선, 야외 활동을 하면 보다 많은 사람들을 만날 수 있는 기회가 생긴다. 공원에 가거나 시내를 돌아다니기만 해도 온갖 종류의 사람들을 만날 수 있다. 두 번째로, 야외 활동을 하면 자연을 즐길 수 있는 기회를 접할 수 있다. 야외에는 항상 시간을 내서 즐기고 싶은 멋진 것들이 너무나 많다.

Exercise 2B p.19

Opinion

I would say that I am partial to spending my free time doing indoor activities.

Reasons

1 I can only do the things I like doing indoors.
2 I prefer more laidback activities to physical ones.

Responding

| Example |

해석

나는 여가 시간이 생기면 실내에서 시간을 보내는 것을 좋아한다. 이유는 다음과 같다. 우선, 실내에서 여가 시간을 보내면 날씨 걱정을 할 필요가 없다. 그래서 비가 오거나 눈이 와도 계획에 차질이 생기지 않는다. 다음으로, 실내 활동은 일반적으로 야외 활동에 비해 안전하다. 따라서 실내에서 어떤 일을 할 때에는 그다지 걱정할 필요가 없다. 야외에 있는 경우라면 종종 안전에 신경을 써야 할 것이다.

Comparing

Sample Response 🎧 01-10

I would say that I am partial to spending my free time doing indoor activities. First of all, I can only do the things I like doing indoors. I enjoy playing the piano, and I can't do that outside. In addition, I prefer more laidback activities to physical ones. For example, I don't really enjoy sports, but I like surfing the Internet. I also enjoy watching television, which is another indoor activity.

해석

나는 실내 활동을 하면서 여가 시간을 보내는 것을 매우 좋아하는 편이다. 우선, 실내에서는 내가 좋아하는 것들을 할 수가 있다. 나는 피아노 치는 것을 좋아하는데, 야외에서는 그럴 수가 없다. 또한 나는 신체 활동보다 느긋한 활동을 더 좋아한다. 예를 들어 나는 스포츠를 그다지 좋아하지 않고 인터넷 서핑을 좋아한다. 또한 텔레비전을 시청하는 것도 좋아하는데, 이 역시 실내 활동에 해당된다.

Unit 03 School I

Exercise 1A p.20

Opinion

I've always believed that it's better to wear school uniforms.

Reasons

1 Students don't get any stress from worrying about their clothes.
2 Uniforms are less expensive than buying a large amount of clothes.

Responding

| Example |

해석

교복에 대해 말하자면, 나는 교복이 좋은 아이디어라고 생각한다. 첫 번째로 교복은 학생들에게 동질감을 가져다 준다. 학생들이 같은 교복을 입으면 교복 때문에 급우들과 더 큰 친밀감을 느끼게 될 것이다. 뿐만 아니라 교복은 애교심을 향상시킬 수 있다. 많은 학생들이 교복을 자랑스럽게 여기는데, 이러한 점은 또 다시 학교에 대한 자부심을 갖도록 만든다.

Comparing

Sample Response 🎧 01-11

I've always believed that it's better to wear school uniforms. In my opinion, if students have school uniforms, they won't get any stress from worrying about their clothes. They don't have to compare their clothes with those of others. All they have to do is wear their uniforms.

In addition, uniforms are less expensive than buying a large amount of clothes. Without uniforms, students need many different clothes to wear every day. So uniforms are much cheaper.

해석

나는 교복을 입는 것이 낫다고 항상 생각해 왔다. 내 생각에는 학생들이 교복을 입으면 옷에 대한 고민 때문에 생기는 스트레스가 사라질 것이다. 자신의 옷과 다른 학생의 옷을 비교할 필요가 없다. 그냥 교복을 입으면 된다. 또한 교복은 여러 벌의 옷을 사는 것보다 비용이 적게 든다. 교복이 없으면 학생들에게는 매일 입어야 할 서로 다른 옷들이 여러 벌 필요하다. 그렇기 때문에 교복이 훨씬 더 비용이 적게 든다.

Exercise 1B p.21

Opinion

In my opinion, schools should allow students to decide what clothes they will wear.

Reasons

1 Choosing their own clothes allows students to be more confident.
2 Students will study better if they are wearing comfortable clothes.

Responding

| Example |

해석

내 생각에 학생들은 자신이 원하는 것을 마음대로 입을 수 있어야 한다. 우선 자신의 옷을 입음으로써 학생들은 자기 자신을 표현할 수 있다. 학생들은 온갖 종류의 옷과 온갖 색상의 옷을 입고 싶어한다. 학교는 학생들이 개인으로서 자기 자신을 표현하는 것을 허용해야 한다. 게다가 교복은 학생들의 개성을 앗아간다. 학생들은 다른 사람이 입은 것과 똑같은 옷을 입고 싶어 하지 않는다. 대신, 교장 선생님이 입으라고 하는 옷이 아니라, 자신들이 좋아하는 유형의 옷을 입고 싶어 한다.

Comparing

Sample Response 🎧 01-12

In my opinion, schools should allow students to decide what clothes they will wear. First, teenagers are very self-conscious about their clothes. Choosing their own clothes will allow students to be more confident since they will like the clothes they are wearing. Students will also study better if they are wearing comfortable clothes. Many school uniforms don't look good and are uncomfortable to wear. Students should not be thinking about their clothes at school. Instead, they should be focusing on their schoolwork. So this is why they should be able to wear any kinds of clothes.

해석
내 생각에 학교는 학생들이 <u>스스로</u> 어떤 옷을 입을지 선택하는 것을 허용해야 한다. 우선 십대들은 자신의 옷에 대해 매우 신경을 쓴다. 학생들은 스스로 자신의 옷을 선택할 수 있다면 자신감이 커질 것인데, 그 이유는 자신이 입고 있는 옷을 좋아할 것이기 때문이다. 또한 학생들은 편안한 옷을 입음으로써 공부도 더 잘 하게 될 것이다. 많은 학교들의 교복들은 예쁘지도 않고 입기에 불편해 보인다. 학생들이 수업 중에 옷에 대한 생각을 해서는 안 된다. 대신 학업에 집중해야 한다. 따라서 이런 이유로 학생들은 어떤 옷이든지 입을 수 있어야 한다.

Exercise 2A ·· p.22

Opinion

In my opinion, students should have many short vacations rather than one long one.

Reasons

1 Students can do numerous seasonal activities during their many short vacations.

2 Students can rest up at various times all throughout the year.

Responding

| Example |

해석
나는 학생들이 한 번의 장기 방학보다 여러 번의 단기 방학을 갖는 것이 더 낫다고 생각한다. 두 가지 이유에서 그렇게 생각한다. 첫째, 장기 방학은 학습 흐름을 차단한다. 일단 학생들이 긴 방학을 보낸 후 다시 학교로 돌아오면 다시 수업에 익숙해지기까지 몇 주가 걸린다. 두 번째로, 여러 번의 단기 방학은 학생들의 스트레스 감소에 도움이 된다. 학교 생활은 많은 스트레스를 줄 수가 있기 때문에 학생들에게 두 달 마다 스트레스를 풀 수 있는 한두 주의 방학을 주는 것은 학생들의 스트레스를 줄일 수 있는 좋은 방법이 된다.

Comparing

Sample Response 🎧 01-13

In my opinion, students should have many short vacations rather than one long one. For one reason, students can do numerous seasonal activities during their many short vacations. This will allow them to enjoy their vacations much more. In addition, by having many short vacations throughout the year, students can rest up at various times. At the end of every semester, students are usually exhausted. However, if they had a short vacation in the middle of the semester, they wouldn't feel this way.

해석
내 생각에 학생들은 한 번의 장기 방학보다 여러 번의 단기 방학을 가져야 한다. 첫 번째 이유로, 여러 번의 단기 방학 동안 학생들은 다수의 계절별 활동을 할 수 있다. 그러면 학생들이 방학을 훨씬 더 재미있게 보낼 것이다. 또한, 1년 동안 많은 단기 방학을 보냄으로써 학생들은 여러 번에 걸쳐 휴식을 취할 수가 있다. 각 학기가 끝날 무렵에 학생들은 보통 녹초가 된다. 하지만 학기 중간에 단기 방학을 가진다면 그렇게 되지 않을 것이다.

Exercise 2B ·· p.23

Opinion

I'd rather have one long vacation than a lot of shorter ones.

Reasons

1 It is possible for students to get rid of all of their stress during this time.

2 Students can have enough time to take up hobbies or other activities.

Responding

| Example |

해석
내 경우에는 몇 번의 단기 방학보다 한 번의 장기 방학이 더 낫다. 장기 방학은 길기 때문에 학생들에게 여러 가지로 도움이 될 수 있다. 우선 학생들은 이러한 방학 동안에 장기간의 여행을 떠날 수 있다. 이러한 여행은 재미있을 뿐만 아니라 때때로 교육적이기도 하다. 실제로 학생들은 이러한 여행에서 학교에서 배우지 못한 것들을 배울 수 있다. 또한 장기 방학 동안에 아르바이트를 하는 것도 가능하다. 이로써 학생들은 미래를 위한 소중한 실무 경험을 쌓게 될 것이다.

Comparing

Sample Response 🎧 01-14

I'd rather have one long vacation than a lot of shorter ones. With a long vacation, it is possible for students to get rid of all of their stress during this time. They can just stay home, play with their friends, or attend a summer camp or someplace similar during this time. All of these activities help get rid of stress. In addition, during a long vacation, students can have enough time to take up hobbies or other activities. Because schoolwork usually keeps students busy, they need a long vacation to do things like learn to play a musical instrument, take dancing lessons, or play a sport.

해석
나는 여러 번의 단기 방학보다 한 번의 장기 방학이 낫다고 생각한다. 장기 방학이 있으면 학생들이 이 기간 동안 모든 스트레스를 날려 버릴 수 있다. 이 기간 동안 그냥 집에서 지낼 수도 있고, 친구들과 놀 수도 있으며, 혹은 여름 캠프와 같은 행사에 참가할 수도 있다. 이러한 모든 활동은 스트레스를 해소시켜 준다. 또한 장기 방학 동안 학생들은 취미 활동이나 기타 활동을 할 수 있는 충분한 시간을 가질 수 있다. 보통 학업 때문에 바쁘기 때문에 악기 연주를 배우고, 댄스 레슨을 받고, 혹은 운동을 하기 위해서는 학생들에게 장기 방학이 필요하다.

Unit 04 Multimedia

Exercise 1A ·· p.24

Opinion

I like to use the Internet more than the library.

Reasons

1 The Internet has the most up-to-date information.

2 It is easier to use the Internet than to use the library.

Responding

| Example |

해석

내 경험상 도서관에서 책을 이용하는 것보다 인터넷을 이용하는 것이 더 낫다. 첫 번째 이유는 인터넷이 더 편리하기 때문이다. 나는 집에 있는 컴퓨터를 이용해서 내가 원하는 모든 정보를 얻을 수 있다. 또한 인터넷에는 보다 많은 정보가 들어 있다. 나는 인터넷으로 전 세계 각지에서 온 정보를 얻을 수 있다. 도서관에서는 그런 일이 불가능하다.

Comparing

Sample Response 🎧 01-15

I like to use the Internet more than the library. For one thing, people are constantly updating the information found on the Internet. So the Internet has the most up-to-date information available. In addition, it is easier to use the Internet than to use the library. You must constantly look for different books in different places in the library, but you can find everything you need off the Internet just by using one computer.

해석

나는 도서관보다 인터넷을 이용하는 것을 좋아한다. 우선 사람들이 인터넷에서 찾을 수 있는 정보를 끊임없이 업데이트한다. 그래서 인터넷에서는 가장 최근의 정보를 얻을 수 있다. 또한 도서관보다 인터넷을 이용하는 것이 더 쉽다. 도서관에서는 계속해서 서로 다른 장소에서 서로 다른 책을 찾아야 하지만, 컴퓨터 한 대만 있으면 인터넷에서 필요한 모든 정보를 찾을 수가 있다.

Exercise 1B ·· p.25

Opinion

In my opinion, it's better to use the library than the Internet.

Reasons

1 A librarian can help me find whatever I'm looking for.

2 Sometimes the books in the library have information that the Internet does not.

Responding

| Example |

해석

내 경우에는 정보가 필요한 경우 도서관에서 책을 이용하는 것이 더 좋다. 우선, 책에 있는 정보들이 더 믿을만하다. 모든 책은 편집자가 검토해서 실수를 찾아낸 것이다. 하지만 인터넷에는 누구라도 정보를 올릴 수가 있다. 인터넷에서 읽을 수 있는 모든 정보를 항상 신뢰해서는 안 된다. 또한 책은 읽기가 더 쉽다. 나는 책을 읽을 때 책을 들고 읽는 것을 좋아한다. 컴퓨터 화면으로 글을 읽는 것은 때때로 불편하다.

Comparing

Sample Response 🎧 01-16

In my opinion, it's better to use the library than the Internet. First of all, a librarian can help me find whatever I'm looking for. This is convenient because it saves me time. When I use the Internet, it is sometimes slow because I am not sure how to find the information that I want. In addition, sometimes the books in the library have information that the Internet does not. Plus, most of my schoolwork only requires information from books in the library, not information from the Internet.

해석

내 생각에는 인터넷보다 도서관을 이용하는 것이 더 낫다. 우선 내가 찾는 것이 무엇이든 사서가 도움을 줄 수 있다. 이는 편리한 일인데, 이로써 시간을 절약할 수가 있다. 인터넷을 이용하는 경우에는 내가 원하는 정보를 어떻게 찾아야 할지 모르기 때문에 때때로 시간이 걸리기도 한다. 또한 인터넷에 나와 있지 않은 정보가 때때로 도서관 책에 나와 있는 경우도 있다. 게다가 대부분의 학교 과제물들은, 인터넷 정보가 아니라, 도서관의 책에 들어 있는 정보들만 요구한다.

Exercise 2A ·· p.26

Opinion

I believe that taking care of the basic needs of people is more important than developing better technology.

Reasons

1 A society with advanced technology will still have problems if it lacks basic needs.

2 Solving people's needs can eventually lead to the development of new technology.

Responding

| Example |

해석

내 생각에는 정부가 사람들의 기본적인 욕구를 충족시키는데 보다 많은 돈을 써야한다. 우선, 인간의 욕구는 기존 기술을 향상시키는 것보다 중요하다. 정부의 첫 번째 의무는 사람들을 돌보는 것이다. 다음으로, 정부가 아닌 민간 단체들이 자체적으로 기술을 개발할 수 있다. 실제로 이러한 단체들은 새로운 기술을 개발하는데 있어서 정부보다 훨씬 더 효과적인 경우가 많다.

Comparing

Sample Response 🎧 01-17

I believe that taking care of the basic needs of people is more important than developing better technology. I have two reasons for feeling this way. First, a society with advanced technology will still have problems if it lacks basic needs. A society is no good if the people using advanced technology don't have enough food to eat. Second, solving people's needs can eventually lead to the development of new technology. Once people have solved their own problems of food, health, and housing, they can devote their energy toward improving technology.

해석

나는 보다 나은 기술을 개발하는 것보다 사람들의 기본적인 욕구를 충족시키는 것이 더 중요하다고 생각한다. 여기에는 두 가지 이유가 있다. 첫째, 첨단 기술을 보유한 사회라도 기본적인 욕구가 충족되지 않으면 여전히 문제를 겪게 될 것이다. 첨단 기술을 사용하는 사람들에게 먹을 식량이 부족하다면 사회는 아무런 소용이 없다. 둘째, 사람들의 욕구를 해결해 주는 것은 결국 새로운 기술 개발로 이어질 수 있다. 사람들이 식량, 건강, 그리고 주거에 관한 문제를 해결하고 나면 자신들의 모든 에너지를 기술 개발에 쏟을 수 있다.

Exercise 2B · p.27

Opinion

In my opinion, priority should be given to developing technology.

Reasons

1 The country with the best technology will be able to dominate in this age of globalization.

2 We should not sacrifice the future for the needs of a small number of people.

Responding

| Example |

해석

나는 정부가 기술 개발에 최대한 많은 돈을 써야 한다고 믿는다. 첫째, 사람들은 정부에 의존하지 않고 스스로를 돌볼 수 있어야 한다. 열심히 일을 하면 자신의 욕구를 충족시킬 수 있다. 정부가 국민들의 사생활에 관여해서는 안 된다. 또한 첨단 기술은 모든 사람들의 삶의 질을 향상시킬 수 있다. 예를 들어 사람들이 더 나은 농법을 개발하면 식량이 보다 저렴해지고 풍부해질 수 있다. 그러면 사람들의 삶의 질이 올라갈 것이기 때문에 사람들은 정부에 의존할 필요가 없다.

Comparing

Sample Response 🎧 01-18

In my opinion, priority should be given to developing technology. For one thing, the country with the best technology will be able to dominate in this age of

globalization. Therefore, our government should invest as much as possible to develop new technology. Second of all, we should not give up on the future for the needs of a small number of people. For the most part, there are few people starving and without homes. The government should not sacrifice the needs of the many for the needs of the few. For these reasons, the government should invest in technology.

해석

내 생각으로는 기술 개발이 우선시되어야 한다. 우선, 최고의 기술을 가진 국가가 이 세계화 시대를 주도하게 될 것이다. 따라서 정부는 새로운 기술을 개발하기 위해 최대한 많이 투자를 해야 한다. 둘째, 소수의 사람들의 욕구를 위해서 미래를 포기해서는 안 된다. 대부분의 경우, 굶어 죽거나 집이 없는 사람들은 거의 없다. 정부가 소수의 욕구를 위해 다수에게 필요한 것을 희생해서는 안 된다. 이런 이유들로 정부는 기술에 투자해야 한다.

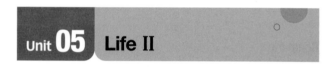

Unit 05 Life II

Exercise 1A · p.28

Opinion

I agree that it's desirable for friends to have different opinions from each other.

Reasons

1 I don't expect everyone to think the same way as me.

2 Debating my friends on their opinions is fun.

Responding

| Example |

해석

나는 그러한 주장에 동의한다. 내 생각으로는 친구들끼리 서로 다른 의견을 가지는 것이 바람직하다. 첫째, 나는 내 친구들로부터 새로운 아이디어 및 신념을 접할 수 있다. 이는 지식을 넓히는데 도움이 된다. 둘째, 나는 나와 다르게 생각하는 사람을 알게 되는 것을 좋아한다. 나는 친구들이 내 신념에 문제를 제기하는 경우 이를 방어하는 것을 좋아한다.

Comparing

Sample Response 🎧 01-19

I agree that it's desirable for friends to have different opinions from each other. For one thing, I don't expect everyone to think the same way as me. The world would be boring if everyone had the same opinions. Next, debating my friends on their opinions is fun. I get to hear their arguments, and I also get to strengthen mine by talking to them. That makes me a better thinker.

나는 친구들끼리 서로 의견이 다른 것이 바람직하다는 점에 동의한다. 우선 나는 모든 사람이 나와 똑같은 방식으로 생각할 것으로 기대하지 않는다. 모든 사람들이 동일한 의견을 가지고 있다면 세상은 지루할 것이다. 다음으로 나는 친구들과 의견에 대해 토론을 하는 것이 재미있다. 그들의 주장을 듣고 그들에게 이야기를 함으로써 내 주장을 강화시킬 수도 있다. 그러면 사고력을 기를 수 있다.

Exercise 1B p.29

Opinion

In my mind, it's not desirable for friends to have different opinions from each other.

Reasons

1 Different opinions lead to many arguments.

2 I don't want to know people who are very different from me.

Responding

| Example |

나는 친구들끼리 서로 의견이 다른 것이 바람직하다고 생각하지 않는다. 따라서 그러한 주장에 동의하지 않는다. 한 가지 이유는 공통으로 가지고 있는 것이 없으면 사람들과 친구가 될 수 없기 때문이다. 서로 의견이 다르기 때문에 같이 할 수 있는 것이 없을 것이다. 또 다른 이유는 종종 나와 의견이 다른 사람들을 친절하게 대하기가 힘들기 때문이다. 나는 내 친구들에게 친절할 수 있지만, 나와 의견이 다른 사람들에게는 친절할 수 없다.

Comparing

Sample Response 🎧 01-20

I disagree with the statement. In my mind, it's not desirable for friends to have different opinions from each other. Let me tell you why. First, different opinions lead to many arguments. I don't want to argue with my friends all the time. That would not be good. Second, I don't want to know people who are very different from me. Instead, I would rather know people who are similar to me. So I think having friends with similar opinions is much better than having friends with different opinions.

나는 그러한 주장에 동의하지 않는다. 내 생각에 친구들끼리 서로 의견이 다른 것은 바람직하지 않다. 그 이유를 말해 보겠다. 첫째, 의견이 다르면 많은 논쟁이 일어난다. 나는 친구들과 항상 말다툼을 하고 싶지는 않다. 그러면 좋지 않을 것이다. 둘째, 나는 나와 크게 다른 사람들을 알고 싶지가 않다. 오히려 나와 비슷한 사람들을 알고 싶다. 따라서 비슷한 생각을 사람들과 친구를 맺는 것이 서로 다른 생각을 가진 사람들과 친구를 맺는 것보다 훨씬 더 좋다고 생각한다.

Exercise 2A p.30

Opinion

I agree with the statement because it's better to work after high school than to attend college.

Reasons

1 A person can take a break from school before returning to studying.

2 Many people need money for tuition since school is so expensive nowadays.

Responding

| Example |

나는 고등학교 졸업 후 1년 동안 일을 하는 것이 바로 대학에 진학하는 것보다 더 좋다는 점에 동의한다. 우선 대학에 가기 전에 돈을 벌 수 있다. 돈을 저축함으로써 이후 대학에 다니는 동안 아르바이트를 하지 않아도 될 것이다. 또한 일을 함으로써 경험을 쌓을 수도 있다. 그러면 대학 졸업 후 일자리를 찾을 때 도움이 될 것이다.

Comparing

Sample Response 🎧 01-21

I agree with the statement because it's better to work after high school than to attend college. One reason is that a person can take a break from school before returning to studying. High school is difficult for most people. So taking a year off can help them recover. A second reason is that many people need money for tuition since school is so expensive nowadays. By saving the money made at a job, a person can help pay all of the school fees in college.

나는 고등학교 졸업 후 대학에 진학하는 것보다 일을 하는 것이 더 낫다는 주장에 동의한다. 한 가지 이유는 다시 학업에 종사하기에 앞서 휴식을 취할 수가 있기 때문이다. 고등학교 시절은 대부분의 사람들에게 힘든 시기이다. 따라서 1년 동안 휴식을 취하면 회복하는데 도움이 될 수 있다. 두 번째 이유는 요즘 등록금이 너무나 비싸서 많은 사람들이 학비로 쓸 돈을 필요로 하기 때문이다. 일을 해서 번 돈을 저축한다면 대학 등록금을 모두 납부할 수 있을 것이다.

Exercise 2B p.31

Opinion

I disagree because I would much rather go straight to college than take a year off after high school.

Reasons

1 I just want to get college over with as quickly as possible.

2 I don't want to get out of the habit of studying.

Responding

| Example |

해석

고등학교 졸업 후 바로 대학에 진학하는 것이 훨씬 더 좋기 때문에 나는 그러한 주장에 동의하지 않는다. 두 가지 이유에서 그렇게 생각한다. 첫째, 휴식을 취한다면 나는 고등학교에서 배운 것들을 잊어 버릴지도 모른다. 따라서 1년을 쉬고 대학에 진학을 하는 것이 내게는 너무나 힘든 일이 될 수 있다. 둘째, 대학을 빨리 마칠 수록 더 빨리 취직을 할 수가 있다. 나는 가능한 빨리 경력을 쌓고 싶다. 따라서 곧장 대학에 진학하는 것을 더 선호한다.

Comparing

Sample Response 🎧 01-22

I disagree because I would much rather go straight to college than take a year off after high school. Let me tell you why. For starters, I just want to get college over with as quickly as possible. College is expensive and difficult, so I want to go straight to it and finish it fast. Additionally, I don't want to get out of the habit of studying. If I take a year off, I could lose my study habits. Then, when I go back to school, I might not get good grades.

해석

고등학교 졸업 후 1년을 쉬는 것보다 바로 대학에 입학하는 편이 더 낫기 때문에 나는 동의하지 않는다. 이유를 설명하겠다. 우선 나는 최대한 빨리 대학을 마치고 싶다. 대학 과정은 비싸고 어렵기 때문에 나는 바로 입학을 해서 빨리 마치고 싶다. 게다가 나는 공부하는 습관을 잊어버리고 싶지 않다. 만약 1년을 쉰다면 나는 공부 습관을 잊어버릴 수도 있다. 그러면 다시 학교로 돌아왔을 때 좋은 성적을 받지 못할 수도 있을 것이다.

Unit 06 School II

Exercise 1A p.32

Opinion

I believe it is best that students only take classes in their majors and related fields.

Reasons

1 Students can become experts in their fields quickly.
2 Students will only use those subjects at their future jobs.

Responding

| Example |

해석

나는 학생들이 전공 및 전공 관련 분야의 수업만 들어야 한다는 점에 동의한다. 우선 학생들은 자신의 전공을 최대한 많이 배워야 한다. 전공 및 전공 관련 분야의 수업만 들음으로써 해당 주제들을 매우 잘 배울 수 있다. 또한 학생들은 자신

의 전공에 집중함으로써 좋은 일자리를 구할 수 있다. 이는 그들이 추후에 성공을 하고 돈을 버는데 도움이 될 것이다.

Comparing

Sample Response 🎧 01-23

I believe it is best that students only take classes in their majors and related fields. First, students can become experts in their fields quickly. My uncle only studied his major at his school, and now he is one of the top people in his field. In addition, students will only use those subjects at their future jobs. My uncle doesn't need knowledge from other subjects to do his job. He only needs to know about his major. So he had no need to study other subjects.

해석

나는 학생들이 전공 및 전공 관련 분야의 수업만 듣는 것이 최선이라고 생각한다. 먼저 학생들이 자신의 분야에서 빠르게 전문가가 될 수 있다. 우리 삼촌은 학교에서 전공만 공부했는데, 현재 자신의 분야에서 최고 중 한 명이다. 또한 학생들은 장래의 직장에서 그러한 과목만을 활용하게 될 것이다. 우리 삼촌은 일을 할 때 다른 과목의 지식을 필요로 하지 않는다. 자신의 전공에 대해서만 알면 된다. 따라서 다른 과목들을 공부할 필요가 없었다.

Exercise 1B p.33

Opinion

I disagree with the statement about what classes students should take.

Reasons

1 It is more interesting to study many different subjects.
2 Students may change their minds about their majors in the future.

Responding

| Example |

해석

나는 학생들이 자신의 전공 및 전공 관련 분야의 수업만 들어야 한다는 점에 동의하지 않는다. 우선 학생들은 여러 종류의 수업을 들음으로써 전인격을 갖춘 사람이 될 수 있다. 이로써 단 하나나 두 개가 아닌, 여러 다양한 분야의 지식을 쌓게 될 것이다. 또한 학생들이 다른 수업에서 배웠던 지식이 나중에 필요할 수도 있다. 예를 들어 다른 분야에서 일자리를 구할 수도 있을 것이다. 그런 경우라면 전공 이외의 과목에 대한 지식이 있어야 할 것이다.

Comparing

Sample Response 🎧 01-24

I disagree with the statement about what classes students should take. In fact, I believe students should take a wide variety of classes. One reason is that it is more interesting to study many different subjects. My sister studied history, art, chemistry, math, and many other subjects at her college. She really loved every subject. In addition, students may change their minds about their majors in the future. In that case, they will need to take classes in other fields.

해석

나는 학생들이 어떤 수업을 들어야 하는지에 관한 그러한 주장에 동의하지 않는다. 실제로 나는 학생들이 다양한 수업을 들어야 한다고 믿는다. 한 가지 이유는 여러 다양한 과목들을 공부하는 것이 보다 흥미롭기 때문이다. 내 여동생은 대학을 다닐 때 역사, 예술, 화학, 수학, 그리고 기타 여러 과목들을 배웠다. 그녀는 정말로 모든 과목을 다 좋아했다. 또한 학생들은 추후에 전공에 관한 자신의 생각을 바꿀 수도 있다. 그런 경우에는 다른 분야의 수업을 들어야 할 것이다.

Exercise 2A ·· p.34

Opinion

Universities definitely cost too much to attend these days.

Reasons

1 Many parents cannot afford to send their children to university.

2 Students do not get enough value for the prices they pay.

Responding

| Example |

해석

나는 요즘 대학 등록금이 너무 높다는 점에 동의한다. 우선 학비가 해마다 계속 오르고 있다. 하지만 학위의 가치는 그대로이다. 이는 학비가 너무 높다는 점을 의미한다. 또한 많은 학생들이 수업료를 납부하기 위해 대출을 받아야만 한다. 심지어 좋은 직장을 가진 부모들조차 학비를 지원할 정도의 충분한 돈을 가지고 있지 못하다. 대학 등록금이 너무 높다는 점은 명백해 보인다.

Comparing

Sample Response 🎧 01-25

Universities definitely cost too much to attend these days. For one thing, many parents cannot afford to send their children to university. My aunt and uncle both have good jobs that pay well. But they could not afford to pay for their two children to go to college. In addition, students do not get enough value for the prices they pay. Too many professors don't teach well. So lots of students don't learn much in their classes. Because they are not getting enough value, it proves that universities are charging too much for tuition.

해석

요즘 대학들은 정말로 너무 높은 등록금을 책정하고 있다. 우선 많은 부모들이 자녀를 대학에 보낼 수 있을 정도로 여유가 있지 못하다. 우리 고모와 고모부는 모두 보수를 많이 주는 좋은 직업을 가지고 있다. 하지만 두 명의 자녀를 대학에 보낼 수 있을 정도로 여유가 있지는 않았다. 또한 학생들은 자신들이 내는 학비

만큼의 가치를 보상받지 못한다. 너무 많은 교수들이 잘 가르치지 못한다. 그래서 많은 학생들이 수업에서 많이 배우지 못한다. 학생들이 충분한 가치를 보상받지 못한다는 점에서, 대학들이 수업료로 너무 많은 비용을 책정하고 있다는 점이 입증된다.

Exercise 2B ·· p.35

Opinion

In my opinion, university tuition does not cost too much money.

Reasons

1 Universities often provide financial aid for students.

2 Only the most exclusive universities are really expensive.

Responding

| Example |

해석

나는 요즘 대학 등록금이 너무 높다고 생각하지 않는다. 따라서 나는 그러한 주장에 동의하지 않는다. 한 가지 이유를 들겠다. 우수한 많은 대학들이 합당한 등록금을 책정하고 있다. 내 사촌은 자신의 고향에 있는 우수한 대학에 입학했다. 그는 그곳 학비가 실제로 낮다고 말했다. 또 다른 이유는 학생들이 받을 수 있는 장학금이 많기 때문이다. 우리 형은 대학에서 장학금을 받았다. 그래서 학비를 전혀 내지 않고 학교를 다녔다.

Comparing

Sample Response 🎧 01-26

In my opinion, university tuition does not cost too much money. I feel that way for two reasons. The first reason is that universities often provide financial aid for students. My sister went to a top school. The school gave her grants that covered half of the tuition. So she didn't have to pay very much money. Additionally, only the most exclusive universities are really expensive. There are plenty of universities that are affordable. They may not be the best ones, but students can still get good educations at them. And the prices at these schools are not high.

해석

내 생각으로, 대학 등록금이 그렇게 높은 것은 아니다. 두 가지 이유에서 그렇게 생각한다. 첫 번째 이유는 대학들이 종종 학생들에게 재정적인 지원을 해 주기 때문이다. 내 여동생은 일류 학교를 다녔다. 그 학교는 여동생에게 등록금의 절반에 해당되는 장학금을 지급했다. 그래서 여동생은 그다지 많은 돈을 낼 필요가 없었다. 또한 초일류 대학들의 학비만 실제로 비쌀 뿐이다. 등록금이 합당한 대학들도 많이 존재한다. 최고의 대학은 아닐 수 있지만, 학생들은 그곳에서 좋은 교육을 받을 수 있다. 그리고 그러한 학교의 등록금은 비싸지 않다.

Unit 07 School Facilities I

Exercise 1 .... p.42

Reading

해석

체육관 확장 관련 회의

체육과에서 체육관을 확장할 계획입니다. 체육관 확장을 위한 가능한 방법을 모색하기 위해 금요일에 공개 회의가 열릴 예정입니다. 안건에는 새로운 웨이트 룸, 트랙, 그리고 수영장 신설이 포함될 것입니다. 오후 7시에 참석하셔서 의견을 밝혀 주시기 바랍니다.

> **Note Taking**
>
> **Topic** Meeting to expand the gym
> **Reason** To discuss weight room, track, and swimming pool

Organization

The Athletic Department will expand the gym. The expansion may include features like a new weight room, a track, and a swimming pool.

Listening

Script 02-05

> **M Student:** The gym is being expanded. I hope the school adds a few more basketball hoops. I hate going to play and finding that all the courts have already been taken.
>
> **W Student:** I think expanding the gym is a waste of money. The gym is big enough. We can use that money elsewhere. For example, the school could buy more library books or give more scholarships to deserving students.

해석

M Student: 체육관이 확장될 예정이네. 나는 학교측이 농구 골대를 몇 개 더 늘려 주면 좋겠어. 농구를 하러 갔는데 이미 모든 농구 코트가 다 차 있으면 너무 싫거든.

W Student: 나는 체육관 확장이 돈 낭비라고 생각해. 체육관은 충분히 크니까. 우리는 그 돈을 다른 곳에 쓸 수 있을 거야. 가령 도서관의 책을 더 구비한다거나 자격이 있는 학생들에게 장학금을 더 지급할 수도 있지.

> **Note Taking**
>
> | **Man** | **Woman** |
> |---|---|
> | **Opinion** Wants the gym to expand | **Opinion** Does not want the gym to expand |
> | **Reason** He wants more basketball hoops in the gym. | **Reason** The gym is already big enough. The school should spend the money elsewhere like for books or scholarships. |

Comparing

Sample Response 02-06

The woman disagrees with the expansion plans for the gym. She thinks the gym is big enough and that the school should spend the money elsewhere, like for purchasing books or offering scholarships.

해석

여자는 체육관 확장 계획에 찬성하지 않는다. 그녀는 체육관이 충분히 크다고 생각하며, 학교측은 그 돈을 다른 곳에, 예컨대 도서 구매나 장학금 지급을 위해 써야 한다고 생각한다.

Exercise 2 .... p.43

Reading

해석

새 방송 장비 구입

방송실이 드디어 장비를 교체합니다. 우리 장비는 너무 오래 되었고 구형입니다. 그래서 기존의 모든 장비를 저렴한 가격에 판매할 것입니다. 이번 달 17일까지 모든 장비를 판매해야 합니다. 장비가 다 팔리기 전에 빨리 오시기 바랍니다.

> **Note Taking**
>
> **Topic** Changing broadcasting studio equipment
> **Reason** Current equipment is old and outdated

Organization

The broadcasting studio is going to replace its current equipment because it is too old and outdated. The studio will sell it at cheap rates because it needs space for the new equipment.

Listening

Script 02-07

> **W Student:** Here's another horrible idea by the school. Instead of building a lounge for the students, which we definitely need, the school is purchasing new studio equipment.
>
> **M Student:** I know. No one ever uses the studio. Talk about a waste of money. The school should have let us vote on this matter.

해석

W Student: 학교에서 또 다시 말도 안 되는 아이디어를 내 놓았어. 학생들에게 절대적으로 필요한 휴게실을 만드는 대신 새 방송 장비를 구매하려고 하는군.

M Student: 나도 알아. 방송실을 이용하는 사람은 아무도 없는데. 돈 낭비일 뿐이지. 학교측은 이 문제에 대해서 투표를 실시해야 해.

✏ Note Taking

Woman	Man
Opinion Thinks the school should not spend the money on the equipment	**Opinion** Thinks the school should not spend the money on the equipment
Reason Wants the school to build a lounge for the students	**Reason** Believes that no one uses the studio

Comparing

Sample Response 🎧 02-08

The woman is not happy with the announcement. She thinks that the money could be put to better use by building a much-needed lounge for the students.

해석

여자는 공지에 불만을 가지고 있다. 그녀는 그 돈이 학생들에게 곡 필요한 휴게실을 짓는데 쓰여야 한다고 생각한다.

Exercise 3 .... p.44

Reading

해석

미대 건물의 리모델링 공사

대학 본부는 미대 건물을 리모델링 하기로 결정했습니다. 학교는 학생들에게 양질의 교육을 제공하는 것에 자부심을 갖고 있기 때문에 미대 건물은 최고 수준의 최신 설비를 갖추게 될 것입니다. 이번 공사로 본교는 계속해서 경쟁력을 갖출 수 있고, 본교 학생들에게 합리적인 비용으로 계속 우수한 교육을 제공하게 될 것입니다.

✏ Note Taking

Topic Renovating the art building

Reason To enable the school to remain competitive with other schools

Organization

The school is planning to renovate the art building in order to stay competitive with other schools in terms of facilities.

Listening

Script 🎧 02-09

W Student: I think it is good that the school is renovating the art building. It needs bigger windows so that more light can get inside. It is too dim and dark in there.

M Student: I completely agree. Everyone knows that lighting is everything, especially when you're painting still lifes or portraits. It would be nice to have walls that aren't so drab, too. They make it hard for me to concentrate whenever I'm there for too long.

해석

W Student: 미대 건물을 리모델링한다니 좋은 일인 것 같아. 건물 안으로 햇빛이 더 많이 들어올 수 있도록 창문이 더 커야 할 거야. 그곳 내부는 너무 어둡고 깜깜하거든.

M Student: 전적으로 동감이야. 특히 정물화나 초상화를 그리는 경우, 조명이 가장 중요하다는 점은 누구나 아는 사실이지. 또한 벽이 너무 칙칙하지 않았으면 좋겠어. 오랫동안 건물 안에 있을 때마다 벽 때문에 집중하기가 힘들어.

✏ Note Taking

Woman	Man
Opinion Is glad the school will renovate the art building	**Opinion** Is glad the school will renovate the art building
Reason Wants the building to have bigger windows to let more light come inside	**Reason** Thinks the building needs better lighting and more colorful walls

Comparing

Sample Response 🎧 02-10

The man is pleased with the announcement. He thinks that the art building needs better lighting so that the art students can paint better. He also wants the walls to be less drab since they make it hard for him to concentrate for a long period of time.

해석

남자는 공지에 대해 만족해한다. 그는 미대 학생들이 그림을 더 잘 그리기 위해서는 미대 건물의 조명이 개선되어야 한다고 생각한다. 또한 벽 때문에 장시간 집중하기가 힘들다는 이유에서 벽이 덜 칙칙해지기를 바란다.

Exercise 4 .... p.45

Reading

해석

전공에 따른 기숙사 배정

기숙사 사무실은 전공에 따라 학생들에게 기숙사를 배정하기로 결정했습니다. 기숙사 사무실은 이로 인해 학교의 학구적 분위기가 개선되고 부적절한 행동이 감소될 것으로 기대합니다. 복수 전공자는 자신이 거주하고 싶은 기숙사를 선택할 수 있습니다.

✏ Note Taking

Topic Placing students in dormitories according to their majors

Reason To improve the academic environment and to decrease inappropriate behavior

Organization

The students will be placed in dormitories depending on their majors because the Residential Life Office feels it will improve the academic environment and decrease inappropriate behavior.

Listening

Script 🎧 02-11

> **W Student**: I don't like this. I like living with students with majors different from mine. When we talk, I learn a lot from students who have different majors. What I mean to say is that we are helping each other.
>
> **M Student**: I agree with you. But now we won't get that chance. We will be deprived of the opportunity to experience new concepts and ideas that we need to be exposed to.

해석

W Student: 이 생각은 마음에 들지 않는데. 나는 나와 전공이 다른 학생들과 지내는 것이 좋아. 대화를 하다 보면 전공이 다른 학생들에게서 많은 걸 배우게 되지. 내 말은, 서로가 도움을 주고 받는다는 거야.

M Student: 나도 그렇게 생각해. 하지만 이제 그럴 일이 없겠군. 우리가 접해야 하는 새로운 개념이나 아이디어를 경험할 기회가 없어질 테니까.

✎ Note Taking

Woman	Man
Opinion Thinks the university is making a bad decision	**Opinion** Thinks the university is making a bad decision
Reason Is possible for students with different majors to help each other	**Reason** Can learn new concepts and ideas by talking to students with other majors

Comparing

Sample Response 🎧 02-12

> The woman dislikes the announcement because she enjoys talking to students with other majors and feels that she can learn from them. She also believes that students can help one another even though their majors are different.

해석

여자는 전공이 다른 학생들과 대화하기를 좋아하고 그들로부터 배울 수 있는 것이 있다고 생각하기 때문에 공지를 반기지 않는다. 또한 그녀는 전공이 달라도 서로에게 도움을 줄 수 있다고 생각한다.

Reading

해석

교내 미술관 폐쇄

등록생의 증가로 학교 당국은 교내에 여러 가지 변화를 주기로 결정했습니다. 이 중 첫 번째는 교내 미술관을 폐쇄하고 이곳을 특별 행정실로 바꾸는 것이 될 것입니다. 현재 미술관에 전시 중인 학생들의 작품은 2주 내에 작가들에 의해 수거되어야 하며, 그렇지 않은 경우에는 이를 처리하기 위해 다른 조치들이 취해질 것입니다.

✎ Note Taking

Topic The closing of the art building
Reason School needs new administrative offices

Organization

It has decided to replace the student art gallery with new administrative offices because of a recent increase in enrollment.

Listening

Script 🎧 02-13

> **M Student**: I totally disagree with this recent decision. One of the most important parts of the school is the art program, and without an art gallery to display their work, how are the art majors supposed to get any recognition?
>
> **W Student**: Well, I think it's a good idea to close down that building. Did you ever think that the school's next move might be to build a bigger and better art gallery?

해석

M Student: 나는 학교의 이러한 최근 결정을 전적으로 반대해. 학교에서 가장 중요한 것 중 하나가 미술 프로그램인데, 미술 작품을 전시할 미술관이 없다면 미술 전공자들이 어떻게 자신을 알릴 수 있겠어?

W Student: 음, 나는 미술관을 폐쇄하는 것이 좋은 아이디어라고 생각해. 학교의 다음 번 조치가 더 크고 좋은 미술관을 짓는 것일 수도 있다는 생각은 해봤니?

✎ Note Taking

Man	Woman
Opinion Disagrees with the school's decision to close the art gallery	**Opinion** Agrees with the school's decision to close the art gallery
Reason Feels that art majors need a place to display their work	**Reason** Is a chance that the school will open a bigger art gallery in the future

Comparing

Sample Response 🎧 02-14

> The man disagrees with the university's announcement. He feels that art majors must be able to have a place to

display their art, which will enable them to be recognized for their work.

해석
남자는 대학측의 공지에 만족해하지 않는다. 그는 미술 전공자들이 자신의 작품으로 알려질 수 있도록 그들이 미술 작품을 전시할 수 있는 장소가 있어야 한다고 생각한다.

Exercise 6 .... p.47

Reading

해석

밝은 조명 금지

천문학과가 불만을 제기함으로써 앞으로는 오후 9시부터 오전 5시까지 교내에서 조명이 사용되지 않을 예정입니다. 천문학과에 의하면 학생들이 별을 잘 관찰할 수 있도록 교내가 더 어두워야 합니다. 이러한 새로운 규정은 이번 주 금요일부터 시행됩니다.

🖉 Note Taking

Topic No more bright lights on campus at night
Reason To allow the Astronomy Department to observe the stars

Organization

The Astronomy Department has complained that the lights are too bright, so students cannot observe the stars properly at night.

Listening

Script 🎧 02-15

M Student: I am so glad that there will not be any more bright lights on campus. Now I can do my astronomy work properly. Plus, the campus is just too bright at night.

W Student: I disagree. The campus isn't safe at night. We need bright lights. The Astronomy Department is being selfish, and the students and faculty are sacrificing the safety of the students so that a few students can look at some stars.

해석
M Student: 교내에서 밝은 조명이 없어지게 된다니 정말 다행이야. 이제 천문학 과제를 제대로 할 수 있겠군. 게다가 학교가 밤에 너무 밝아.

W Student: 난 그렇게 생각하지 않는걸. 밤에는 학교가 안전하지 않아. 천문학과가 이기적으로 행동하고 있고, 소수의 학생들이 별을 관찰할 수 있도록 학생 및 교직원들이 학생들의 안전을 희생시키고 있어.

🖉 Note Taking

Man	Woman
Opinion Agrees with the school's decision	**Opinion** Disagrees with the school's decision
Reason Will be able to do work and thinks the school is too bright at night	**Reason** Need brighter lights to ensure the safety of the students

Comparing

Sample Response 🎧 02-16

The man agrees with the university's announcement because he needs to do his astronomy homework correctly. In addition, he thinks the campus is too bright at night, so it should be darker.

해석
남자는 천문학 과제를 제대로 해야 하기 때문에 학교측의 공지에 만족해한다. 또한 그는 학교가 밤에 너무 밝기 때문에 더 어두워져야 한다고 생각한다.

Unit 08 Cafeterias & Computer Labs

Exercise 1 .... p.48

Reading

해석

교내 식당 개선안

교내 식당의 음식의 질이 낮다는 다수의 불만이 제기되었기 때문에 대학측은 교내 식당의 스타일을 바꿀 계획입니다. 다음 학기를 시작으로 학생들은 따뜻한 음식을 먹을 수 있고, 스스로 샌드위치를 만들어 먹을 수도 있으며, 샐러드 바를 이용할 수도 있고, 그리고 파스타와 피자도 먹을 수 있을 것입니다. 이로써 학생들이 매일 선택할 수 있는 음식들이 훨씬 더 많아질 것입니다.

🖉 Note Taking

Topic Making improvements to the school cafeteria
Reason Complaints about the quality of the food

Organization

The school has received many complaints about the low quality of the cafeteria's food, so it is going to make many improvements to it next semester.

Listening

Script 🎧 02-17

W Student: This is going to be great. I can't wait to see the new cafeteria. I can't stand the food that it serves now, but it looks like we will have lots of different choices. Now, we'll be able to eat something different every day.

M Student: It sounds nice, but I bet that the cafeteria is going to be really crowded next semester. I don't have much time to eat because of my classes, so if it's crowded, I'll either have to skip lunch or eat really quickly.

해석

W Student: 이번 일은 정말 멋진걸. 새로운 구내 식당이 너무 기대돼. 지금 파는 음식은 참을 수가 없지만, 다양한 선택을 할 수 있을 것으로 보여. 이제 날마다 다른 음식을 먹을 수 있을 거야.

M Student: 좋은 소식이긴 한데, 분명 다음 학기엔 식당이 사람들로 정말 바글바글할 거야. 난 수업 때문에 식사를 할 시간이 많지 않아서 만약 식당이 붐빈다면 점심을 거르거나 아니면 정말 빨리 식사를 해야 할 거야.

Note Taking

Woman	Man
Opinion Is excited about the new cafeteria	**Opinion** Is not excited about the new cafeteria
Reason Wants to have different choices of food and to eat something different daily	**Reason** Thinks it will be too crowded, so he will not have much time to eat

Comparing

Sample Response 🎧 02-18

The woman is excited about the improvements to the cafeteria. She does not like the food it now serves, and she wants to have more food choices. That way, she can eat different foods every day.

해석

여자는 교내 식당의 개선안에 들떠 있다. 그녀는 교내 식당에서 파는 음식을 좋아하지 않으며, 선택할 수 있는 음식이 더 많아지기를 바란다. 그러면 매일 다른 음식을 먹을 수가 있다.

Exercise 2 .... p.49

Reading

해석

음식점 이전

점점 많아지는 학생들을 수용하기 위해 새 교내 식당의 별관 공사가 다음 주 초에 시작될 것임을 학생 및 교직원들께 알려 드립니다. 여러분의 편의를 위해 공사 기간 중에는 몇몇 스낵 코너가 학생 센터로 이전될 예정입니다. 대학 당국은 이로 인해 교내의 모든 학생들이 보다 편리하게 식사를 할 수 있을 것으로 기대합니다.

Note Taking

Topic Relocation of food vendors to the student center
Reason To make getting food more convenient

Organization

The school is currently extending the cafeteria. So during the construction period, it will relocate several vendors to make it more convenient for students and staff to get food.

Listening

Script 🎧 02-19

M Student: I'm really pleased that the school is relocating some vendors to the student center. Now, it's going to be much easier to get some food. Plus, the cafeteria is so noisy with all of that construction. I don't want to eat there when there is so much noise.

W Student: Yeah, but the problem is that now the student center is going to be even more crowded than before. There are just too many people there all of the time, and this is going to make it even worse.

해석

M Student: 학교에서 몇몇 스낵 코너를 학생 센터로 옮긴다니 정말 기쁘군. 이제 식사하기가 훨씬 쉬워질 거야. 게다가 교내 식당은 공사 때문에 너무 시끄럽고. 그렇게 시끄러운 곳에서 식사를 하고 싶지는 않아.

W Student: 그래, 하지만 문제는 이제 학생 센터가 이전보다 훨씬 더 복잡해질 거라는 점이야. 거기에는 항상 사람들이 너무 많은데, 이번 일로 상황이 더 악화되겠지.

Note Taking

Man	Woman
Opinion Is pleased with the university's action	**Opinion** Is not pleased with the university's action
Reason Will be easier to get food and will not be so noisy at the student center	**Reason** Will be too crowded at the student center

Comparing

Sample Response 🎧 02-20

The man is pleased with the university's announcement. He thinks that it will be a lot easier to get food. He also does not want to eat at the cafeteria because the construction will make it too noisy. The student center will be much less noisy.

해석

남자는 대학의 공지에 만족해한다. 그는 식사를 하는 것이 훨씬 더 쉬워질 것이라고 생각한다. 그는 또한 공사 때문에 너무 시끄러워서 교내 식당에서 식사하는 것을 원하지 않는다. 학생 센터는 훨씬 덜 시끄러울 것이다.

Reading

해석

컴퓨터 전공자 채용 공고

새 컴퓨터실에서 파트타임으로 일할 소수의 학생 직원을 모집합니다. 이번 일자리는 컴퓨터 과학이나 컴퓨터 공학 전공자들만 지원이 가능합니다. 컴퓨터실은 24시간 운영되며, 얼마 전에 개방을 했기 때문에 학생들은 어떤 시간에도 근무를 할 수 있습니다. 학생 직원은 컴퓨터 사용법을 학생들에게 알려 주고 문제가 발생하면 문제를 해결하는 일을 하게 될 것입니다.

✎ Note Taking

Topic Part-time employees to be hired at the computer laboratory

Reason Lab has just opened and needs many employees

Organization

Student employees at the new computer laboratory will work there twenty-four hours a day. They will have to show students how to use the computers and fix any problems with the computers.

Listening

Script 🎧 02-21

W Student: I'm so happy that the new computer laboratory is going to hire students majoring in computers. It seems that the old lab has students working there who don't know a thing about computers. When my computer breaks down, they just can't fix it.

M Student: You are so right. I use the computer lab a lot because it's near my department. I don't know anything about computers, but the workers should. Sometimes it takes them forever to figure out what's wrong with my computer when something bad happens.

해석

W Student: 새 컴퓨터실에서 컴퓨터 전공자를 채용할 계획이라니 너무 다행이야. 기존 컴퓨터실에서는 컴퓨터를 전혀 모르는 학생들이 일을 하는 것 같아. 컴퓨터가 고장이 나도 고치지를 못해.

M Student: 맞는 말이야. 우리 학과 건물에서 가까워서 나도 컴퓨터실을 많이 이용하는 편이지. 나는 컴퓨터에 대해서 아는 것이 없지만 직원들은 알아야 하잖아. 때때로 문제가 발생하면 컴퓨터에 뭐가 잘못되었는지 알아내기까지 시간이 한참 걸린다니까.

✎ Note Taking

Woman	**Man**
Opinion Is happy about the new computer laboratory	**Opinion** Is happy about the new computer laboratory
Reason Students at the old laboratory are not computer majors and cannot fix problems	**Reason** Does not know much about computers, and current employees cannot help him very well

Comparing

Sample Response 🎧 02-22

The woman is pleased with the announcement to hire computer majors. She uses the old computer laboratory, but the employees there are not computer majors. So when her computer has a problem, they cannot repair it.

해석

여자는 컴퓨터 전공자를 채용한다는 공고에 기뻐한다. 그녀는 기존 컴퓨터실을 이용하는데, 그곳 직원들은 컴퓨터 전공자들이 아니다. 그래서 컴퓨터에 문제가 생기는 경우 고칠 수가 없다.

Reading

해석

컴퓨터실 운영 시간

컴퓨터실을 이용하는 사람들이 너무 많기 때문에 모든 사람들이 컴퓨터를 충분히 이용하지 못하고 있습니다. 다음 주 월요일인 10월 12일부터 학생들이 컴퓨터를 이용하기 위해서는 예약을 해야 합니다. 학생들은 한 번에 두 시간 동안만 컴퓨터를 이용할 수 있습니다. 이번 규정에는 예외가 없습니다.

✎ Note Taking

Topic Making reservations to use computers

Reason Too many students and not enough machines

Organization

There are too many students using the computers, but there are not enough machines for all of the students.

Listening

Script 🎧 02-23

W Student: I'm really not pleased with this decision. I have a lot of time off between classes, so I like to spend it at the computer center. I don't know why we need reservations. Most of the time when I go there, the center is not even half full.

M Student: Well, I usually go in the evening, when it's packed with students. And not everyone is doing work. Some students are just playing games or chatting with their friends. I think that this is a good idea because it will give everyone a fair chance to use the computers.

해석

W Student: 난 이번 결정이 정말 마음에 들지 않아. 나는 수업 사이에 비는 시간이 많아서 컴퓨터실에서 시간을 보내는 편이야. 왜 예약을 해야하는지 모르겠어. 거기에 가면 대부분의 경우 컴퓨터실이 반도 안 차 있지 않아.

M Student: 음, 나는 학생들로 꽉 차 있는 저녁 시간에 주로 가는 편이야. 그런데 모든 학생들이 공부를 하고 있지는 않아. 어떤 학생은 게임을 하거나 친구들과 채팅만 하고 있지. 나는 이번 결정이 모든 학생들에게 컴퓨터를 사용할 공평한 기회를 준다는 점에서 좋은 아이디어라고 생각해.

Woman	Man
Opinion Dislikes the school's decision	**Opinion** Likes the school's decision
Reason Is no need for reservations since computer center is usually half full	**Reason** Not all students use computers for work so should give everyone a fair chance

Comparing

Sample Response 🎧 02-24

The woman dislikes the school's decision. She often goes to the computer center in between classes, and it is usually half full then. So she does not think she needs a reservation.

해석

여자는 학교의 결정을 마음에 들어 하지 않는다. 그녀는 수업 중간에 종종 컴퓨터실에 가는데, 이때 그곳은 보통 절반 정도만 차 있다. 그래서 그녀는 예약이 필요하다고 생각하지 않는다.

Exercise 5 ·· p.52

Reading

해석

컴퓨터 강좌 개설

본교에서 주로 홈페이지 디자인 및 제작을 다루는 컴퓨터 강좌가 개설될 예정입니다. 이 강좌의 목표는 기본적인 컴퓨터 프로그래밍에 관해 배울 수 있는 기회를 학생들에게 제공하는 것입니다. 이 강좌는 모든 전공자에게 개방될 것이며, 컴퓨터 사용 경험도 요구하지 않습니다.

Topic Opening of new computer class
Reason To give students an opportunity to learn basic computer programming

Organization

The class will let students in all majors learn about basic computer programming.

Listening

Script 🎧 02-25

M Student: This new class sounds awesome. I don't know a thing about computers, so it will be nice to learn with some other beginners. I'd love to learn to make a webpage.

W Student: I don't know. This class sounds like it doesn't really belong at a university. If people want to learn about web design, they can learn it elsewhere. But the school shouldn't be offering such easy classes as this one.

해석

M Student: 이번 신규 강좌는 멋진걸. 나는 컴퓨터에 관해서 아무것도 모르기 때문에 다른 초보자들과 같이 배우게 되면 좋을 것 같아. 웹 페이지 만드는 법을 정말 배우고 싶어.

W Student: 난 잘 모르겠어. 이 강좌는 대학측이 개설할 성격의 수업은 아닌 것처럼 들려. 웹 디자인에 대해 배우고 싶으면 다른 곳에서 배울 수 있잖아. 학교측이 이처럼 쉬운 강좌를 개설해서는 안 되지.

Man	Woman
Opinion Approves of the new class	**Opinion** Disapproves of the new class
Reason Wants to learn how to make a webpage	**Reason** Thinks it is not an appropriate university class

Comparing

Sample Response 🎧 02-26

The woman disapproves of the new class. She thinks that the new class is too easy and should not be taught at the school. She believes that students who want to learn webpage design should do it somewhere else.

해석

여자는 새로운 강좌에 불만을 나타낸다. 그녀는 새 강좌가 너무 쉽기 때문에 학교에서 이를 가르쳐서는 안 된다고 생각한다. 그녀는 웹 디자인을 배우고 싶은 학생들은 다른 곳에서 배워야 한다고 생각한다.

Exercise 6 ·· p.53

Reading

해석

더 이상 교내 식당에서 학생증이 필요하지 않습니다

대학 경찰의 결정 및 표준 안전 정책에 따라 교내 식당에서는 더 이상 학생들에게 학생증 제시를 요구하지 않을 것입니다. 이번 변경 조치로 여러분의 식사 시간이 보다 즐거워지기를 기대합니다.

Topic Showing ID card is no longer necessary
Reason A change in security policy

Organization

The school canceled its policy because the campus police were satisfied that standard security measures were met and no longer required it.

Listening

Script 🎧 02-27

W Student: I like the fact that we will be able to get into the cafeteria much more quickly now. It was so annoying to have to show one of the employees there our student IDs.

M Student: Well, I disagree. What if someone stole your student ID from you? Someone could be walking around using your name. It seems to me that the school is sacrificing safety for speed.

해석

W Student: 이제 교내 식당에 훨씬 빨리 들어갈 수 있게 되어서 좋아. 그곳 직원 중 한 명에게 학생증을 제시해야 하는 것은 정말 성가신 일이었어.

M Student: 글쎄, 나는 생각이 달라. 만약 누군가가 네 학생증을 훔친 경우에는 어떻게 될까? 누군가가 네 이름을 도용해서 돌아다닐 수도 있어. 내게는 학교 측이 신속성을 위해 안전을 희생시키고 있다고 보여지는 걸.

📝 Note Taking

Woman	Man
Opinion Likes the new policy	**Opinion** Dislikes the new policy
Reason Can get into the cafeteria much more quickly now	**Reason** Is worried about someone stealing his ID and using his name

Comparing

Sample Response 🎧 02-28

The woman likes the new policy. She says that the lines to get into the cafeteria are too long, so now they should move faster. She also doesn't like having to show her ID to any of the workers there.

해석

여자는 새로운 정책을 반긴다. 그녀는 교내 식당으로 들어가는 길이 너무 길었는데, 이제는 더 빨리 이동할 수 있을 것이라고 말한다. 또한 그녀는 그곳 직원에게 자신의 학생증을 제시해야만 한다는 점도 좋아하지 않는다.

Unit 09 School Events & Policies

Exercise 1 .... p.54

Reading

해석

교내 영화 상영

본교 체육관에서 영화가 상영될 예정입니다. 주중에는 오후 9시에 영화가 시작됩니다. 주말에는 오후 11시에 영화가 시작됩니다. 모든 분들을 환영합니다. 학교측은 학생들이 양질의 오락을 즐기기를 바라기 때문에 관람료는 무료입니다.

📝 Note Taking

Topic Showing movies in the gymnasium

Reason University wants students to have access to quality entertainment

Organization

The school will show movies in the gymnasium in order to try to entertain the students.

Listening

Script 🎧 02-29

M Student: Why is the school showing movies on campus? Students should be doing other things, such as sports or club activities. There are plenty of things to do. We don't need movies in the gym, too.

W Student: I think it's a good idea. After all, we need something to do besides go to parties. In addition, movie tickets are expensive these days. It'll be nice to save some money.

해석

M Student: 왜 학교에서 영화를 상영하려고 할까? 학생들은 스포츠나 동아리 활동 등을 통해 다른 활동들을 해야 해. 할 것들이 많이 있어. 체육관에서 영화를 상영할 필요는 없잖아.

W Student: 난 좋은 아이디어라고 생각해. 어찌되었든 파티에 가는 것 말고도 할 수 있는 일이 필요하니까. 게다가 요즘에는 영화 관람료도 비싸잖아. 돈을 아낄 수 있으면 좋지.

📝 Note Taking

Man	Woman
Opinion Thinks movies on campus are a bad idea	**Opinion** Thinks movies on campus are a good idea
Reason Believes there are already many different activities to do	**Reason** Wants to have a fun activity to do and wants to save on movie tickets

Comparing

Sample Response 🎧 02-30

The man does not like the university's decision. He thinks that the students should do activities like play sports or be involved in clubs instead of just watching movies.

해석

남자는 대학측의 결정을 반기지 않는다. 그는 학생들이 영화를 관람하는 대신 스포츠나 동아리 활동과 같은 다른 활동을 해야 한다고 생각한다.

Exercise 2 .... p.55

Reading

해석

과외 프로그램 폐지

유감스럽게도 학생 과외 프로그램이 폐지되었습니다. 이로 인해 불편을 겪게 될 학생들에게 유감을 표합니다. 프로그램은 자원봉사 학생의 부족으로 폐지되었습니다. 하지만 학교측은 현재 활동하고 있는 개인 과외 교사들이 계속해서 학생들을 도와 주기를 바랍니다.

Topic The abolishing of the student tutoring program
Reason Are not enough student volunteers

Organization

The program is being canceled because there are not enough student volunteers to tutor those students who need help.

Listening

Script 🎧 02-31

W Student: We can't cancel the tutoring program. That program is really valuable. Several of my friends have gotten tutored, and their grades went up a lot after that. It really helps so many students improve their grades.

M Student: I totally agree with you. I got tutored in math there last year, and I brought my grade up from a C to a B+ after just a month or so. It's a shame that there are not enough student volunteers for that program.

해석

W Student: 과외 프로그램을 폐지해서는 안 돼. 그 프로그램은 정말로 가치가 있어. 내 친구들 중 여러 명이 과외를 받는데 그 후에 성적이 크게 올랐거든. 많은 학생들의 성적 향상에 정말로 도움이 되고 있다고.

M Student: 전적으로 동감이야. 나도 작년에 거기에서 수학 과외를 받았는데, 불과 약 한 달 후에 성적이 C에서 B+로 올랐어. 그 프로그램에 자원봉사 학생이 부족하다는 건 정말 안타까운 일이야.

Woman	Man
Opinion Disapproves of the school's decision	**Opinion** Disapproves of the school's decision
Reason Helps many students improve their grades	**Reason** Has personal experience with the success of the program

Comparing

Sample Response 🎧 02-32

The woman disagrees with the school's decision. She knows many students whose grades have improved because of the program. She also knows that it is helpful to lots of students.

해석

여자는 학교의 결정에 불만족해한다. 그녀는 그 프로그램 덕분에 성적이 오른 학생들을 많이 알고 있다. 그녀는 또한 그 프로그램이 많은 학생들에게 도움이 된다는 점도 알고 있다.

Exercise 3 .... p.56

Reading

해석

교내 방송 프로그램의 변화

학교측은 방송 프로그램을 확대할 예정입니다. 프로그램 강화를 위해 외부 인사도 초빙할 것입니다. 뿐만 아니라 방송 프로그램 수도 늘릴 계획입니다. 이 프로그램들은 더 일찍 시작하고 더 늦게 끝날 것입니다. 이로써 프로그램에 보다 많은 광고가 유치될 것이며, 그 결과 방송 프로그램으로 더 많은 기금이 모일 수 있을 것입니다.

Topic Expanding the broadcasting program
Reason To attract more advertisers and to help the broadcasting program raise funds

Organization

The broadcasting program will expand by adding more programs to the air. It will also get more advertisers, which will help it raise more money.

Listening

Script 🎧 02-33

W Student: I like this idea. The school has some really good shows, and it will be nice to have some more programs get on the air. Some of the students are really talented, so they should have their own shows.

M Student: I agree. Plus, it's nice that they will be raising their own money. That way, the school can spend more money on facilities that are more important, like the library and some of the science laboratories.

해석

W Student: 난 이 아이디어가 마음에 들어. 학교측은 정말로 좋은 프로그램을 갖추고 있는데, 방송되는 프로그램이 더 많아진다면 좋을 것 같아. 학생들 중 일부는 정말로 재능이 뛰어나기 때문에 그들이 자기 자신만의 프로그램을 진행하게 될 거야.

M Student: 나도 그렇게 생각해. 게다가 학생들이 스스로 기금을 마련하게 될 것이라는 점도 좋은 일이지. 그러면 학교측은 도서관 및 과학 연구실 같은 보다 중요한 시설에 더 많은 돈을 쓸 수 있을 거야.

Woman	Man
Opinion Likes the school's decision	**Opinion** Likes the school's decision
Reason Thinks there should be more programs since many students are very talented	**Reason** Broadcasting Department can support itself so school spends more on other facilities

Comparing

Sample Response 🎧 02-34

The woman agrees with the school's decision to expand the broadcasting program. She thinks that some of the shows are good, so there should be more of them. She also believes many students on the programs are talented, so she would like for them to have their own shows.

해석

여자는 방송 프로그램을 확대하겠다는 학교측의 결정에 찬성한다. 그녀는 몇몇 방송 프로그램들이 훌륭하기 때문에 그러한 프로그램이 더 많아져야 한다고 생각한다. 그녀는 또한 프로그램과 관련된 많은 학생들이 재능을 갖추고 있기 때문에 그들이 자신만의 프로그램을 진행하기를 바란다.

Exercise 4 .... p.57

Reading

해석

의료 센터 오픈

학교에서 교내 의료 센터를 오픈할 예정입니다. 학생들은 무료로 건강 검진 및 의료 서비스를 받을 수 있습니다. 이 센터는 의료비를 감당하기가 힘든 학생 혹은 건강 보험에 가입되어 있지 않은 학생들에게 큰 도움이 될 것입니다.

> **✎ Note Taking**
>
> **Topic** The opening of a school medical center
> **Reason** To provide services for all students at no cost

Organization

It is opening the medical center to allow students to get medical care at no cost.

Listening

Script 🎧 02-35

M Student: I'm so happy that the school is finally opening up a medical center. I broke my leg last year and had to pay a few thousand dollars in medical bills. In fact, I'm still in debt. I could have used some of those free services.

W Student: I agree. With hospital costs rising these days, it's a good thing that the school recognizes that many students can't pay those prices. Now when I'm sick, I'll actually go to see the doctor instead of just staying home and waiting to get better.

해석

M Student: 학교측이 마침내 의료 센터를 열게 돼서 정말 기쁘군. 나는 작년에 다리가 부러져 의료비로 수천 달러를 내야만 했어. 사실 아직도 갚고 있는 중이지. 의료 센터의 무료 서비스를 이용할 수 있었다면 좋았을 텐데.

W Student: 동감이야. 요즘에는 병원비가 올라서 많은 학생들이 그러한 비용을 감당하지 못한다는 걸 학교측이 알게 되어 다행이야. 이제 몸이 아프면 집에 머물면서 낫기만 바라는 대신 진료를 받으러 가야겠어.

> **✎ Note Taking**
>
> | **Man** | **Woman** |
> |---|---|
> | **Opinion** Is pleased with the school's action | **Opinion** Is pleased with the school's action |
> | **Reason** Is still in debt from a past accident and wants to have free services | **Reason** Will now be able to go to the doctor when she is sick |

Comparing

Sample Response 🎧 02-36

The man is happy with the school's decision to open the medical center. He states that he had to pay thousands of dollars in medical fees when he broke his leg and that he is still in debt. He would like to have access to free medical care.

해석

남자는 의료 센터를 열기로 한 학교측의 결정에 기뻐한다. 그는 자신의 다리가 부러졌을 때 의료비로 수천 달러를 내야 했으며 아직까지 빚을 다 갚지 못했다고 말한다. 그는 무료로 의료 서비스를 이용할 수 있기를 바란다.

Exercise 5 .... p.58

Reading

해석

자원봉사 활동

이제 모든 학생들은 졸업 전에 지역 봉사 활동에 참여해야 합니다. 본교는 지역 사회에 대한 학생들의 참여도를 높이기 위해 이번 정책을 실시하게 되었습니다. 자세한 사항을 원하거나 필요한 절차를 밟고자 하는 학생들은 자원봉사 센터에 문의하시기 바랍니다. 담당 직원이 모든 질문에 친절하게 답변해 줄 것입니다.

> **✎ Note Taking**
>
> **Topic** Students are required to perform community service before graduating
> **Reason** To get students more involved in the community

Organization

All students must perform some kind of volunteer activity to be more involved in the local community.

Listening

Script 🎧 02-37

W Student: I can't believe that the school is making us do volunteer work before we graduate. I've got a full load of classes and also have two part-time jobs. When am I supposed to find the time to do volunteer work?

M Student: I agree with you. Plus, people should do volunteer work because they want to, not because they have to. There are going to be many unhappy students doing volunteer work. I don't think that is going to help community relations very much.

해석

W Student: 학교에서 우리보고 졸업하기 전에 자원봉사 활동을 하라고 하다니 믿을 수가 없네. 난 수업도 꽉 채워서 듣고 있는데, 아르바이트도 두 개나 하고 있어. 자원봉사 활동을 할 수 있는 시간을 어디서 찾아야 하지?

M Student: 나도 네 말에 동의해. 게다가 자원봉사는 사람들이 원해서 하는 것이지, 해야 하기 때문에 하는 것이 아니잖아. 자원봉사 활동으로 기분이 상하는 학생들이 많겠군. 이렇게 한다고 해서 지역 사회와의 관계가 크게 좋아질 것 같지는 않아.

✏ **Note Taking**

Woman	Man
Opinion Dislikes the school's new regulation	**Opinion** Dislikes the school's new regulation
Reason Is already very busy and does not have time to do volunteer work	**Reason** Thinks people should volunteer because they want to and not be forced into doing it

Comparing

Sample Response 🎧 02-38

The woman dislikes the university's decision. She says that she has a full class load and also works two part-time jobs, so she does not have any time to volunteer.

해석

여자는 학교의 결정을 반기지 않는다. 그녀는 자신이 수업을 꽉 채워 듣고 있고 두 개의 아르바이트를 하고 있기 때문에 자원봉사를 할 수 있는 시간이 없다고 말한다.

Exercise 6 .... p.59

Reading

해석

난방 정책 변경

다음 주 월요일 부로 전기 요금을 줄이고 비용 절감을 위해 본교의 모든 강의실의 난방 장치가 오후 5시 정각에 가동이 중지될 것입니다. 오후 5시 이후에 수업이 있는 교수님께서는 수업이 끝날 때까지 교실의 난방 장치를 끄지 말아 달라고 건물 관리실에 요청하실 수 있습니다.

✏ **Note Taking**

Topic Turning off the heat in classrooms
Reason To save electricity and to reduce costs

Organization

The school will be turning of the heat because it wants to save electricity and also because it wants to reduce the amount of money it spends on electricity.

Listening

Script 🎧 02-39

W Student: Can you believe that the school will be turning off the heat in the classrooms in the evening? A lot of students study in these classrooms in the evening when there are no lectures going on in them. Now, they're going to freeze.

M Student: Yeah, you're right. Since the library is so crowded, we don't have any choice but to study in empty classrooms, especially because the dorms are so noisy. I also have a study group that meets late at night in a classroom.

해석

W Student: 학교측이 저녁에 강의실의 난방 장치를 끌 것이라는 점이 말이 되니? 많은 학생들이 저녁 시간에 비어 있는 강의실에서 공부를 하고 있어. 이제 얼어 죽게 생겼군.

M Student: 그래, 네 말이 맞아. 도서관에 사람이 많아서 빈 강의실에서 공부하는 것 외에는 선택지가 없는데, 특히 기숙사가 시끄러울 때가 그래. 게다가 나는 밤늦게 강의실에서 모임을 갖는 스터디 그룹에도 속해 있어.

✏ **Note Taking**

Woman	Man
Opinion Disagrees with the school's decision	**Opinion** Disagrees with the school's decision
Reason Thinks lots of students study in classrooms in the evening	**Reason** Cannot study in library because it is crowded and has a study group that meets at night in a classroom

Comparing

Sample Response 🎧 02-40

The woman disagrees with the school's decision. She thinks that many students study in empty classrooms in the evening, but now they are going to be very cold.

해석

여자는 학교의 결정에 반대한다. 그녀는 많은 학생들이 저녁에 빈 강의실에서 공부를 하고 있지만, 이제 추위를 크게 느끼게 될 것이라고 생각한다.

Unit 10 School Systems

Exercise 1 .... p.60

Reading

해석

신관 개관

본교는 어젯밤에 드디어 최신 건물을 개관했습니다. 이곳에서는 수면 장애 및 수면 부족이 기억에 미치는 영향에 관한 연구가 진행될 것입니다. 또한 이곳에는 새로운 학생 의료 센터가 들어설 예정입니다. 학생들은 정상적인 병원비를 지불하고 의료 센터의 서비스를 받을 수 있습니다.

✏ **Note Taking**

Topic Opening of a new school facility

Reason To conduct research and to house a student health center

Organization

The university opened a facility that will conduct medical research and which also has a health center for students.

Listening

Script 🎧 02-41

M Student: It sounds like this new research and health center is a waste of money. After all, the research that will be conducted there won't really help too many people. In addition, the health center won't provide cheap rates for students. That's not good.

W Student: You're completely right. If there's going to be a health center on campus, the school should give students a discounted rate. Not all of us have health insurance, so we won't be able to afford to pay for health care there.

해석

M Student: 이번에 개관한 연구 및 의료 센터는 돈 낭비처럼 보여. 결국 거기서 진행되는 연구가 많은 사람들에게 그다지 도움이 되지 않을 거고. 게다가 의료 센터는 학생들에게 저렴한 요금을 적용하지도 않잖아. 도움이 안 돼.

W Student: 정말 맞는 말이야. 교내에 의료 센터가 들어설 예정이라면 학교측이 학생들에게 할인 요금을 적용해야지. 우리 모두가 의료 보험을 든 것도 아니어서 그곳 의료비를 감당할 수 없을 거야.

✏ **Note Taking**

Man	Woman
Opinion Dislikes the new facility	**Opinion** Dislikes the new facility
Reason Is a waste of money since research is not important and health center will be expensive	**Reason** Cannot afford to visit health center since it is too expensive without insurance

Comparing

Sample Response 🎧 02-42

The man dislikes the new facility and considers it a waste of money. He says that the research it will conduct is not very helpful and that the health center's rates are not cheap.

해석

남자는 새 시설에 불만을 나타내고 그것이 돈 낭비라고 생각한다. 그는 그곳에서 진행되는 연구가 그다지 도움이 되지 않으며 의료 센터의 요금은 저렴하지 않다고 생각한다.

Exercise 2 .... p.61

Reading

해석

재활용 프로그램 폐지

대학측은 2년 후에 재활용 프로그램을 폐지할 예정입니다. 많은 학생들이 재활용의 중요성에 대해 언급하면서도 분리수거함 중 거의 사용되는 것이 없습니다. 지금부터 학생들은 쓰레기를 교내 곳곳에서 찾아볼 수 있는 쓰레기통에 버려주시기 바랍니다.

✏ **Note Taking**

Topic Cancelation of the university's recycling program

Reason Is not being used by most students

Organization

The program is being canceled since almost none of the students ever recycles.

Listening

Script 🎧 02-43

M Student: It's about time the school cancels the recycling program. What a waste of time. I never once saw anyone recycle a single bottle or glass. Those bins are just taking up valuable space all around campus.

W Student: I think it's a shame the school is canceling the program. The environment is important, so we should think about recycling. The school ought to promote some environmental awareness campaigns to encourage more people to recycle.

해석

M Student: 학교측이 재활용 프로그램을 폐지해야 할 때가 되었어. 시간 낭비일 뿐이지. 나는 병이나 유리를 분리수거함에 넣는 사람을 한 번도 본 적이 없어. 분리수거함들은 교내 여기저기에서 소중한 공간만 차지할 뿐이야.

W Student: 나는 대학측이 재활용 프로그램을 폐지하려고 해서 안타깝다고 생각하는데. 환경은 중요하기 때문에 우리는 재활용에 대해 생각해야 해. 학교측이 환경 의식을 고취시키는 캠페인을 벌여서 보다 많은 사람들로 하여금 재활용을 하도록 해야 할 거야.

Man	**Woman**
Opinion Approves of the program's cancelation	**Opinion** Disapproves of the program's cancelation
Reason Thinks program is waste of time and bins take up valuable space	**Reason** Should think about the environment and promote environmental awareness campaigns

Comparing

Sample Response 🎧 02-44

The man approves of the university canceling the program. He says that he has never seen anyone on campus recycle anything, and he thinks that the recycling bins on campus just take up a lot of space.

해석

남자는 재활용 프로그램을 철회하기로 한 대학측에 찬성한다. 그는 자신이 교내에서 재활용하는 사람을 본 적이 없다고 말하며, 교내의 분리수거함들이 많은 공간만 차지할 뿐이라고 생각한다.

Exercise 3 ⋯⋯⋯⋯⋯⋯⋯⋯⋯⋯⋯⋯⋯⋯⋯⋯⋯ p.62

Reading

해석

버스 노선 신설

본교 학생들에게 큰 도움을 줄 새로운 버스 노선이 신설되었습니다. 학생들의 쇼핑을 편리하게 할 수 있도록 이제 93번 버스가 학교에서부터 New Horizons 쇼핑몰까지 학생들을 데려다 줄 것입니다. 이 버스는 30분 간격으로 운행되며 학생들은 학생증을 제시할 경우 1달러의 요금만 내면 됩니다.

Topic Introduction of new bus line
Reason Enable students to get to a shopping mall easily

Organization

The bus will go from the university to the New Horizons Shopping Mall.

Listening

Script 🎧 02-45

W Student: I can't wait to take the number 93 bus. It's so annoying to have to pay for a taxi after I do all of my shopping. Now, I can save a lot of money by taking the bus.

M Student: You're right. Plus, maybe more students will take the bus, which will help take care of the environment. There will be fewer cars on the road, too.

해석

W Student: 93번 버스를 탈 날이 정말 기다려져. 쇼핑을 한 후에 택시비를 내는 것은 정말 짜증나는 일이거든. 이제 그 버스를 타면 돈을 꽤 절약할 수가 있겠어.

M Student: 맞는 말이야. 게다가 아마도 더 많은 학생들이 버스를 탈 테니까 환경에도 도움이 될 거야. 도로에 자동차들도 줄어들겠지.

Woman	**Man**
Opinion Is pleased with the announcement	**Opinion** Is pleased with the announcement
Reason Will not have to take taxi and can save money now	**Reason** Will help the environment and result in fewer cars on the road

Comparing

Sample Response 🎧 02-46

The woman is pleased with the announcement about the new bus. She likes to go shopping but has to take a taxi back to school from the mall. Since that is expensive, now she can save money by taking the bus.

해석

여자는 신규 버스 노선에 관한 대한 공지에 만족해한다. 그녀는 쇼핑을 좋아하지만 쇼핑몰에서 학교로 돌아올 때 택시를 타야 한다. 택시 요금이 비싸기 때문에, 이제 그녀는 버스를 이용함으로써 돈을 절약할 수 있다.

Exercise 4 ⋯⋯⋯⋯⋯⋯⋯⋯⋯⋯⋯⋯⋯⋯⋯⋯⋯ p.63

Reading

해석

기숙사 휴게실의 변경 사항

Weston 홀의 모든 기숙사생들은 휴게실의 공용 TV의 철거 문제를 논의하기 위한 회의에 참석해 주시기 바랍니다. 많은 학생들이 휴게실의 대형 TV 때문에 시끄러워서 휴식을 취하기가 힘들다고 생각합니다. TV 철거에 대한 찬반 의견을 가진 학생들은 이번 주 목요일 저녁 7시에 본인의 생각을 발표할 수 있습니다.

Topic Removal of television from dormitory lounge
Reason Is too loud and disturbing

Organization

Some students say that the television is too loud and also does not let students relax while they are in the lounge.

Listening

Script 🎧 02-47

M Student: I cannot believe the school is thinking of taking away the television. I don't have one in my room, so that's the only place that I get to watch anything. Plus, it's a lounge, not a study area. Students can study in their rooms if they want peace and quiet.

W Student: Well, not everyone likes to watch television. And you can do many things in the lounge besides just study. I like to play games there and talk to my friends, but we can't do that if the TV is on too loud.

해석

M Student: 학교측이 TV를 없애려고 하다니 믿을 수가 없군. 내 기숙사 방에는 TV가 없어서 뭔가를 볼 수 있는 장소는 그곳뿐이야. 게다가 거긴 휴게실이지 공부방이 아니라고. 학생들이 휴식과 안정을 원한다면 자기 방에서 공부하면 되잖아.

W Student: 음, 모두가 TV 시청하는 걸 좋아하는 것은 아니야. 그리고 휴게실에서는 공부 외에도 여러 가지를 할 수가 있어. 나는 거기서 게임하는 것과 친구들하고 대화하는 것을 좋아하는데, TV 소리가 너무 크면 그럴 수가 없더라고.

✎ **Note Taking**

Man	**Woman**
Opinion Disagrees with removing the television	**Opinion** Agrees with removing the television
Reason Does not have a TV in room so watches in the lounge	**Reason** Likes to do things other than watch TV in the lounge

Comparing

Sample Response 🎧 02-48

The man disagrees with removing the television. He does not have a TV of his own, so he needs to watch the one in the lounge. He also thinks that students should not study in the lounge but in their rooms. This way, the television will not bother them.

해석

남자는 TV 철거에 동의하지 않는다. 그는 자신의 방에 TV가 없기 때문에 휴게실에서 TV를 보아야 한다. 또한 그는 학생들이 휴게실이 아니라 자신의 방에서 공부해야 한다고 생각한다. 그렇게 하면 TV가 그들을 방해하지 않을 것이다.

Exercise 5 ··· p.64

Reading

해석

과외 프로그램의 변경 사항

다음 달부터 학생들이 과외 교습을 보다 편리하게 받을 수 있도록 학생 과외 프로그램에서 온라인 과외 프로그램이 제공될 예정입니다. 학생들이 로그인을 하고 과외 교사에게 질문을 하면, 과외 교사가 즉각적으로 답변을 해 줄 것입니다. 또한 카메라가 있는 학생들은 비디오 링크로 과외를 받을 수가 있을 것입니다. 이로써 기숙사에 머물면서 본인의 컴퓨터를 이용해 과외를 받을 수 있을 것입니다.

✎ **Note Taking**

Topic Changes in the university's tutoring program
Reason To make tutoring more convenient for students

Organization

Students can ask questions online and get immediate answers and also get tutored by a video link with their personal computers.

Listening

Script 🎧 02-49

W Student: Why does everything have to be done with computers? I'm not comfortable using them, and one of the things that I need tutoring for is computer technology.

M Student: Well, I'm pretty happy with the changes. I hate leaving my room in the evening, so now I can get tutored easily. In addition, I sometimes just have a simple question to be answered. So this new program should really help me out a lot.

해석

W Student: 왜 모든 것이 컴퓨터랑 연결되어야 하지? 나는 컴퓨터 사용이 익숙하지 않아서 과외가 필요한 과목 중 하나가 컴퓨터 기술이야.

M Student: 음, 나는 이번 변경 사항이 꽤 만족스러워. 저녁에는 방에서 나가기가 정말 싫은데, 이제 쉽게 과외를 받을 수가 있게 되었어. 게다가 때로는 간단한 질문에 대한 답이 필요할 때도 있어. 그래서 이번에 신설되는 프로그램이 내게는 정말로 큰 도움이 될 것 같아.

✎ **Note Taking**

Woman	**Man**
Opinion Dislikes the changes	**Opinion** Likes the changes
Reason Is not comfortable with computers	**Reason** Can get tutored easily and can sometimes just ask simple questions

Comparing

Sample Response 🎧 02-50

The woman dislikes the changes in the announcement. She does not know very much about computers and does not like using them either.

해석

여자는 공지의 변경 사항에 대해 불만을 나타낸다. 그녀는 컴퓨터를 잘 모르기 때문에 컴퓨터를 이용하는 것 또한 좋아하지 않는다.

Exercise 6 ··· p.65

Reading

해석

도서관 운영 시간

기말고사 준비를 보다 더 잘 할 수 있도록, 학생회의 일부 위원들이 도서관의 운영 시간 연장에 대해 논의를 하고자 합니다. 이 기간 동안 도서관이 24시간 개방되어야 한다는 의견에 동의하시면 이번 주 수요일 저녁 9시에 도서관 회의실로 오시기 바랍니다. 도서관의 운영 시간을 변경하고자 하는 학생들의 모임이 마런될 예정입니다. 오셔서 여러분의 의견을 밝혀 주시기 바랍니다.

Organization

Final exams are coming up, so the students want to be able to stay in the library all day and night long so that they can study more.

Listening

Script 🎧 02-51

M Student: I sure hope that the library agrees to extend its hours. I need to study in there for as long as possible. My roommate goes to bed early, so I can't stay up late at night in my dorm studying.

W Student: Yeah, plus, I sometimes need to look at some books and journals from the library. It will be really nice if we can have access to them at any time of the day.

해석

M Student: 도서관측이 운영 시간 연장에 찬성해 주면 정말 좋겠어. 나는 그곳에서 최대한 오래 공부를 해야 해. 룸메이트가 일찍 자는 편이라 기숙사에서는 밤 늦게까지 공부를 할 수가 없거든.

W Student: 그래, 게다가 나는 때때로 도서관에서 책이나 정기 간행물을 찾아봐야 할 때가 있어. 하루 중 언제라도 그런 것들을 찾아볼 수 있다면 정말로 좋을 것 같아.

✏ Note Taking

Man	Woman
Opinion Likes the announcement	**Opinion** Likes the announcement
Reason Wants to study in the library since his roommate goes to bed early	**Reason** Needs books and journals and wants to look at them anytime

Comparing

Sample Response 🎧 02-52

The man likes the announcement. He feels that he should study at the library for as long as possible. In other words, he cannot study in his dorm room because his roommate goes to bed early, so he needs another place to study late at night.

해석

남자는 공지를 반긴다. 그는 자신이 최대한 오랫동안 도서관에서 공부해야 한다고 생각한다. 즉 룸메이트가 일찍 자기 때문에 기숙사에서 늦게까지 공부를 할 수가 없어서 그에게는 밤 늦게까지 공부를 할 수 있는 또 다른 장소가 필요하다.

Unit 11 School Facilities II

Exercise 1 ⋯⋯⋯⋯⋯⋯⋯⋯⋯⋯⋯⋯ p.66

Reading

해석

새로운 기숙사 건설

본교에서 이번 봄에 새로운 기숙사에 대한 공사가 시작될 예정입니다. 이곳은 Deacon 홀 뒤에 위치하게 될 것입니다. 이 기숙사는 200개의 방을 갖추게 될 것입니다. 이러한 방에는 1인실, 2인실, 그리고 3인실이 포함됩니다. 이로써 보다 많은 학생들이 학교 밖이 아닌 교내에서 지낼 수 있을 것입니다.

✏ Note Taking

Topic Building a new dormitory

Reason To allow more students to live on campus

Organization

The school is going to build a new dormitory. It will have 200 rooms, including singles, doubles, and triples.

Listening

Script 🎧 02-53

W Student: The school is going to build another new dorm? Don't we already have enough of them? The school should spend more money on academic buildings. We need a new science building with modern labs.

M Student: I disagree with you. I don't think we have enough dorms on campus. I have to live off campus this year, and I don't like it. My home is far from school and costs more than a dorm room. I want more dormitories on campus.

해석

W Student: 학교측이 기숙사를 또 건설한다고? 이미 충분히 있지 않니? 학교측은 학과 건물에 더 많은 돈을 써야 해. 현대적인 실험실을 갖춘 과학관이 필요하다고.

M Student: 나는 네 말에 동의하지 않아. 나는 교내에 기숙사가 충분하지 않다고 생각해. 나는 올해 캠퍼스 밖에서 지내야 하는데, 그건 마음에 들지 않는 일이야. 집이 학교에서 멀리 떨어져 있고 기숙사보다 방값도 비싸. 나는 교내에 기숙사가 더 많으면 좋겠어.

✏ Note Taking

Woman	Man
Opinion Doesn't want another dorm	**Opinion** Would like more dorms on campus
Reason She wants a new science building with modern labs instead.	**Reason** He lives off campus and doesn't like it. His home is far from school and more expensive than a dorm room.

Comparing

Sample Response 🎧 02-54

The man agrees with the plan to build a new dorm. He lives off campus because there are not enough dorm rooms, and he doesn't like it. His home is far from school and more expensive than a dorm room. He wants more dormitories on campus.

해석

남자는 새 기숙사를 건설하려는 계획을 찬성한다. 그는 기숙사 방이 충분하지 않아서 학교 밖에서 지내고 있는데, 그러한 상황이 마음에 들지 않는다. 그의 집은 학교에서 멀리 떨어져 있고 기숙사 방보다 방값이 더 비싸다. 그는 교내에 기숙사가 더 많아지기를 바란다.

Exercise 2 .... p.67

Reading

해석

도서관이 확장됩니다

Jefferson 도서관이 곧 확장될 예정입니다. 규모를 현재의 두 배로 확대시키기 위해 도서관에서 공사가 진행될 것입니다. 추후에는 더 많은 도서, 잡지, 그리고 컴퓨터가 배치될 수 있을 것입니다. 도서관은 가을 학기 동안 폐쇄될 예정입니다. 공사는 12월에 마무리될 것입니다.

🖊 Note Taking

Topic Expanding the size of the school library
Reason To double the size to hold more books, journals, and computers

Organization

The library is going to expand. This will double the size of the library and let it hold more books, journals, and computers. However, it will close for construction during the fall semester.

Listening

Script 🎧 02-55

M Student: Can you believe it? The library is going to be closed during the fall semester due to construction. The library is already big enough. And most people use e-books, so we don't need a bigger library.

W Student: I agree with you. It's going to be hard for me to do research this fall. My grades might fall if I can't visit the library. I don't understand why the school is doing this.

해석

M Student: 믿을 수 있니? 도서관이 공사 때문에 가을 학기 동안 폐쇄될 거래. 도서관은 지금도 충분히 큰데 말이야. 그리고 대부분의 학생들이 전자책을 사용하기 때문에 도서관이 더 클 필요가 없어.

W Student: 나도 네 말에 동의해. 이번 가을에 조사를 하는 일이 힘들어질 거

야. 도서관에 가지 못하면 내 성적은 떨어질 수도 있어. 왜 학교측이 이런 일을 하려는지 이해가 안 가.

🖊 Note Taking

Man	Woman
Opinion Thinks the school should not expand the library	**Opinion** Thinks the school should not expand the library
Reason The library is big enough already. People use e-books, so the library doesn't need to expand.	**Reason** She will have a hard time doing research when the library is closed. She might get lower grades.

Comparing

Sample Response 🎧 02-56

The woman is not pleased with the announcement. She does not like the fact that the library will close during the fall semester. She thinks doing research will be hard, and she believes her grades will fall.

해석

여자는 공지를 반기지 않는다. 그녀는 도서관이 가을 학기 동안 문을 닫을 것이라는 사실이 마음에 들지 않는다. 그녀는 조사를 하는 일이 힘들어 질 것이라고 생각하고 자신의 성적이 떨어질 것이라고 믿는다.

Exercise 3 .... p.68

Reading

해석

화학과 폐지

학교측은 화학과를 폐지하기로 결정했습니다. 현재 화학을 전공하는 학생이 거의 없기 때문에 해당 학과를 유지할 필요가 없습니다. 현재 화학을 전공 중인 학생들은 전공을 바꾸거나 다른 학교로 전학을 가야 합니다. 정보가 더 필요한 경우에는 학생처장실로 연락을 주시기 바랍니다.

🖊 Note Taking

Topic Closing the Chemistry Department
Reason There are few students who are majoring in chemistry now.

Organization

There is no need to have the department since few students are currently majoring in chemistry.

Listening

Script 🎧 02-57

W Student: I can't believe the school is going to close the Chemistry Department. I'm a pre-med student, and I need to take several chemistry classes. I may have to transfer to another school.

M Student: I'm sorry to hear that, but I agree with the decision. I took a chemistry class once, but it only had eleven students. My other classes have more than twice that number. The school can use the money it saves on more popular majors like economics.

해석

W Student: 학교측이 화학과를 폐지하려고 한다니 믿기지가 않아. 나는 의예과 학생이라서 화학 수업을 몇 개 들어야만 해. 다른 학교로 전학을 가야 할지도 모르겠군.

M Student: 그런 이야기를 들으니 유감이지만 나는 이번 결정에 찬성이야. 화학 수업을 한 번 들은 적이 있는데, 학생이 11명뿐이었어. 다른 수업에는 그 두 배 이상의 학생들이 있는데 말이야. 학교측은 남는 돈을 경제학과와 같은 인기 있는 다른 전공 과목에 쓸 수 있을 거야.

✎ Note Taking

Woman	Man
Opinion Is unhappy the school will close the Chemistry Department	**Opinion** Agrees with the school's decision
Reason She needs to take several chemistry classes because she is a pre-med student.	**Reason** The chemistry class he took once had few students. He wants the school to spend the money on more popular majors.

Comparing

Sample Response 🎧 02-58

The man supports the decision to close the Chemistry Department. He took a chemistry class one time, but it had few students. Other classes he has taken had at least twice the number of students. He thinks the school can spend the money it saves on popular majors such as economics.

해석

남자는 화학과를 폐지한다는 결정을 지지한다. 그는 화학 수업을 한 번 들었는데, 그때 수강생이 거의 없었다. 그가 들었던 다른 수업에는 최소 그 두 배의 학생들이 있었다. 그는 학교측이 경제학과 같은 인기 있는 전공 과목에 남는 돈을 쓸 수 있을 것이라고 생각한다.

Exercise 4 .... p.69

Reading

해석

미술관에서 학생들을 위한 전시회가 열립니다

교내 미술관에서 학생 예술가들을 위한 전시회가 개최될 예정입니다. 전시회는 4월 10일부터 23일까지 계속됩니다. 모든 학생들이 자신의 작품을 제출하여 심사를 받을 수 있습니다. 작품은 유명한 지역 예술가들이 심사할 것입니다. 심사위원에 의해 선정된 상위 5개 작품에는 상금이 지급됩니다.

✎ Note Taking

Topic Holding an exhibition for student artists
Reason To let famous local artists view the work and to have the top five entries receive prizes

Organization

It will hold an exhibition that all students may submit work for consideration to be displayed. Several famous local artists will view the work. And the top five entries will receive prizes.

Listening

Script 🎧 02-59

W Student: Isn't this great? I'm so pleased that the art gallery will be holding an exhibition. I hope that my work gets approved. I'd love for some famous artists to check out my work.

M Student: I think this is a great opportunity. I'm not an artist, but lots of students here paint. Many of them are really talented. They just need a chance to get discovered. Having their work displayed at the exhibition can help them.

해석

W Student: 멋지지 않아? 미술관에서 전시회를 한다니 정말 기뻐. 내 작품이 통과되었으면 좋겠어. 유명한 화가들이 내 작품을 심사하면 정말 좋을 것 같아.

M Student: 나도 좋은 기회가 될 것이라고 생각해. 나는 그림을 그리지 않지만 이곳 많은 학생들이 그림을 그리고 있지. 그중 다수는 정말로 소질이 뛰어나. 인정을 받을 수 있는 기회가 필요할 뿐이지. 전시회에 작품을 전시한다면 그들에게 도움이 될 수 있을 거야.

✎ Note Taking

Woman	Man
Opinion Is pleased with the decision by the art gallery	**Opinion** Thinks this is a great opportunity for student artists
Reason She hopes her work is selected. She wants some famous artists to view her work.	**Reason** He thinks many students are talented artists. They just need a chance to be discovered.

Comparing

Sample Response 🎧 02-60

The woman is very pleased with the announcement by the art gallery. She plans to submit her work for consideration to be displayed at the exhibition. She says that she hopes her work can be viewed by some famous artists.

해석

여자는 미술관의 공지 내용에 매우 만족해한다. 그녀는 전시회에서 자신의 작품을 전시하기 위해 작품을 제출해서 심사를 받으려고 한다. 그녀는 자신의 작품이 유명 예술가들에 의해 심사를 받게 되기를 희망한다고 말한다.

Reading

해석

학교 신문의 발행 기간 단축

용지 및 잉크 가격의 상승과 비용 절감의 필요성 때문에 학교 신문이 더 이상 매일 발행되지는 않을 것입니다. 대신 월요일, 수요일, 그리고 금요일에 발행될 예정입니다. 인터넷으로는 여전히 일주일 내내 신문을 볼 수 있습니다. 신문은 학생, 교수진, 그리고 교직원들에게 계속해서 무료로 제공될 것입니다.

Note Taking

Topic The reduced number of days the school newspaper is printed

Reason To save money due to the rising costs of paper and ink

Organization

It will no longer be printed daily. Instead, due to the rising costs of paper and ink, it will be printed three days a week on Monday, Wednesday, and Friday.

Listening

Script 🎧 02-61

W Student: I'd say that this is a smart decision by the school. Not many students even read the printed version of the paper. So I'd say that it's a waste of money even to print the paper one day a week.

M Student: I completely disagree with you. I love to read the school newspaper at breakfast every day. It gives me up-to-date news about school events. The online version is not very good. I would much rather read the printed version.

해석

W Student: 학교측이 현명한 결정을 내렸다고 말하고 싶군. 인쇄된 형태의 신문을 읽는 학생은 많지 않아. 그래서 나는 일주일에 하루만 신문을 발행하는 것조차 돈 낭비라고 말하고 싶어.

M Student: 나는 네 말에 전적으로 동의하지 않아. 나는 매일 아침을 먹으면서 학교 신문을 읽는 것이 정말 좋거든. 신문은 학교 행사에 관한 최신 소식을 알려 주지. 온라인 신문은 그다지 좋지가 않더라고. 나로서는 인쇄된 형태의 신문을 읽는 것이 훨씬 좋아.

Note Taking

Woman	Man
Opinion Agrees with the decision to reduce the number of days the paper is printed	**Opinion** Disagrees with the decision to print the paper less often
Reason She says that few students read the printed version. She also thinks it's a waste of money to print the paper.	**Reason** He reads the newspaper at breakfast every day. He thinks the online version is not good and prefers the printed version.

Comparing

Sample Response 🎧 02-62

The man disagrees with the decision to print the school newspaper less often. First, he says that he likes reading the paper at breakfast every day. Next, he points out that the online version is poor. So the printed version is much better for him.

해석

남자는 학교 신문의 발행 기간을 단축하겠다는 결정에 반대한다. 우선 그는 자신이 매일 아침 식사를 하면서 신문을 읽는 것을 좋아한다고 말한다. 다음으로 그는 온라인 신문이 좋지 않다고 지적한다. 따라서 그에게는 인쇄된 형태의 신문이 훨씬 더 낫다.

Reading

해석

리모델링 공사로 인한 Harper 홀 폐쇄

올해 혹독한 겨울 날씨로 인해 Harper 홀이 피해를 입었습니다. 이 건물은 보수 공사를 위해 현재 폐쇄된 상태입니다. 보수 공사는 봄 학기 내내 진행될 것으로 예상됩니다. Harper 홀의 모든 수업 장소는 다른 건물들로 이전될 것입니다. 새로운 교실에 대한 리스트는 해당 학과에서 확인하시기 바랍니다.

Note Taking

Topic The closing of Harper Hall for the spring semester

Reason To repair the building after it suffered damage from severe winter weather

Organization

The building suffered damage due to severe winter weather. The building is closed for repairs.

Listening

Script 🎧 02-63

W Student: Oh, no! This is terrible. Half of my classes are in Harper Hall. I just checked the new schedule, and I'm going to have to go to Whittaker Hall for my classes. That building is on the other side of campus.

M Student: I understand how you feel. But the school made the right decision. The building isn't safe, so it needs to be repaired. What if the roof collapsed when students were in class? It's inconvenient for some people, but the repairs need to be made.

해석

W Student: 오, 이런! 큰일이군. 내 수업 절반은 Harper 홀에서 이루어져. 내가 새로운 스케줄을 조금 전에 확인해 봤는데, 수업을 받으러 Whittaker 홀까지 가야만 하더라고. 그 건물은 캠퍼스 반대편에 있는데 말이야.

M Student: 네가 어떤 기분인지 이해할 수 있어. 하지만 학교측은 올바른 결정을 내린 거야. 그 건물은 안전하지 않기 때문에 보수 공수가 이루어져야 해. 학

생들이 수업을 듣고 있을 때 지붕이 무너지면 어떻게 되겠어? 몇몇 사람들에게 는 불편한 일이겠지만 보수 공사는 진행되어야 한다고.

> ✏ Note Taking
>
> | Woman | Man |
> |---|---|
> | **Opinion** Disagrees with the school's decision | **Opinion** Agrees with the school's decision |
> | **Reason** Half of her classes are in Harper Hall. Now, she has to go to a different building on the other side of campus. | **Reason** He understands that it's inconvenient for some students. However, the building needs to be repaired since it isn't safe right now. |

Comparing

Sample Response 🎧 02-64

The man agrees with the decision by the school to close Harper Hall. He says that while it is inconvenient for some students, the building isn't safe. Therefore, it should be repaired before something bad happens when students are in the building.

해석

남자는 Harper 홀을 폐쇄하겠다는 학교측의 결정을 지지한다. 그는 몇몇 학생들이 불편해할 수는 있지만 그 건물은 안전하지 않다고 말한다. 따라서 학생들이 그 건물에 있을 때 불행한 일이 생기기 전에 보수 공사가 이루어져야 할 것이다.

Unit 12 School Life

Exercise 1 .... p.72

Reading
해석

이번 겨울 방학에는 학생들이 기숙사에 머물 수 없습니다

12월 23일부터 1월 18일까지 이번 겨울 방학에는 학생들이 기숙사에서 지내는 것이 허용되지 않습니다. 이 기간 동안 각 기숙사에서 소규모 보수 공사가 진행될 예정입니다. 모든 학생들은 12월 22일 자정까지 기숙사 방에서 퇴실해야 합니다. 입실은 1월 18일 오후 1시에 가능합니다.

> ✏ Note Taking
>
> **Topic** No students in dormitories during winter break
> **Reason** To allow minor renovations to be conducted

Organization

Minor renovations will be conducted in the school's dormitories. As a result, students may not stay in their dorm rooms during winter break.

Listening
Script 🎧 02-65

> **M Student**: Can you believe this? The dorms are going to be closed this winter break. I always stay at school during the holidays, but now I can't. I'm not sure what I will do for a month this winter.
>
> **W Student**: I'm sorry for your inconvenience, but I understand the school's policy. I read about the renovations. The dorms will be much nicer when we return for the spring semester. So I'm rather pleased about this.

해석

M Student: 믿을 수 있어? 기숙사가 이번 겨울 방학 동안 폐쇄될 예정이야. 나는 휴일이면 항상 학교에서 지내는데, 이제 그럴 수가 없게 되었군. 이번 겨울 한 달 동안 어떻게 해야 할지 잘 모르겠어.

W Student: 네가 불편을 겪게 되어 유감이지만, 나는 학교측의 방침이 이해가 가. 나는 보수 공사에 대한 글을 읽어 봤어. 우리가 봄에 다시 돌아올 때에는 기숙사가 훨씬 더 좋아져 있을 거야. 그래서 이번 일이 꽤 마음에 들어.

> ✏ Note Taking
>
> | Man | Woman |
> |---|---|
> | **Opinion** Dislikes the announcement | **Opinion** Approves of the announcement |
> | **Reason** Always stays at school during winter break, but now has to find another place to stay | **Reason** Thinks the renovations will make the dormitories much nicer for the students |

Comparing

Sample Response 🎧 02-66

The woman approves of the announcement by the school. She says that she knows what kinds of renovations will happen in the dormitories. She points out that the dorms will be much nicer for the students when they return to school.

해석

여자는 학교측의 공지 내용을 지지한다. 그녀는 기숙사에서 어떤 종류의 보수 공사가 진행될 것인지 알고 있다고 말한다. 그녀는 학생들이 학교로 돌아올 때 기숙사가 학생들에게 훨씬 더 좋은 곳이 될 것이라고 주장한다.

Exercise 2 .... p.73

Reading
해석

기숙사 내에서의 소음 감소

학생들의 여러 불만 제기에 따라 현재 새로운 소음 규정이 교내 기숙사에 적용되고 있습니다. 오후 9시부터 오전 7시까지 기숙사 내 학생들은 학생들이 공부를 하고 수면을 취할 수 있도록 정숙해야 합니다. 이는 시끄러운 음악 소리, 고함, 함성, 그리고 다른 학생들을 방해할 수 있는 소음이 금지된다는 점을 의미합니다. 이러한 규정을 위반하는 학생들에게는 벌금이 부과될 것입니다.

Topic A new noise regulation in the school dormitories
Reason To make the dormitories quiet for students to study and sleep

Organization

They must be quiet from 9:00 PM to 7:00 AM. So they may not play loud music, yell, shout, or make noises that can disturb other students.

Listening

Script 🎧 02-67

M Student: What kind of new regulation is this? We have to be quiet in the dorms for nearly half the day now. I can't believe the school is trying to tell students what to do. The dorms aren't even that loud.

W Student: I disagree with you, Mark. In my dorm, students play music and have parties until after midnight. It's hard for me to focus on my studies in my dorm room. And the library is too far away for me to visit at night. I'm glad the school is doing something about the noise level.

해석
M Student: 이게 도대체 무슨 종류의 새 규정이지? 이제 거의 하루의 절반 동안 기숙사에서 조용히 지내야만 하겠군. 학교측이 학생들에게 이래라저래라 하려고 한다니 믿기지가 않아. 심지어 기숙사가 그렇게 시끄럽지도 않은데 말이야.

W Student: 나는 네 말에 동의하지 않아, Mark. 우리 기숙사에서는 학생들이 자정 이후까지 음악을 틀고 파티를 열거든. 기숙사에서는 공부에 집중하기가 힘들어. 그리고 도서관은 너무 멀리 떨어져 있어서 밤에 가기가 힘들고. 나는 학교측이 소음 수준에 대해 무언가 조치를 취하려고 한다는 점이 마음에 들어.

✏ Note Taking

Man	Woman
Opinion Disagrees with the decision to restrict noise	**Opinion** Is glad the school is restricting the noise level in the dorms
Reason He dislikes the school telling students what to do and thinks the dorms are not very loud.	**Reason** She says that students make too much noise even after midnight. So she can't concentrate on her studies in her own room.

Comparing

Sample Response 🎧 02-68

The woman is glad that the school made the announcement about the new regulation in the dorms. She says that students in her dorm have loud parties until after midnight. She cannot concentrate on her studies in her dorm room. And the library is not close enough to her to visit at night.

해석
여자는 학교측이 기숙사의 새로운 규정에 대해 공지를 해서 기뻐한다. 그녀는 자신의 기숙사에 있는 학생들이 자정 이후까지 시끄러운 파티를 연다고 말한다. 그녀는 기숙사 방에서 공부에 집중할 수가 없다. 그리고 도서관은 그녀가 밤에 갈 수 있을 정도로 가까이에 있지 않다.

Exercise 3 .... p.74

Reading

해석

교내 안전 요원의 감축

올해 대학 예산이 감소되었습니다. 따라서 더 이상 다수의 안전 요원을 고용할 수가 없게 되었습니다. 평소 20명이었던 것과 달리 이제 10명의 요원들이 상시 근무를 할 것입니다. 밤에는 친구들과 함께 교내를 돌아다닐 것을 학생들에게 권고합니다.

✏ Note Taking

Topic Reducing the number of safety officers on campus
Reason To compensate for the decrease in the school's budget

Organization

The school will have ten safety officers on duty now. This is a reduction from the twenty that are currently on duty.

Listening

Script 🎧 02-69

W Student: This is a really bad decision by the school. The school is making the campus unsafe for everyone by reducing the number of safety officers. Crime on campus is almost surely going to increase now.

M Student: I know what you mean. One of my friends was assaulted recently, but a safety officer was nearby and caught the person responsible. Lots of my friends are going to be too frightened to go out at night now.

해석
W Student: 학교측이 정말로 잘못된 결정을 내렸군. 학교측은 안전 요원의 수를 줄여서 캠퍼스가 모두에게 안전하지 못한 곳으로 만들고 있어. 이제 교내 범죄가 거의 틀림없이 증가하게 될 거야.

M Student: 무슨 말인지 알아. 내 친구 중 한 명도 최근에 폭행을 당했지만 안전 요원이 근처에 있어서 범인을 붙잡았지. 이제는 많은 친구들이 너무 무서워서 밤에 나가지 못하게 되겠군.

Woman	Man
Opinion Is unhappy with the school's decision	**Opinion** Disagrees with the school's decision
Reason Thinks that the campus will be unsafe and that crime will increase	**Reason** Says that a friend was assaulted but that a safety officer helped his friend and adds that many of his friends will be scared to go outside at night

Comparing

Sample Response 🎧 02-70

The man disagrees with the school's decision to reduce the number of safety officers on campus. He points out that one of his friends was assaulted on campus. However, a safety officer stopped the crime. In addition, he thinks some of his friends will be too scared to go out at night now.

해석

남자는 교내 안전 요원의 수를 줄이겠다는 학교측의 결정에 반대한다. 그는 자신의 친구 중 한 명이 교내에서 폭행을 당했다고 지적한다. 하지만 안전 요원이 범죄를 제지했다. 게다가 그는 자신의 몇몇 친구들이 이제는 너무 무서워서 밤에 밖으로 나가지 못할 것이라고 생각한다.

Exercise 4 ·· p.75

Reading

해석

총장님과의 저녁 식사

Jason Milo 대학 총장님과 저녁 식사를 함께 하고 싶으신가요? 다음 주를 시작으로 학생들은 총장님과 매주 월요일과 목요일 저녁에 식사를 할 수가 있습니다. 그분과 10명의 학생들이 저녁마다 식사를 하면서 학교 및 현안에 대한 이야기를 나눌 수 있습니다. 신청을 원하면 총장실을 방문해 주십시오.

✏ Note Taking

Topic Letting students have dinner with the university president

Reason To let students talk with the president about school and current affairs

Organization

They can apply to have dinner with the university president. They can eat with him and also talk to him about school and current affairs.

Listening

Script 🎧 02-71

M Student: What a silly idea. Why would I want to have dinner with the school president? I'm sure that not many students are going to apply to this program.

W Student: I disagree with you. I'm going to apply to have dinner with him. I would like to ask him some questions about the school. For example, maybe I can convince him to get the school to hire more sociology teachers.

해석

M Student: 참으로 어리석은 아이디어로군. 내가 왜 총장님과 함께 저녁을 먹으려고 하겠어? 이번 프로그램에 지원하는 학생들은 분명 그다지 많지 않을 거야.

W Student: 나는 그렇게 생각하지 않아. 나는 그분과의 저녁 식사를 신청할 거야. 학교에 대해 몇가지 질문을 하고 싶거든. 예를 들어 내가 그분을 설득시켜서 학교측이 사회학 교수님들을 더 많이 고용하도록 만들 수도 있을 거야.

✏ Note Taking

Man	Woman
Opinion Thinks the idea is silly	**Opinion** Likes the idea of having dinner with the president
Reason Believes very few people would want to have dinner with the president	**Reason** Wants to talk to the president about the school

Comparing

Sample Response 🎧 02-72

The woman is pleased with the announcement that students can have dinner with the school president. She says that she wants to ask him some school-related questions. For instance, she could ask him to hire more sociology professors.

해석

여자는 학생들이 대학 총장과 저녁 식사를 할 수 있다는 공지 내용을 반긴다. 그녀는 자신이 총장에게 학교와 관련된 몇 가지 질문을 하고 싶다고 말한다. 예를 들어 그녀는 총장에게 사회학 교수를 더 많이 고용해 달라고 요청할 수 있을 것이다.

Exercise 5 ·· p.76

Reading

해석

신입생의 밀플랜

가을 학기를 시작으로 모든 신입생들은 일주일에 최소 14번의 식사를 할 수 있는 밀플랜을 구입해야 합니다. 이는 신입생들이 하루에 충분한 양의 식사를 할 수 있도록 하기 위한 것입니다. 이러한 방침은 기숙사에서 생활하는 모든 학생들에게 적용됩니다. 자택에서 생활하는 학생들은 이번 프로그램에 대해 면제를 신청할 수 있습니다.

Organization

It has been decided that all freshmen must have meal plans for fourteen or more meals per week. This will guarantee that students get enough food to eat.

Listening

Script 🎧 02-73

W Student: I like this new school policy. I know a lot of students who don't have meal plans here. They are constantly hungry during the day, and this affects their studies.

M Student: I don't see it that way. When I was a freshman, I rarely ate at any of the dining halls. The food just isn't good there. Instead, I ate at restaurants on and around campus. A meal plan will be a waste of money for some students.

해석

W Student: 이 새로운 학교 방침은 마음에 드는걸. 나는 이곳에서 밀플랜을 가지고 있지 않은 학생들을 많이 알고 있어. 그들은 하루 동안 항상 배고픔을 느끼는데, 이러한 점이 그들의 학업에 영향을 미치고 있지.

M Student: 나는 그렇게 생각하지 않아. 내가 신입생이었을 때 나는 학교 식당 중 어디에서도 거의 식사를 거의 하지 않았어. 그곳 음식이 별로였거든. 대신 교내 안팎의 레스토랑에서 식사를 했지. 몇몇 학생들에게는 밀플랜이 돈 낭비가 될 거야.

Comparing

Sample Response 🎧 02-74

The man dislikes the new policy that freshmen must have meal plans of fourteen or more meals a week. He points out that he rarely ate in the dining halls as a freshman. He ate elsewhere because the food is bad. For some freshmen, the meal plan will be a waste of money.

해석

남자는 신입생들이 일주일에 14번 이상 식사를 할 수 있는 밀플랜을 구입해야 한다는 새로운 방침에 반대한다. 그는 자신이 신입생이었을 때 학교 식당에서 거의 식사를 하지 않았다는 점을 지적한다. 그는 그곳 음식이 형편없었기 때문에

다른 곳에서 식사를 했다. 일부 신입생들에게 밀플랜은 돈 낭비가 될 것이다.

Exercise 6 .... p.77

Reading

해석

신설 장학금

몇몇 후한 기부자들 덕분에 학생들에게 제공될 새로운 장학금들이 신설되었습니다. 각 장학금은 각기 다른 금액으로 지급되며 등록금으로 사용됩니다. 이러한 장학금은 가정 형편이 아니라 학업 성적에 따라 지급됩니다. 신청을 원하는 경우에는 학생처장 사무실로 오시기 바랍니다.

Organization

The scholarships pay various amounts of money for tuition. Students can receive scholarships based upon their academic performance.

Listening

Script 🎧 02-75

M Student: You know, I'm happy that the school has new scholarships. But they should be need-based scholarships, not ones based on academics. I need a scholarship, but I don't have the best grades.

W Student: I disagree with you. Students who do well at school should be rewarded even if they don't need the money. These scholarships will make students study harder to improve their grades.

해석

M Student: 너도 알겠지만 나는 새로운 장학금이 마련되어 기뻐. 하지만 성적 장학금이 아니라 재정 지원 장학금이 되어야 해. 나도 장학금이 필요한데, 성적이 가장 우수하지는 않거든.

W Student: 나는 네 말에 동의하지 않아. 필요하지 않더라도 학교 성적이 좋은 학생들이 돈을 받아야 해. 이런 장학금 때문에 학생들이 성적을 올리려고 더 열심히 공부하게 될 테니까.

Comparing

Sample Response 🎧 02-76

The woman likes the announcement of new scholarships. She believes that giving scholarships based on grades is a good idea. It rewards students who do well at school. She thinks students will study harder to improve their grades now.

해석

여자는 신설된 장학금에 관한 공지를 반긴다. 그녀는 성적에 기반해서 장학금을 주는 것이 좋은 아이디어라고 생각한다. 이로써 학교 성적이 우수한 학생들에게 보상이 돌아갈 것이다. 그녀는 이제 학생들이 성적을 높이기 위해 더 열심히 공부할 것이라고 생각한다.

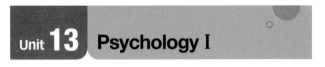

Unit 13 Psychology I

Exercise 1 .... p.84

Reading

해석

몰입

몰입이란 사람들이 자신이 하는 일에 완전히 집중할 때 일어나는 정신 상태이다. 몰입의 효과로서 집중력, 참여도, 그리고 성취감을 들 수 있다. 몰입의 상태에 있으면 마치 자신이 막대한 창의력을 지닌 것처럼 느껴진다. 몰입에서 빠져 나오면 이전 정신 상태가 사라짐으로써 종종 우울함을 느끼게 된다.

> ✎ **Note Taking**
>
> **Flow** A mental state of concentration resulting in senses of focus, involvement, and success
> **Positive effect** Can feel creative with flow
> **Negative effect** May feel depressed without flow

Organization

Flow is a mental phenomenon that occurs when people concentrate fully on the task at hand.

Listening

Script 🎧 03-05

> **M Professor:** Take my friend Ken for example. Ken was a successful architect who experienced a state of flow while designing buildings. But when he retired, he was suddenly deprived of this sensation. He retired with plenty of money and time to enjoy a leisurely lifestyle, but he was plagued by nightmares, insomnia, and depression because of the loss of flow from his work.

해석

M Professor: 제 친구인 Ken을 예로 들어보겠습니다. Ken은 건물을 설계하는 동안 몰입의 상태를 경험했던 성공적인 건축가였어요. 하지만 은퇴를 하자 갑자기 그러한 감정을 잃어 버렸죠. 은퇴를 했을 때 여유로운 삶을 즐길 수 있는 돈과 시간은 많았지만 일에서 느꼈던 몰입이 사라졌기 때문에 악몽, 불면증, 그리고 우울증에 시달렸습니다.

> ✎ **Note Taking**
>
> **Ken** Was successful architect who designed buildings
> **Result** When retired, suffered from nightmares, insomnia, and depression

Comparing

Sample Response 🎧 03-06

One of the professor's friends was a successful architect. When he was designing buildings, he often entered a state of flow. Flow occurs when someone concentrates on something, and it often results in an excess of creativity. This was true of the professor's friend. In addition, when his friend retired, he no longer experienced flow, so he suffered from nightmares, insomnia, and depression. All of these are common when people are not experiencing flow.

해석

교수의 친구 가운데 한 사람은 성공한 건축가였다. 건물 설계를 하고 있을 때 그는 종종 몰입의 상태에 들어갔다. 몰입은 무엇인가에 집중할 때 일어나며, 종종 창의력이 과다하게 나타나는 결과로 이어진다. 이는 교수의 친구의 경우에도 해당되었다. 게다가 친구가 은퇴를 했을 때 그는 더 이상 몰입을 경험하지 못했고, 이 때문에 악몽, 불면증, 그리고 우울증을 겪었다. 이 모두는 몰입을 경험하지 못할 때 흔히 일어나는 현상이다.

Exercise 2 ·· p.85

Reading
해석

행동적 스크립트

행동적 스크립트는 누군가 익숙한 상황을 마주할 때 일어나는 행동이다. 일련의 행동들은 습관 및 연습을 통해 획득된다. 이는 새로운 상황을 파악하는데 소요되는 시간 및 정신적인 노력을 절약시켜 준다.

> 🖊 Note Taking
>
> **Behavioral script** Actions taken when one encounters a familiar situation
> **Result** Can save a person time and mental effort

Organization

A behavioral script is a pattern of actions that a person follows when he comes across a situation he is familiar with.

Listening
Script 🎧 03-07

M Professor: I needed to learn a new song, but I was having trouble memorizing the verses. So I thought back in my memory to a song that I once learned using behavioral script. The way I did it was that I repeated each verse a corresponding number of times. For example, I repeated the first one once, the second one twice, and the third one three times. I repeated this with the new song and learned it easily.

해석

M Professor: 저는 새로운 노래를 배워야 했는데, 가사를 외우는 것이 힘들었어요. 그래서 행동적 스크립트를 이용해서 예전에 익혔던 노래에 대한 기억을 떠올렸죠. 제가 한 것은 각 절을 해당 수만큼 반복해서 부르는 것이었어요. 예를 들어 1절은 한 번, 2절은 두 번, 그리고 3절은 세 번을 반복해서 불렀죠. 저는 새로운 노래도 이렇게 반복해서 불러서 쉽게 가사를 익힐 수 있었습니다.

> 🖊 Note Taking
>
> **Problem** Could not memorize verses in song
> **Solution** Used behavioral script and repeated verses multiple times to remember song

Comparing
Sample Response 🎧 03-08

The professor mentions that he was having trouble memorizing a song. He could not remember the verses. So he thought about a method he had used earlier to memorize a different song. He used behavioral script by repeating the verses a certain number of times. Behavioral script involves actions a person takes when doing something very familiar. It is a way a person can act without having to think much. Once the professor used this method, he easily memorized the song.

해석

교수는 자신이 노래를 외우는데 어려움이 있었다고 말한다. 그는 가사를 외울 수가 없었다. 그래서 그는 다른 노래를 암기하기 위해 더 이전에 사용했던 방법을 떠올렸다. 그는 특정 횟수로 각 절을 반복해서 부름으로써 행동적 스크립트를 이용했다. 행동적 스크립트는 매우 익숙한 것을 할 때 사람들이 하는 행동과 관련이 있다. 이는 크게 생각을 하지 않고 행동을 취하는 방법이다. 교수는 이 방법을 사용해서 쉽게 노래를 암기했다.

Exercise 3 ·· p.86

Reading
해석

전위

전위는 어떤 개인이 자신의 감정을 옮겨 놓는 심리학적인 효과이다. 그러한 감정을 위험하거나 받아들일 수 없는 대상으로부터 안전하거나 받아들일 수 있는 대상으로 보내 버린다. 이에 관한 한 가지 예는 친구에게 화가 날 때 베개를 때리는 것이다.

> 🖊 Note Taking
>
> **Displacement** Is transfer of feelings
> **Example** When a person punches pillow instead of friend

Organization

Displacement is transferring one's feelings away from something that could be dangerous or harmful to something that is safe and less harmful.

Listening
Script 🎧 03-09

M Professor: One year, my parents forgot to wish me a happy birthday. I was hurt and angry but too proud to remind them. Later that day, the phone rang. I picked up the phone, and it was someone who'd dialed the wrong number. Normally, I would just politely tell the person that he had the wrong number. But this time, I displaced my anger and screamed at the person even though he had made an innocent mistake.

해석

M Professor: 어느 해에 부모님께서 깜빡 잊으시고 제 생일을 축하해 주지 않으셨습니다. 저는 상처를 받고 화가 났지만, 자존심 때문에 먼저 알려 드리지 않았죠. 그날 늦게 전화가 울렸습니다. 저는 전화기를 집어 들었는데, 잘못 걸려온 전화였어요. 평소라면 정중하게 그 사람에게 전화를 잘못 걸었다고 말했을 것입니다. 하지만 이때에는, 그 사람이 모르고 한 실수였음에도 불구하고, 저는 제 분노를 그에게 돌려서 소리를 질렀습니다.

🖉 Note Taking

Problem Professor's parents forgot his birthday
Action Got telephone call but was wrong number
Result Yelled at person who had called

Comparing

Sample Response 🎧 03-10

One time, the professor's parents forgot about his birthday. That same day, a person called his house, but he had the wrong number. Instead of being polite, the professor yelled at the person. This was an example of displacement. Instead of getting angry at his parents, the professor yelled at someone on the other end of the phone line. He transferred his feelings away from his parents to someone that he did not even know.

해석

한 번은 교수의 부모님이 교수의 생일을 잊어 버렸다. 같은 날 어떤 사람이 그의 집에 전화를 했는데, 전화번호가 잘못되어 있었다. 교수는 예의 바르게 행동하는 대신 그 사람에게 소리를 질렀다. 이것은 전위의 사례였다. 교수는 부모님께 화를 내는 대신 전화 상대방에게 소리를 질렀다. 자신의 감정을 부모로부터 알지도 못하는 사람에게 옮겨 놓은 것이었다.

Exercise 4 .... p.87

Reading
해석

인상 관리

인상 관리란 다른 사람이 자신을 어떻게 생각하는지를 조절하려는 행동이다. 이는 특히 첫인상을 남기고자 할 때 흔히 나타난다. 이러한 행동은 자신이 원하는 바와 같이 생각되도록 자신의 복장과 매너를 드러낼 때 나타난다.

🖉 Note Taking

Impression management Involves trying to control people's opinions of self
Example Dress and act according to way one wants to be thought of

Organization

Impression management is trying to control the way people think of themselves by dressing and acting according to the image they want to project.

Listening

Script 🎧 03-11

W Professor: When I first began working at this university, the dean asked me to drive him to a meeting the next day. That night, I went home, washed my car, and cleaned the inside. I was hoping to impress the dean. I even bought a classical music CD, which I don't normally listen to, so that we could listen to it in the car.

해석

W Professor: 제가 이 대학에서 첫 근무를 시작했을 때, 그 다음날 학장님께서 회의 장소까지 자신을 차로 태워다 달라고 부탁하셨어요. 그날 밤 저는 집으로 가서 세차를 하고, 실내도 청소했죠. 학장님께 좋은 인상을 남기고 싶었거든요. 차 안에서 들을 수 있도록 평소에는 잘 듣지도 않는 클래식 음악 CD까지 사 두었죠.

🖉 Note Taking

Situation Professor had to drive dean to meeting next day
Action Cleaned car and bought classical music CD to listen to in car

Comparing

Sample Response 🎧 03-12

The professor was going to drive the dean to a meeting the next day. So before she took him, she cleaned her car and bought a classical music CD to listen to while they were driving. This is an example of impression management. The professor tried to control the image that she presented to the dean. She wanted to look clean and cultured, so she tried to control the way that he thought of her.

해석

교수는 다음날 학장을 회의 장소까지 태워다 줄 예정이었다. 그래서 그를 태우기 전에 세차를 하고 이동 중에 들을 수 있도록 클래식 음악 CD도 구입했다. 이는 인상 관리의 예이다. 교수는 학장에게 비춰지는 자신의 이미지를 조절하고자 했다. 그녀는 깔끔하면서도 교양 있어 보이고 싶었기 때문에 그녀에 대한 학장의 인상을 조절하려고 했다.

Exercise 5 .... p.88

Reading
해석

집단 사고

집단 사고란 개인들이 집단의 구성원으로 타인의 결정에 영향을 미치는 과정이다. 이 과정은 구성원들간의 구두 및 비구두에 의한, 혹은 암묵적인 의사소통과 관련이 있다. 집단 사고는 전체적으로 집단의 발전에 기여하는 기준 및 가치관의 공유를 포함된다. 집단 사고에서는 집단 전체의 필요에 따라 일부 개별적인 아이디어나 감정이 억압된다. 집단 사고는 해당 그룹에게 종종 최선의 결과를 가져다 준다.

✏ Note Taking

Group thinking When individuals affect others' choices as group members

Action Suppress some individual thoughts or feelings to serve group

Result Usually helps group in best possible way

Organization

Group thinking occurs when members of a group abandon their own individual ideas to take on group thoughts or ideas to serve the group better.

Listening

Script 🎧 03-13

M Professor: I was once on a software development team at a computer company. There were many times when the individual decisions I made concerning the software we were developing were not the best possible decisions. So when we were together as a group, we communicated very clearly about our shared values and standards. This helped me produce better software products than I would have if I'd just done it alone.

해석

M Professor: 예전에 저는 컴퓨터 회사에서 소프트웨어 개발팀에서 일을 했습니다. 개발 중인 소프트웨어와 관련해서 제가 개인적으로 내린 결정이 최선의 결정이 아니었던 때가 많았어요. 그래서 팀을 이루어 함께 일하면서 우리는 우리의 공통된 가치관과 기준에 대해 아주 분명하게 의사소통을 했죠. 그로 인해 저는 혼자서 했을 경우 얻게 될 제품보다 더 나은 소프트웨어 제품을 생산할 수 있었습니다.

✏ Note Taking

Problem Professor often made individual decisions that were not ideal

Solution Communicated group's shared values and standards

Result Produced better software products

Comparing

Sample Response 🎧 03-14

The professor mentioned that he had once produced software for a company, but his ideas were not that good. So his group had meetings to explain their shared values and standards. This let the professor create better software. In group thinking, people must follow the group's thoughts as a whole. This is what the professor did. He stopped thinking as an individual and began to follow the group's ideas. The result was that the group as a whole was greatly improved.

해석

교수는 자신이 한때 한 회사의 소프트웨어를 생산했지만 자신의 아이디어가 그다지 좋지는 않았다고 말한다. 그래서 그의 팀은 공동의 가치관과 기준을 설명하기 위해 회의를 가졌다. 이로써 교수는 더 나은 소프트웨어를 만들 수 있었다. 집단 사고에서 사람들은 전체 집단의 사고를 따라야 한다. 바로 교수가 했던 일이다. 그는 독자적으로 생각하는 것을 멈추고 집단의 아이디어를 따르기 시작했다. 그 결과 그 집단 전체가 커다란 발전을 이루었다.

Exercise 6 .... p.89

Reading

해석

초두 효과

초두 효과는 어떤 사람이나 사물에 대한 이후의 인상이 첫인상과 모순되는 경우에도 첫인상을 믿는 경우에 나타난다. 이 효과는 첫인상이 가장 지속적인 인상이라는 점을 입증한다. 이는 긴 단어 목록을 읽는 사람의 예에서 명확히 드러날 수 있다. 초두 효과에 따르면 사람들은 목록의 중간에 있는 단어보다 목록의 시작 부분에 있는 단어들을 더 잘 기억하는 경향이 있다.

✏ Note Taking

Primacy effect Happens when people let first impressions guide them even though they have been contradicted by later impressions

Example When person reads long list of words, is more likely to remember words from beginning than from middle

Organization

The primacy effect is the phenomenon of people allowing their first impressions of a person or thing to guide them even though later events may oppose this impression.

Listening

Script 🎧 03-15

W Professor: In my early days at this university, I was a research assistant. On my first research assignment, I worked really hard and got some great results. My boss, Professor Osgood, decided I was a great researcher even though some of my later work for him was not so good. In contrast, my coworker had trouble on his first research assignment. A mistake he made caused a huge loss of data. Afterward, he worked twice as hard and was a better researcher than me. But because of his mistake, which gave Professor Osgood a poor first impression of him, he never got the credit he deserved for being a better researcher than me.

W Professor: 제가 이 대학에 처음 왔을 때 저는 연구 조교였어요. 첫 번째 연구 과제에서 정말 열심히 일했고 좋은 결과를 얻었죠. 제 지도 교수님이셨던 Osgood 교수님께서는 그 이후에 제가 했던 연구가 그다지 좋지 못했음에도 불구하고 저를 뛰어난 연구자라고 생각하셨어요. 그와는 반대로 제 동료는 첫 번째 연구 과제를 할 때 어려움을 겪었습니다. 그가 저지른 한 가지 실수 때문에 데이터가 크게 손상되었죠. 그 후 그는 두 배로 열심히 일했고 저보다 더 뛰어난 연구자가 되었어요. 하지만 Osgood 교수님께 좋지 않은 첫인상을 가져다 준 실수 때문에 저보다 나은 연구 성과에 대해 마땅히 받아야 할 신임을 결코 얻지 못했습니다.

✎ Note Taking

Professor's action Did great work on first project but not on later work, yet Professor Osgood always had good thoughts of her

Coworker's action Performed badly on first project but later did better research than professor, yet Professor Osgood never had good impression of him

---

Comparing

Sample Response 🎧 03-16

The professor mentions that her first work with Professor Osgood yielded great results but that her later work was not good. Still, Professor Osgood always thought highly of her. Her coworker, on the other hand, performed poorly on his first assignment. Professor Osgood had a poor first impression of him, and even though his later work was much better, the professor never changed his mind about him. This relates to the primacy effect in that people are often guided by their first impressions even if later events should make them change their minds. This is exactly what happened to the professor and her coworker with regards to Professor Osgood.

해석

교수는 Osgood 교수와의 첫 번째 연구에서 좋은 결과를 냈지만 이후의 연구들은 좋지 못했다고 말한다. 하지만 Osgood 교수는 항상 그녀를 높이 평가했다. 한편 그녀의 동료는 자신의 첫 번째 과제에서 좋은 성과를 내지 못했다. Osgood 교수는 그에 대해 좋지 못한 첫인상을 갖게 되었고 이후에 그의 연구가 훨씬 뛰어났음에도 교수는 그에 대한 자신의 생각을 바꾸지 않았다. 이는 비록 나중에 일어난 일이 사람들의 생각을 바꾸어야 하지만 사람들이 종종 첫인상에 좌우되다는 점에서 초두 효과와 관련이 있다. 이것이 바로 Osgood 교수와 관련해서 교수와 교수의 동료에게 일어났던 일이다.

Exercise 1 .... p.90

Reading

해석

공급과 수요

공급과 수요라는 개념은 미시 경제학의 기본 모델이다. 이는 시장의 제품에 대한 생산자와 소비자 사이의 상호 작용을 설명하며 가격과 판매량에 기반한다. 이 모델은 주어진 재화나 용역의 공급과 수요의 증가 및 감소 사이의 상호 관계를 살펴보는데 이용된다.

✎ Note Taking

Supply and demand The interaction between producers and consumers for goods based on price and sales

Use Look at correlations between increases and decreases in supply and demand of item or service

---

Organization

It is the basic model of microeconomics, which describes the interaction between consumers and producers for marketplace goods.

Listening

Script 🎧 03-17

W Professor: We can understand a lot about supply and demand by looking at a situation in Victorian England during the 1800s. Even though the supply of bread dropped and the price went up, the demand remained the same. This was due to the fact that even the more expensive bread was still cheaper than meat.

해석

W Professor: 1800년대 빅토리아 시대의 영국의 상황을 살펴봄으로써 공급과 수요에 대한 많은 것을 이해할 수 있습니다. 빵 공급이 감소하고 빵 가격이 상승했지만 수요는 변함이 없었어요. 가격이 훨씬 비싼 빵이라고 해도 여전히 고기보다는 더욱 저렴하다는 사실 때문에 그런 것이었죠.

✎ Note Taking

Situation Victorian England saw bread supply drop while price increased but demand was same

Reason Bread was still cheaper than meat

Comparing

Sample Response 🎧 03-18

The professor mentions how, in Victorian England, the bread supply dropped while bread got more expensive, yet the demand for bread remained the same. She mentions that it was due to the fact that expensive bread was still cheaper than meat. This relates to supply

---

and demand because it shows how producers and consumers interact in the marketplace.

해석

교수는 빅토리아 시대의 영국에서 빵 공급이 감소하면서 빵이 비싸졌지만 어떻게 빵에 대한 수요가 변함이 없었는지를 설명한다. 그녀는 비싼 빵도 고기보다는 여전히 싸다는 사실 때문에 그랬다고 설명한다. 이는 시장에서 생산자와 소비자가 어떻게 상호 작용을 하는지 보여 주기 때문에 공급과 수요와 관련이 있다.

Exercise 2 ································· p.91

Reading

해석

인지 부조화

인지 부조화는 양립불가능하거나 모순적인 두 가지 사고를 동시에 지니는 사람에게 나타나는 현상으로 정의된다. 어떤 사람이 자신의 아버지가 좋은 사람이라고 생각하는데 아버지가 나쁜 행동을 하는 것을 보는 경우, 그 사람은 인지 부조화를 경험할 가능성이 높다.

> ✎ Note Taking
>
> **Cognitive dissonance** Holding of two incompatible or contradictory thoughts at same time
> **Example** When one thinks father is good man but sees father doing something bad

Organization

Cognitive dissonance is the holding of two thoughts or opinions that are incompatible or contradict one another.

Listening

Script 🎧 03-19

> **W Professor**: When I was in high school, I wanted to play this video game all the time even though I knew I should study chemistry. I experienced a mental problem since I was caught between what I wanted and what I knew I should do. To solve this problem, I told myself that I wanted to be a sociologist and therefore didn't need to get a high grade in chemistry. Once I decided this, I felt much better.

해석

W Professor: 제가 고등학교를 다닐 때 저는 화학 공부를 해야 한다는 걸 알면서도 항상 비디오 게임을 하고 싶어 했어요. 제가 하고 싶은 것과 해야 하는 것 사이에서 고민을 하다가 정신적인 문제를 겪게 되었죠. 이러한 문제를 해결하기 위해, 저는 제 자신에게 나는 사회학자가 되고 싶기 때문에 화학 점수를 잘 받을 필요가 없다고 말했습니다. 일단 이렇게 생각을 하자 마음이 훨씬 편해졌어요.

> ✎ Note Taking
>
> **Situation** Professor wanted to play game instead of studying chemistry
> **Problem** Had cognitive dissonance between what should do and what wanted to do
> **Result** Decided to be sociologist so did not need high chemistry grade

Comparing

Sample Response 🎧 03-20

> The professor says that she once wanted to play a video game yet recognized that she had to study for a chemistry test. She knew what she had to do and what she wanted to do. She decided to become a sociologist since sociologists do not need to do well in chemistry class. During this event, the professor suffered from cognitive dissonance. She had two contradictory views that she held at the same time.

해석

교수는 자신이 한때 비디오 게임을 하고 싶어했지만 화학 시험 공부를 해야한다는 점을 깨달았다고 말한다. 그녀는 자신이 해야 하는 일과 자신이 하고 싶은 일이 무엇인지 알았다. 사회학자는 화학 성적이 뛰어날 필요가 없었기 때문에 그녀는 사회학자가 되기로 결심했다. 이러한 일을 겪는 동안 교수는 인지 부조화를 겪었다. 그녀는 두 개의 모순되는 견해를 동시에 가지고 있었다.

Exercise 3 ································· p.92

Reading

해석

신뢰성

신뢰성이란 어떤 사람의 말이나 행동을 다른 사람들이 믿는 정도를 말한다. 신뢰성에는 세 가지 주요 요소가 존재한다. 역량, 신용, 그리고 활기이다. 신뢰성은 정치 및 언론 분야에서 매우 중요한 것으로 여겨진다.

> ✎ Note Taking
>
> **Credibility** Extent to which person's statements or actions are believed by others
> **Aspects** Competence, trustworthiness, and dynamism

Organization

Credibility is the degree to which other people believe the statements or actions of another.

Listening

Script 🎧 03-21

> **W Professor**: Jessica Miller was the manager of a financial company when she decided to run for mayor on a platform that she would help the city solve its budget crisis. But election polls showed that despite her

competence, she was not a popular candidate. So she watched a video of one of her speeches and realized she was not making eye contact with her audience. This fact seemed to be damaging her credibility. Once she corrected this problem, her popularity rose, and she was elected mayor.

해석

W Professor: 제시카 밀러는 시의 재정 위기를 타개하는데 일조하겠다는 공약으로 시장 출마를 결심했던 당시 금융 회사의 관리자였어요. 하지만, 그녀의 능력에도 불구하고, 선거 결과 그녀는 인기 있는 후보가 아니라는 점이 밝혀졌죠. 그래서 그녀는 자신의 연설 중 하나를 담은 비디오를 보았는데, 자신이 청중들과 눈을 마주치지 않고 있다는 점을 깨달았어요. 이러한 사실은 그녀의 신뢰성에 타격을 주는 것처럼 보였습니다. 이러한 문제를 고치자 그녀의 인기는 올라갔고, 그녀는 시장에 당선되었죠.

📝 Note Taking

Situation Manager of financial company ran for mayor
Problem Was unpopular candidate since lost credibility from not making eye contact with audience
Result Corrected problem and won election

Comparing

Sample Response 🎧 03-22

Jessica Miller was running for mayor in a city. Even though she had a financial background and the city had financial problems, she was an unpopular candidate. She realized she was not making eye contact with her audience. That was damaging her credibility, which is the extent to which people trust another person. When she started making eye contact, she gained credibility, and then she won the election.

해석

제시카 밀러는 시장 선거에 출마하고 있었다. 그녀는 금융과 관련된 경력을 가지고 있었고 시는 재정 위기를 겪고 있었음에도 불구하고 그녀는 인기 있는 후보가 아니었다. 그녀는 자신이 청중들과 시선을 마주치지 않았다는 점을 깨달았다. 이로써 그녀의 신뢰성이 타격을 입었는데, 신뢰성이란 사람들이 다른 사람을 믿는 정도이다. 그녀가 사람들과 눈을 맞추기 시작하자 그녀는 신뢰성을 얻었고 선거에서 승리했다.

Exercise 4 .... p.93

Reading

해석

구매자의 후회

구매자의 후회는 어떤 제품을 구입한 뒤 후회를 하는 경우에 일어나는 감정 상태이다. 이는 보석, 자동차, 그리고 부동산 같은 고가의 제품을 구매한 후에 가장 흔히 나타난다. 하지만 이로 인해 느끼게 되는 기분은 구매의 정당화나 설득 과정을 통해 사라질 수 있다.

📝 Note Taking

Buyer's remorse Emotion person feels after purchasing expensive item
Easing of feelings By justification of purchase or persuasion

Organization

Buyer's remorse is a feeling of regret a person gets after purchasing something expensive.

Listening

Script 🎧 03-23

M Professor: Okay . . . Here is an example. On my thirty-first birthday, I bought an expensive new car. A few days later, though, I called the salesman who sold me the car to discuss the possibility of returning it. But the salesman was quick to remind me of the reasons I'd told him I wanted to buy the car. He also sent me a thank-you letter. This simple gesture put my buyer's remorse to rest.

해석

M Professor: 좋아요… 한 가지 사례를 들어보죠. 저는 31번째 생일에 값비싼 새 자동차를 샀습니다. 그런데 며칠 후 저는 자동차를 팔았던 영업 사원에게 전화를 걸어 반품이 가능한지 논의했어요. 하지만 그 영업 사원은, 제가 그에게 말했던, 제가 차를 사고 싶다고 한 이유들을 재빨리 상기시켜 주었습니다. 또한 제게 감사의 편지도 보내 주었어요. 이러한 간단한 행동이 저의 구매자의 후회를 잠재워 주었습니다.

📝 Note Taking

Situation Bought expensive new car but wanted to return it
Result Salesman convinced him to keep car and sent thank-you letter

Comparing

Sample Response 🎧 03-24

The professor tells the class that he purchased an expensive new car on his birthday but soon felt bad about it. He wanted to return it, so he called the salesman. The professor was experiencing buyer's remorse, which is a feeling of regret a person gets after buying something expensive. However, people can be persuaded not to feel buyer's remorse. This is what the salesman did. He convinced the professor that he had bought the car for good reasons and sent him a thank-you note. The professor then decided to keep the car.

해석

교수는 학생들에게 자신의 생일날 자신이 값비싼 차를 구매했지만 곧 그에 대해 후회를 했다고 말한다. 그는 반품을 하려고 영업 사원에게 전화를 했다. 교수는 구매자 후회를 경험하고 있었는데, 이는 고가의 제품을 구매한 후에 겪는 후회를 말한다. 하지만 사람들은 구매자의 후회를 겪지 않도록 설득을 당할 수도 있다.

이것이 바로 영업 사원이 했던 일이다. 그는 교수에게 교수가 합당한 이유로 자동차를 구매했다는 점을 확신시켰고, 그에게 감사 카드를 보냈다. 그러자 교수는 자동차를 계속 갖고 있기로 결심했다.

Exercise 5 ··· p.94

Reading

해석

광고의 과장

많은 광고들이, 제조사가 소비자들이 구매를 바라는, 제품의 효과를 과장하는 잘못을 저지른다. 광고에서는 종종 제품이 크게 과장된 품질이나 크기를 지니고 있는 것으로 묘사된다. 이러한 과장된 광고에서 보이는 효과를 원하는 사람들은 때때로 실제로 원하지 않거나 필요하지 않은 제품들을 구매하게 된다. 그 후 자신이 허황된 광고에 속았다는 점에 분노를 느낄 수도 있다. 어떤 경우에는 이러한 과장된 광고가 허위 광고로 간주되기도 하는데, 이는 종종 범죄로 여겨진다.

🖉 Note Taking

Exaggeration in advertising Shows products having qualities or sizes that are exaggerated
Positive result Makes people want effects seen in advertisements
Negative result Makes people feel angry because of deception in advertisement

Organization

It occurs when advertisements greatly exaggerate the size or qualities of a product.

Listening

Script 🎧 03-25

W Professor: Last week, I saw a vacuum advertised as being the ultimate floor cleaner. It was supposed to be capable of removing all dirt, even carpet stains. I was so excited that I rushed out and bought one even though it was really expensive. I immediately took it home and tried to remove a stain in my carpet that I hated. Did it remove the stain? No way! I tried a few times, but it didn't work very well. So I tried to return it. But since I'd already used it a few times, the store refused to take it back.

해석

W Professor: 지난주에 저는 최고의 바닥 청소기라고 광고되는 진공청소기를 보았습니다. 모든 먼지와 심지어는 카펫의 얼룩까지도 제거할 수 있다고 광고를 하더군요. 저는 너무 흥분한 나머지, 가격이 상당히 비쌌지만, 바로 나가서 구매를 했습니다. 곧바로 집으로 가져와서는 제가 싫어하는 카펫의 얼룩을 없애려고 했죠. 얼룩이 없어졌을까요? 전혀 그렇지 않았습니다! 몇 차례 시도해 보았지만 그다지 효과가 없었어요. 그래서 반품을 하려고 했죠. 하지만 제가 이미 몇 차례 사용을 했다는 이유로 매장에서는 반품을 거부하더군요.

🖉 Note Taking

Situation Professor purchased vacuum cleaner advertised as being best
Problem Did not remove stain in professor's carpet
Result Professor could not return product to store

Comparing

Sample Response 🎧 03-26

The professor mentions that she saw an advertisement about the ultimate vacuum cleaner. Supposedly, it could get the dirt and even stains out of anything. So she purchased the vacuum cleaner and tried to remove a stain in her carpet. Unfortunately, the advertisers had exaggerated about the quality of the product, so she could not get the stain out. When she found out that the vacuum cleaner's capabilities had been exaggerated, she tried to return it, but she could not.

해석

교수는 최고의 진공청소기 광고를 보았다고 말한다. 추측하건대 먼지 및 어떤 얼룩도 제거할 수 있을 것이었다. 그래서 그녀는 그 진공청소기를 구매해서 카펫의 얼룩을 제거하려고 했다. 불행히도 광고업체는 제품의 품질을 과장했고, 따라서 그녀는 얼룩을 제거할 수 없었다. 그녀는 진공청소기의 성능이 과장되었다는 것을 깨닫고 환불을 받으려 했지만 그럴 수가 없었다.

Exercise 6 ··· p.95

Reading

해석

향기

잘 혼합된 향기에서 나는 달콤한 냄새는 사람들의 마음에 매우 긍정적인 방식으로 영향을 미칠 수 있다. 이러한 사실 때문에 향기는 종종 마케팅에서 이용된다. 쇼핑몰에서 사람들을 푸드코트로 유인하기 위해 사용되는 한 가지 향기는 시나몬 빵을 구울 때 나는 향기이다. 과학자들은 이러한 인기 있는 냄새가 사람들을 배고프게 만든다는 점을 밝혀냈다. 일단 푸드코트로 들어오면 사람들은 시나몬 빵 이외의 제품에 돈을 쓸 수도 있지만, 이들을 그곳으로 데리고 온 것은 다름 아닌 냄새였다.

🖉 Note Taking

Fragrance Can affect people's minds in positive ways
Use Smell of baking cinnamon buns can attract people to food courts

Organization

Good smells are used to attract people into situations in which they will spend money.

Listening

Script 🎧 03-27

W Professor: Today, I want to talk about perfumes used

in marketing with highly successful results. In this case, we'll talk about the effect of women's perfume on men and women. That's right. It has a double effect. When entering a department store, you may notice that the scent of women's fragrance in the women's and men's clothing departments is very strong. The reason is that the smell induces people of both genders to spend money in the hope of attracting a mate.

해석

W Professor: 오늘은 마케팅에 사용되어 대단히 성공적인 결과를 낸 향수에 대해 이야기하고자 합니다. 이번 경우, 여성들의 향수가 남성과 여성에게 미치는 영향에 대해 살펴보도록 하죠. 맞습니다. 이중적인 효과가 있어요. 백화점에 들어가면 여성복과 남성복 매장에 여성 향수의 향이 아주 강한 것을 알 수 있을 거예요. 그 이유는 그러한 냄새가 남녀를 불문하고 상대방을 유혹하기 위한 바람으로 돈을 쓰도록 유인하기 때문입니다.

✏ Note Taking

Use of fragrance Are fragrances of women's perfumes in clothing sections of department stores
Result Induces men and women to spend money

Comparing

Sample Response 🎧 03-28

The professor mentions that both the men and women's clothing sections in department stores smell strongly of perfume. This smell actually makes both men and women spend more money on clothes since they are hoping to find a mate. This shows how fragrance is used as a marketing tactic. Just like certain smells can make people hungry and cause them to buy food, other smells can make people purchase different products.

해석

교수는 백화점에서 남성복 매장과 여성복 매장에서 강한 향수 냄새가 난다고 언급한다. 이러한 냄새는 남성과 여성 모두 자신의 상대를 찾기를 바라기 때문에 이들이 옷에 더 많은 돈을 쓰도록 만든다. 이는 어떻게 향기가 마케팅 전략으로 이용되는지 보여 준다. 어떤 냄새는 사람들을 배고프게 만들어서 음식을 구입하도록 만드는가 하면, 어떤 냄새는 사람들로 하여금 다양한 제품을 구매하도록 만들 수 있다.

Unit 15 Architecture & Arts

Exercise 1 ·· p.96

Reading

해석

균형의 중요성

실내 장식은 사용자의 생활 방식에 맞추기 위해 실내를 장식하는 예술이다.

이는 주위 벽에 사용되는 색상의 통일성과 대비 사이의 균형을 맞추는 것에 초점을 둔다. 항상 디자인 이론은 실내 장식에서 지루하지 않으면서도 너무 어지럽지 않은 균형을 찾으려고 한다.

✏ Note Taking

Importance of balance Find balance between unity and contrast of colors
Result Seek look that is neither boring nor busy

Organization

It is important to keep balance in a room so that the look is neither too boring nor too busy.

Listening

Script 🎧 03-29

W Professor: So you have to be very careful about the colors. After all, if you overdo the unity, the room will look solid and boring. But if you have too much contrast, it can become too busy, which will confuse people. This skill is sort of like picking up some apples in both of your hands and trying to match two of them with the same weight.

해석

W Professor: 그래서 색상에 관해 매우 주의해야 합니다. 결국 통일성을 너무 강조하다 보면 실내가 너무 단조롭고 지루해 보일 거예요. 하지만 너무 많이 대비를 시키면 너무 어지럽게 보일 수 있는데, 이러면 사람들이 혼란을 느끼게 될 것입니다. 이러한 기술은 양손에 사과 몇 개를 집어 들고 무게를 맞추려는 노력과 비슷하다고 할 수 있어요.

✏ Note Taking

Unity If overdone, room looks solid and boring
Contrast Too much makes room busy and confusing

Comparing

Sample Response 🎧 03-30

The professor talks about the use of colors. She states that if there is too much unity, a room will look boring. However, if there are too many colors, this will create contrasts that will make a room look too busy and will confuse people. This is related to the importance of balance because the person must be careful neither to make the room too busy nor to make the room too boring.

해석

교수는 색상의 사용에 대해 말한다. 그녀는 만약 통일성이 지나치면 실내가 지루하게 보일 것이라고 주장한다. 하지만 색상들이 너무 많으면 대비가 생겨서 실내가 너무 어지럽게 보이고 사람들이 혼란을 느끼게 될 것이다. 이러한 점은, 실내를 너무 어지럽거나 너무 지루하게 보이지 않도록 신경을 써야 하기 때문에, 균형의 중요성과 관련이 있다.

Reading

해석

영화 평론

영화 평론은 영화의 상업적 성공에 막대한 영향을 미칠 수 있다. 평론가들은 새로운 영화를 시청한 후 텔레비전, 인쇄물, 인터넷, 그리고 라디오와 같은 다양한 매체를 통해 자신의 의견을 나타낸다. 이러한 평론가들의 의견에 따라 소비자들이 새로운 영화를 볼 것인지, 보지 않을 것인지를 선택하는 경우가 많다. 심지어 과거 영화에 대한 평론에 따와 스튜디오 및 제작자들이 어떤 영화를 제작할지를 결정할 수도 있다.

✎ Note Taking

Film criticism Is offered by critics on variety of media
Result Can determine consumers' choices of movies

Organization

Film criticism can not only affect which movies people go to see but also which movies studios and producers decide to film.

Listening

Script 🎧 03-31

M Professor: Consider the movie *Waterworld*. At the time, it was the most expensive movie ever made. It starred two of the biggest actors in Hollywood. It had all of the makings of a great success. But the critics who saw the movie hated it and published their negative criticism in various mass media. Their reviews helped make the movie a commercial and critical failure.

해석

M Professor: *워터월드*라는 영화를 살펴봅시다. 이 영화는 당시 가장 많은 제작비가 든 영화였어요. 할리우드에서 가장 거물인 두 배우를 출연시켰죠. 대대적인 성공에 필요한 모든 요소를 다 갖추고 있었습니다. 하지만 영화를 본 평론가들은 영화를 마음에 들어 하지 않았고, 다양한 대중 매체에서 부정적인 의견을 나타냈어요. 그들의 리뷰 때문에 영화는 상업적으로, 그리고 평론상으로도 실패작이 되었습니다.

✎ Note Taking

Prediction *Waterworld* believed to be future success
Problem Was disliked by critics, who published negative reviews
Result Became commercial and critical failure

Comparing

Sample Response 🎧 03-32

Waterworld was a movie with an enormous budget and famous actors. Almost everyone predicted success for it. However, there were many negative reviews of it. These film reviews were published in many kinds of mass media. Once people read the reviews, they chose not to go, which showed the power of film criticism. Because of the negative reviews, *Waterworld* failed as a movie.

해석

*워터월드*는 엄청난 예산을 쏟아 붓고 유명한 배우를 출연시킨 영화였다. 거의 모든 사람들이 영화가 성공할 것이라고 예상했다. 하지만 부정적인 평론들이 많이 쏟아졌다. 이러한 영화 리뷰는 여러 종류의 대중 매체에서 발표되었다. 사람들은 리뷰를 읽고 영화를 보지 않기로 결심했는데, 이는 영화 평론의 힘을 보여 주는 것이었다. 부정적인 리뷰 때문에 *워터월드*는 실패작이 되었다.

Reading

해석

과장법

과장법은 과장이라고도 불리는 문학적 장치이다. 과장법을 사용함으로써 작가는 사건이나 캐릭터를 강조하여 이들에게 극적인 또는 희극적인 효과를 부여할 수 있다. 과장법은 과장된 표현이므로 이를 글자 그대로 받아들여서는 안 된다.

✎ Note Taking

Hyperbole Also called exaggeration
Use Can emphasize events or characteristics to make them more dramatic or funnier

Organization

Hyperbole is a literary method that uses exaggeration to make things more dramatic or funnier.

Listening

Script 🎧 03-33

W Professor: The writer wants to say that the lady in this story walked so far that now she is incredibly tired. But instead of just writing that, he writes, "She walked so far that by the end, she couldn't walk another step." Now, this lady was not handicapped. If she had to, she actually could have walked farther. But the author is exaggerating in order to describe how tired she was.

해석

W Professor: 작가가 소설 속의 여인이 너무 많이 걸어서 지금은 믿을 수 없을 정도로 피곤하다고 말하고 싶어합니다. 하지만 그냥 그렇게 글을 쓰는 대신 "그녀는 너무 많이 걸어서 결국 한 발짝도 뗄 수 없었다."고 씁니다. 자, 이 여인에게 장애가 있지는 않았어요. 만약 걸어야만 했다면 사실 더 걸을 수도 있었을 거예요. 하지만 작가는 그녀가 얼마나 피곤했는지 묘사하기 위해 과장을 하고 있습니다.

✎ Note Taking

Situation Writer wants to show how tired woman was from walking
Solution Writes that woman could not walk any farther, thereby using hyperbole

Comparing

Sample Response 🎧 03-34

The professor describes a woman in a story by a writer. She had been walking very far, and the writer wanted to emphasize that. So the writer wrote that she could not walk another step. This is an example of hyperbole, which is exaggerating something to give it a dramatic or comedic effect. Since the woman could have walked farther, the writer's statement is not true. However, like all hyperbole, readers should not take the statement literally. They should realize the author is emphasizing a point.

해석

교수는 어떤 작가가 쓴 소설 속 여인을 묘사한다. 그녀는 너무 많이 걸었는데, 작가는 그 점을 강조하고 싶어한다. 그래서 작가는 그녀가 단 한 발자국도 뗄 수가 없었다고 쓴다. 이는 과장법의 예로, 과장법이란 극적인 또는 희극적인 효과를 내기 위해 무엇인가를 과장하는 것이다. 그 여자는 더 걸을 수도 있었기 때문에 작가의 말은 사실이 아니다. 그럼에도 불구하고, 모든 과장법에서와 마찬가지로, 독자들은 그러한 말을 글자 그대로 받아들여서는 안 된다. 작가가 어떤 점을 강조하고 있다는 사실을 깨달아야 한다.

Exercise 4 .... p.99

Reading

해석

즉흥 예술

즉흥 예술은 공연자가 사람들이 예술로 바라보기를 바라는 공연, 이벤트, 혹은 상황 등을 말한다. 즉흥 예술은 전통적인 예술과 크게 다르다. 이는 1950년대에 시작되었다. 이는 버려진 건물, 버스, 그리고 공원을 포함하여 다양한 장소에서 예술가들이 실시했던 특이한 이벤트들을 설명하기 위해 사용되었다.

> ✎ Note Taking
>
> **Art happenings** Are performances, events, or situations different from traditional art
> **Locations** Often occur in unusual places like abandoned buildings, buses, and parks

Organization

An art happening is an unusual event, performance, or situation whose creator wants people to think of it as art.

Listening

Script 🎧 03-35

M Professor: Two artists walked into the middle of a cafeteria at lunchtime. They had a canvas and paint. They immediately began dipping their hands in the paint and painting "I Love" on the canvas. Then, they began painting the same words on each other's bodies. People were confused at first since this kind of thing doesn't usually happen in the cafeteria. But soon, some people realized that it was a spontaneous art happening.

해석

M Professor: 두 명의 예술가가 점심 시간에 식당 한가운데로 걸어 들어갔습니다. 캔버스와 물감을 갖고 있었고요. 그들은 곧바로 페인트에 손을 담그고는 캔버스에 "I Love"라고 쓰기 시작했어요. 그런 다음, 서로의 몸에 같은 단어들을 쓰기 시작했습니다. 보통 식당에서 이런 종류의 공연이 이루어지지는 않기 때문에 사람들은 처음에 당황해 했죠. 하지만 곧 몇몇 사람들이 그것이 자발적인 즉흥 예술이라는 것을 알아차렸습니다.

> ✎ Note Taking
>
> **Situation** Artists painted "I Love" on canvas and bodies while in cafeteria
> **Result** Confused people at first until some recognized it as art happening

Comparing

Sample Response 🎧 03-36

The professor mentions that a couple of artists walked into a cafeteria and began painting "I Love" both on canvas and their bodies. This was an instance of an art happening. Art happenings are unusual events or performances that often take place in atypical places. This is what the artists were doing. They were creating an art happening.

해석

교수는 두 명의 예술가가 식당으로 걸어 들어가서 캔버스와 서로의 몸에 "I Love"라고 썼다고 말한다. 이는 즉흥 예술의 사례이다. 즉흥 예술은 전형적이지 않은 장소에서 주로 이루어지는 특이한 이벤트나 공연을 말한다. 예술가들이 했던 것이 바로 이것이다. 그들은 즉흥 예술을 하고 있었던 것이다.

Exercise 5 .... p.100

Reading

해석

연결숏

영화 제작에서 연결숏은 장면을 전환시키는 숏이다. 전환은 보통 시간의 흐름이나 장소의 변화를 나타낸다. 하지만 연결숏은 등장 인물 혹은 존재의 상태에 극적인 변화를 나타내기 위해서도 사용될 수 있다. 가장 많이 사용되는 연결숏은 회전하는 시계, 달력에서 찢어지는 페이지, 그리고 기차나 자동차와 같은 질주하는 차량 등에 관한 것이다. 흔히 사용되는 또 다른 연결숏은 지도 위의 한 지점에서 다른 지점으로 그어지는 선에 대한 숏이다.

> ✎ Note Taking
>
> **Bridging shot** Is film shot that makes transition
> **Examples** Spinning clock, pages coming off calendar, or speeding vehicles like trains and cars
> **Other example** Line being drawn from point to point on map

Organization

A bridging shot is a film shot that is used to make a transition from one scene to another in a movie.

Listing

Script 🎧 03-37

W Professor: When the two main characters break up, we suddenly see the pages of a calendar tearing away. This expresses the passage of time that they are apart from one another. Later, the man tries to find his ex-girlfriend, and he learns that she's in Paris. Then, we see the wheels of a train spinning. This dramatic effect shows that he's speeding to Paris in search of his love.

해석

W Professor: 두 명의 등장 인물이 헤어질 때 갑자기 달력의 페이지들이 찢겨 나가는 것을 보게 됩니다. 이는 서로 헤어져 있는 시간의 흐름을 나타내죠. 그 후 남자는 옛 여자 친구를 찾으려고 하다가 그녀가 파리에 있다는 점을 알게 됩니다. 그러면 돌고 있는 기차의 바퀴가 보입니다. 이러한 극적인 효과는 그가 연인을 찾아 파리로 가고 있음을 보여 줍니다.

✎ Note Taking

First movie scene Pages of calendar tearing away show time passing after breakup
Second movie scene Wheels of train spinning show man speeding to Paris to find ex-girlfriend

Comparing

Sample Response 🎧 03-38

The professor discusses a movie in which, in one scene, pages of a calendar tear off to show time passing after a couple breaks up. Later, there are wheels turning on a train to show the man heading to Paris to find his ex. These are both examples of bridging shots. Directors use bridging shots to show the passage of time in film and to make transitions from one scene to another.

해석

교수는 한 장면에서 커플이 헤어진 후 시간의 흐름을 나타내기 위해 달력이 찢겨 나가는 영화에 대해 이야기한다. 이후에는 옛 연인을 찾아 파리로 향하는 남자를 나타내기 위해 회전하는 기차 바퀴가 등장한다. 이들은 모두 연결숏의 예이다. 감독들은 연결숏을 이용하여 영화에서 시간의 흐름을 나타내거나 한 장면에서 다른 장면으로 장면을 전환시킨다.

Exercise 6 ·· p.101

Reading

해석

아웃사이더 예술가

아웃사이더 예술가는 전통적인 문화의 경계 밖에서 예술 작품을 만드는 사람이다. 이러한 예술가 중 많은 이들이 독학을 한 사람들로 순수 미술 기법을 정식으로 교육받은 적이 없다. 이들 예술가들은 종종 주류 예술계의 바깥에서 활동하며 보통 독특한 기법과 재료들을 사용한다.

✎ Note Taking

Outsider artist Person working outside boundaries of traditional art
Definition Is self-taught and employs unique techniques and materials

Organization

Outsider artists are self-taught individuals who do not create traditional art and who also use unique methods and materials to create their art.

Listening

Script 🎧 03-39

M Professor: Today, I want to tell you about an artist named Henry Roger. He had no connection to the mainstream art community whatsoever. He also never received any formal training. His pictures employed a unique style. One example of the uniqueness of his style can be illustrated by the time he needed to portray the human figure in one of his works. But he was so isolated that he had no way to study the human figure. So he simply cut out pictures of children from a newspaper and pasted them on to his paintings.

해석

M Professor: 오늘은 헨리 로저라는 예술가에 대해 논의하고자 합니다. 그는 주류 예술계와는 전혀 관련이 없었어요. 또한 정식으로 교육을 받은 적도 없었죠. 그의 그림에는 독특한 스타일이 적용되었습니다. 그의 독특한 스타일에 대한 한 가지 예는 그가 자신의 작품 중 하나에서 인간의 모습을 그려야 했을 무렵에 찾아볼 수 있습니다. 그는 너무 고립되어 있어서 인간의 모습을 연구할 방법이 없었어요. 그래서 그는 신문에서 아이 사진들을 잘라내고 그 사진을 자기 그림에 붙였습니다.

✎ Note Taking

Henry Roger Man unconnected to art community
Method Cut out pictures of children and pasted them on to canvas when needed human figures

Comparing

Sample Response 🎧 03-40

The professor describes Henry Roger as a man unconnected to the art world. He never studied formally and had a unique style, which are two characteristics of outsider artists. He also used unique methods. For example, when he needed to use human figures in paintings, he merely cut out pictures of children and attached them to his paintings. This is another way in which he was an outsider artist since they often use original methods in their artwork.

해석

교수는 헨리 로저를 예술계와 연관이 없었던 사람이라고 설명한다. 그는 한 번도 정식으로 공부를 한 적이 없었고 독특한 스타일을 가지고 있었는데, 이러한 점은 아웃사이더 예술가의 두 가지 특징이다. 그는 또한 독특한 기법을 사용했다. 예를 들어 그가 그림에서 인간의 모습을 나타내야 했을 때 그는 아이의 사진을 잘라내서 이를 자기 그림에 붙였다. 이러한 측면에서도 그는 아웃사이더 예술가였는데, 그 이유는 아웃사이더 예술가들이 종종 자신의 작품에서 독창적인 방법을 사용하기 때문이다.

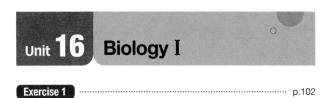

Unit 16 Biology I

Exercise 1 .... p.102

Reading
해석

위장

위장은 생물체가 자신을 둘러싼 주위 환경과 어울리는 방법이다. 동물들은 포식자들을 피하기 위해 위장을 한다. 일부 동물들은 자기를 잡아먹으려는 다른 동물들을 피하기 위해 자신의 색을 바꿔 위장을 한다.

> **✎ Note Taking**
>
> **Camouflage** Used to blend in with environment
> **Method** Can change colors to hide from predators

Organization
Camouflage is a method, such as changing colors, which animals use to blend in with their environment.

Listening
Script 🎧 03-41

> **W Professor**: Okay, class, have you ever seen a cuttlefish swimming in a tank? Have you seen one change its body color instantly? Isn't that cool? These animals are able to control their bodies to camouflage themselves. That's amazing, isn't it? By using various pigments in their bodies, cuttlefish can alter the colors of their bodies to match their environment. Not only cuttlefish but also other species of fish can alter their bodies' colors by eating different foods.

해석

W Professor: 좋아요, 여러분, 수조 안에서 헤엄치는 오징어를 본 적이 있나요? 순식간에 몸 색깔을 바꾸는 것을 보았나요? 멋지지 않아요? 이 동물들은 위장을 하기 위해 신체를 조절할 수 있습니다. 놀랍죠, 그렇죠? 신체 내의 다양한 여러 색소를 사용함으로써 오징어는 환경과 비슷하게 신체의 색깔을 바꿀 수가 있어요. 오징어뿐만 아니라 다른 종의 어류들도 다양한 먹이를 먹음으로써 신체의 색깔을 바꿀 수가 있습니다.

> **✎ Note Taking**
>
> **Cuttlefish** Can change color of bodies instantly
> **Method** Use pigments to change colors
> **Other fish** Can change colors depending upon food eaten

Comparing
Sample Response 🎧 03-42

> The professor discusses the cuttlefish and how it can instantly change the color of its body to match its environment. It does this by using various pigments in its body. The cuttlefish uses this ability as camouflage. Many animals use camouflage to blend in with their environment when they are hiding from predators. One common method of camouflage is changing colors, which is exactly what the cuttlefish does.

해석

교수는 오징어에 대해, 그리고 오징어가 어떻게 순식간에 주변 환경과 비슷하게 자신의 신체의 색깔을 바꿀 수 있는지 이야기한다. 오징어는 신체 내의 다양한 색소를 이용해 그렇게 한다. 오징어는 이러한 능력을 이용하여 위장을 한다. 많은 동물들이 포식자로부터 몸을 숨길 때 위장을 사용해서 주변 환경과 어우러진다. 위장의 한 가지 흔한 방법은 색깔을 변화시키는 것으로, 이것이 바로 오징어의 위장 방법이다.

Exercise 2 .... p.103

Reading
해석

수면의 중요성

수면은 대부분의 동물들에게 필요한 휴식 시간이다. 수면을 취하는 동물들은 움직임이 줄어들고 빛이나 소리에 대한 반응이 느려진다. 인간은 몇 단계의 수면을 경험한다. 이러한 단계 중 일부에서는 잠재 의식이 매우 활발해진다. 인간은 뇌의 인지 기능을 유지하기 위해 규칙적으로 수면을 취해야 한다. 인간이 필요한 양의 수면을 취하지 못하는 경우에는 신체의 능력이 급격히 저하된다.

> **✎ Note Taking**
>
> **Sleep effects** Reduced movements and slower reactions
>   to light and sound
> **Importance of sleep** Lets brain function, and body will
>   suffer without it

Organization
Humans require sleep in order to maintain their brains' cognitive functions.

Listening
Script 🎧 03-43

> **M Professor**: You know, it's really important to get enough sleep. The average human needs six to eight hours of sleep every twenty-four hours to maintain peak

cognitive performance. A good example is a simple test that was done in which the study subjects had to type the numeric combination 96478 over and over on a keyboard. The group's typing was much more accurate in the morning after eight hours of sleep than it was in the afternoon, when they became tired, or after a night of only four hours of sleep.

해석

M Professor: 아시다시피 충분한 수면을 취하는 것은 정말로 중요합니다. 일반적인 사람은 최상의 인지 기능을 유지하기 위해 24시간마다 6시간에서 8시간의 수면을 필요로 하죠. 한 가지 좋은 예는, 실험 대상자들이 키보드로 96478이라는 숫자 조합을 반복해서 타이핑해야 했던 실험에서 실시되었던, 간단한 테스트입니다. 이 그룹의 타이핑은, 이들이 피곤해지는 오후 시간이나 밤에 불과 4시간의 수면을 취한 후보다, 8시간 수면을 취한 다음날 오전에 훨씬 더 정확했습니다.

✎ Note Taking

Sleep Need six to eight hours every twenty-four to function properly
Test Involved typing numbers over and over
Result More accurate in morning after good sleep than when had less sleep

Comparing

Sample Response 🎧 03-44

The professor discusses a test that had the subjects type the numbers 96478 over and over again on a keyboard. The results showed that the people who got eight hours of sleep were very accurate in the morning but less so in the afternoon. They also did poorly when they only got about four hours of sleep. This shows how important sleep is. A typical human requires six to eight hours of sleep every day, or the person's cognitive functions will suffer. This is exactly what happened during the test.

해석

교수는 피실험자들에게 키보드로 96478이라는 숫자 조합을 계속 타이핑하게 했던 실험에 대해 이야기한다. 그 결과 8시간의 수면을 취한 사람들은 아침에 매우 정확한 타이핑을 했지만, 오후에는 정확도가 떨어졌다. 또한 불과 4시간만 수면을 취했을 때에도 정확도가 떨어졌다. 이러한 점은 수면이 얼마나 중요한지 보여 준다. 일반적인 사람에게는 매일 6시간에서 8시간의 수면이 필요한데, 그렇지 않으면 인지 기능이 저하될 것이다. 이것이 바로 실험에서 일어났던 일이다.

Exercise 3 ·· p.104

Reading

해석

생태계

생태계는 관계 시스템을 형성하고 있는 생물과 무생물로 이루어진 집단이다. 생태계 내에서 특정 종이 사라지면 새로 형성된 종들이 그 자리를 대신한다. 이러한 지속적인 과정은 생활 주기라고 불린다. 생태계 내의 생활 주기가 깨지면 생태계 자체가 소멸할 수 있다. 생활 주기가 깨지지 않은 상태로 남아 있으면 생

태계는 살아남아 무한히 번성할 것이다.

✎ Note Taking

Ecosystem Is group of living creatures and nonliving features that have relationships
Results If lifecycle breaks, ecosystem may die, but it will flourish if lifecycle does not break

Organization

An ecosystem is an area that features both living and nonliving parts that have formed various relationships with one another.

Listening

Script 🎧 03-45

W Professor: You will find some of the most amazing and resilient of the Earth's ecosystems in the ocean. Have you heard of the case where an oil tanker spilled oil all over the Great Barrier Reef? The oil poisoned many fish, which soon died. This large quantity of dead fish decomposed and, in turn, became algae. Now, when algae form in such large quantities over a reef, they can be deadly since they block the sunlight, thus killing the reef. But there was another species of algae-eating fish that actually protected the reef by consuming the excess algae. It's a tough ecosystem that can adapt to an oil spill.

해석

W Professor: 지구의 생태계 중 가장 놀라우면서도 탄력적인 생태계들은 바다에서 찾을 수 있습니다. 그레이트 배리어 리프에서 유조선의 기름이 유출되던 사고를 들어본 적 있나요? 기름이 많은 물고기들을 오염시켜 곧 죽게 만들었죠. 이 엄청난 양의 물고기 사체들은 부패되었고, 이는 다시 해조류가 되었습니다. 자, 산호초 위에 다량의 해조류가 형성되면서 햇빛을 차단시키자 이들은 치명적인 것이 되었고, 그 결과 산호초는 죽어가고 있었어요. 하지만 해조류를 잡아먹는 또 다른 어종이 나타나 넘쳐나는 해조류를 먹어 치움으로써 실제로 산호초를 보호해 주었습니다. 기름 유출 사고에도 적응할 수 있는 강인한 생태계인 것이죠.

✎ Note Taking

Problem Oil spill killed fish in Great Barrier Reef
Result Fish decomposed and became algae, which can kill reef by blocking sunlight
Solution Algae-eating fish ate all algae and protected reef

Comparing

Sample Response 🎧 03-46

The professor talks about an oil spill in the Great Barrier Reef. The oil killed countless fish, which then decomposed and became algae. Unfortunately, algae can often kill reefs. But there were algae-eating fish in the reef, so they ate all of the algae and saved the reef. This shows how an ecosystem works. All of the creatures in an ecosystem have various relationships with one another. Since the lifecycle of the reef was not broken, it did not die but instead prospered.

해석

교수는 그레이트 배리어 리프에서 일어났던 기름 유출 사고에 대해 말한다. 기름으로 인해 수많은 물고기들이 죽었고, 이들은 이후 부패되어 해조류가 되었다. 안타깝게도 해조류는 종종 산호초를 죽게 만들 수 있다. 하지만 산호초에 해조류를 먹는 어종이 있었기 때문에 이들이 해조류를 모두 먹어 치워 산호초를 구했다. 이는 생태계가 어떻게 작용하는지 보여 준다. 생태계 내의 모든 생물은 서로 다양한 관계를 형성하고 있다. 산호초의 생활 주기가 깨지지 않았기 때문에 산호초는 죽지 않고 번성할 수 있었다.

Exercise 4 .... p.105

Reading

해석

공생

공생은 서로 다른 두 생물이 공동체의 구성원으로서 함께 살아가는 방식이다. 공생 관계는 이러한 관계를 맺고 있는 생물 중 최소한 한쪽에 유익한 것이어야 한다. 자연 전체에 많은 공생 관계가 존재한다.

✏ Note Taking

Symbiosis Is way in which two different organisms live together

Result Must have beneficial relationship for at least one organism

Organization

Symbiosis is a relationship between two organisms that live together and in which at least one of the organisms benefits from the relationship.

Listening

Script 🎧 03-47

M Professor: A good example is the relationship between the clownfish and the sea anemone. The clownfish lives within the tentacles of the sea anemone and protects it from fish that eat anemones. The sea anemone is capable of stinging fish to kill them, but the clownfish has adapted to the anemone's ability. It has mucus on its body that protects it from the anemone's tentacles.

해석

M Professor: 좋은 예는 흰동가리와 말미잘 사이의 관계입니다. 흰동가리는 말미잘의 촉수 안에서 살면서 말미잘을 잡아먹는 물고기로부터 말미잘을 보호해 주죠. 말미잘에게는 물고기를 쏘아 죽일 수 있는 능력이 있지만 흰동가리는 이러한 말미잘의 능력에 적응해 있어요. 신체에 말미잘의 촉수로부터 자신을 보호해 주는 점액이 있습니다.

✏ Note Taking

Example Clownfish and sea anemone have symbiotic relationship

Relationship Clownfish lives within sea anemone tentacles and protects it from predators

Adaptation Clownfish has mucus to protect self from sea anemone

Comparing

Sample Response 🎧 03-48

The professor describes the symbiotic relationship between the clownfish and the sea anemone. The clownfish lives within the sea anemone's tentacles and protects the anemone from predators. The anemone can use its tentacles to stun fish, but the clownfish is immune to them. This is a symbiotic relationship because the two species live together. In addition, the anemone clearly benefits from the relationship because the clownfish protects it and keeps other fish from eating it.

해석

교수는 흰동가리와 말미잘 사이의 공생 관계에 대해 설명한다. 흰동가리는 말미잘의 촉수 안에서 살며 포식자로부터 말미잘을 보호해 준다. 말미잘은 촉수를 사용해 물고기를 기절시킬 수 있지만 흰동가리는 이들에 대한 면역력을 가지고 있다. 이 두 종이 함께 살아가기 때문에 이것은 공생 관계이다. 또한 흰동가리는 말미잘을 보호하고 다른 물고기들이 말미잘을 잡아먹지 못하도록 하기 때문에, 말미잘이 이러한 관계로부터 혜택을 받는다는 점은 명확하다.

Exercise 5 .... p.106

Reading

해석

진사회성

일부 동물들은 번식 과정에 있어서 종 내에서 분업을 할 수 있다. 이를 진사회성이라고 부른다. 이러한 과정은 생식 능력이 없는 구성원들을 번식시켜 이루어지는데, 이들은 생식 능력이 있는 구성원들을 위해 특별한 역할을 수행한다. 진사회성을 지닌 흔히 볼 수 있는 종은 개미, 꿀벌, 그리고 말벌이다.

✏ Note Taking

Eusociality Is specializing of species through reproduction

Method Breed sterile members to perform tasks for reproductive members

Species Ants, bees, and wasps

Organization

Eusocial species are able to reproduce sterile members that perform various tasks for the reproductive members.

Listing

Script 🎧 03-49

W Professor: A good example of a eusocial creature is the termite, or white ant. These insects self-organize by using swarm intelligence. There are reproductive individuals of both sexes as well as sterile members, which are the workers and the soldiers. This fact makes them eusocial since the sterile workers and the soldiers are genetically differentiated from the egg-laying queens and the fertile males of the species.

해석

W Professor: 진사회성을 지닌 동물의 좋은 예는 흰개미, 즉 하얀색 개미입니다. 이 곤충은 집단 지능을 사용해서 스스로 조직을 형성하죠. 일개미와 병정개미와 같이 생식 능력이 없는 구성원뿐만 아니라 생식 능력이 있는 암수의 개체들도 존재합니다. 이러한 사실로 인해 이들은 진사회성을 띄는데, 그 이유는 생식 능력이 없는 일개미와 병정개미들이 알을 낳는 여왕개미와 생식 능력이 있는 수캐미들과 유전적으로 다르기 때문입니다.

✎ Note Taking

Termites Organize through swarm intelligence
Sterile members Workers and soldiers that serve reproductive members
Fertile members Egg-laying queens and some males

Comparing

Sample Response 🎧 03-50

The professor lectures about termites. Termites organize themselves into sterile and fertile members. The sterile members are the workers and the soldiers while the fertile members are the queens and various males. Termites are a eusocial species because they reproduce both sterile and fertile members. In addition, the sterile members perform specific tasks to serve the fertile members of the group.

해석

교수는 흰개미에 대한 강의를 하고 있다. 흰개미는 자신들을 생식 능력을 가진 구성원과 생식 능력이 없는 구성원들로 구분한다. 생식 능력이 없는 구성원은 일개미와 병정개미이고, 생식 능력이 있는 구성원은 여왕개미와 다양한 수캐미이다. 흰개미는 생식 능력이 없는 구성원과 생식 능력이 없는 구성원들을 모두 낳기 때문에 진사회성을 띄는 종이다. 또한 생식 능력이 없는 구성원은 무리 내 생식 능력이 있는 구성원들을 돕기 위한 특별한 임무를 수행한다.

Exercise 6 .... p.107

Reading

해석

모방

모방은 스스로를 다른 종류의 생물처럼 보이도록 변장하는 동물의 능력이다. 포식자들을 속여 자신이 잡아먹기에 좋지 않다고 생각하게 만들거나, 먹이로 하여금 자기들이 해로운 포식자가 아니라고 생각하게 만들기 위해 모방을 한다.

✎ Note Taking

Mimicry Is ability of animals to disguise selves as other organisms
Result Can deceive predators or trick prey

Organization

Mimicry is the ability of animals to appear to be other animals in order to deceive both predators and prey.

Listening

Script 🎧 03-51

M Professor: Stick and leaf insects mimic other objects in their environment to disguise themselves in order to avoid predators that eat them. One amazing stick insect actually has the body structure and coloring of a stick that is found growing from a plant or young tree. Another leaf insect has also adapted itself to mimic very closely a leaf that grows on a tree in its immediate environment.

해석

M Professor: 대벌레와 잎벌레는 자신들을 잡아먹는 포식자들을 피하기 위해 주변에 있는 사물을 모방해 몸을 숨깁니다. 실제로 한 놀라운 대벌레는 식물이나 어린 나무에서 자라는 나뭇가지 형태의 신체 구조와 색깔을 지니고 있습니다. 또한 주위 나무에서 자라는 나뭇잎을 매우 비슷하게 모방할 수 있도록 적응한 잎벌레도 있죠.

✎ Note Taking

Stick insect Appears to be stick of tree or plant
Leaf insect Appears to be leaf on tree

Comparing

Sample Response 🎧 03-52

The professor discusses both stick and leaf insects. One stick insect looks just like a stick from a plant or tree. In addition, one leaf insect appears to be a leaf from a tree that grows in its environment. These insects engage in mimicry to hide themselves. By using mimicry and disguising themselves as other organisms, they can hide from predators that would otherwise eat them.

해석

교수는 대벌레와 잎벌레에 대해 이야기한다. 어떤 대벌레는 식물이나 나무의 가지와 똑같은 모양을 하고 있다. 게다가 어떤 잎벌레는 주위에서 자라는 나뭇잎처럼 보인다. 이러한 곤충들은 모방을 해서 몸을 숨긴다. 이들은 모방을 하고 스스로를 다른 생물처럼 보이도록 위장함으로써 그렇지 않을 경우 자신을 잡아먹을 수도 있는 포식자들로부터 몸을 숨길 수 있다.

Unit 17 Business

Exercise 1 ···························· p.108

Reading
해석

앰비언트 광고

앰비언트 광고는 게릴라 마케팅으로도 알려져 있다. 이는 놀라움과 감정에 의존한다. 앰비언트 광고는 종종 예상치 못한 장소에 게시된다. 이로써 보다 눈에 띄기가 쉽다. 그 결과 사람들은 광고판에 있는 일반적인 광고보다 앰비언트 광고를 훨씬 더 주목하는 경향이 있다.

✏ Note Taking

Ambient advertising A form of advertising that relies on surprise and emotions
Action Put ads where they are not expected
Result Noticed by people much more than other ads

Organization

Ambient advertising is advertising that relies on surprise and emotions by putting ads in places where people do not expect them.

Listening
Script 🎧 03-53

M Professor: I take the subway to school every day. This morning, I received a huge shock when I was taking the escalator to go down to catch the subway. At the bottom of the escalator, there was an ad for a donut store. There was a huge picture of delicious-looking donuts. It was a shocking place for an ad. But it worked. When I arrived at the station near the school, I went right to that store and bought half a dozen donuts.

해석
M Professor: 저는 매일 지하철을 타고 학교에 옵니다. 오늘 아침, 저는 지하철을 타려고 내려가기 위해 에스컬레이터에 있다가 크게 놀랐어요. 에스컬레이터 바닥에 도넛 매장의 광고가 있었기 때문이었죠. 맛있어 보이는 거대한 도넛 사진이 있었습니다. 전혀 예상치 못한 장소에 광고가 있었죠. 하지만 효과가 있었어요. 저는 학교 근처의 역에 도착했을 때 바로 그 매장에 가서 도넛 6개를 구입했습니다.

✏ Note Taking

Subway station Professor saw big ad for donut store at the bottom of the escalator
Result Bought some donuts when he arrived at the station

Comparing
Sample Response 🎧 03-54

The professor says that this morning on his way to school, he was surprised at the subway station. At the bottom of the escalator, there was a big ad for a donut shop. He says that it made him hungry for donuts. So he bought six of them when he arrived at his destination. The sign was an example of ambient advertising. It relies on surprise and emotions. It also puts ads in unusual places to make people notice them.

해석
교수는 오늘 아침 학교로 가는 중에 지하철에서 놀랐다고 말한다. 에스컬레이터 바닥에 거대한 도넛 매장 사진이 있었다. 그는 사진 때문에 도넛이 먹고 싶었다고 말한다. 그래서 목적지에 도착해서 6개의 도넛을 구입했다. 그러한 표시는 앰비언트 광고의 한 예이다. 이는 놀라움과 감정에 의존한다. 또한 사람들이 주목할 수 있도록 특이한 장소에 광고를 게시한다.

Exercise 2 ···························· p.109

Reading
해석

미스터리 쇼퍼

일부 기업들은 종종 자신의 직원들이 제공하는 고객 서비스의 품질을 확인한다. 미스터리 쇼퍼를 고용해서 그렇게 할 수 있다. 미스터리 쇼퍼들이 매장을 방문한다. 그런 다음 직원들과 소통을 한다. 이들은 소통한 내용을 기록하고 긍정적인 측면과 부정적인 측면을 목록으로 작성한다. 이로써 관리자들은 자신의 직원들이 얼마나 일을 잘하고 있는지 알 수 있다.

✏ Note Taking

Mystery shoppers Visit businesses and interact with staff members at them
Result Can determine how well employees are doing

Organization

Mystery shoppers are people who visit businesses and record their interactions with the staff. This lets managers know which employees are doing well and which are not.

Listening
Script 🎧 03-55

W Professor: My brother owns a restaurant. He had heard from some of his friends that a few of the members of the serving staff were treating customers poorly. So here is what he did. He hired some people to visit his restaurant. He told them to make requests of the staff and then to evaluate the staffers. These mystery shoppers were great. They told my brother which servers were good and which ones were bad. My brother fired the rude workers and replaced them with better ones.

50

W Professor: 제 남동생은 식당을 소유하고 있어요. 동생은 몇몇 친구로부터 일부 서빙 직원들이 고객들을 잘 응대하지 않는다는 이야기를 들었습니다. 그래서 그가 했던 일을 알려 드리죠. 동생은 사람들을 몇 명 고용해서 자신의 식당을 방문하도록 했습니다. 직원들에게 요청을 한 후 직원들을 평가해 달라고 그들에게 말을 했죠. 이 미스터리 쇼퍼들은 굉장했어요. 그들은 제 동생에게 어떤 서빙 직원이 우수하고 어떤 서빙 직원이 그렇지 못한지 말해 주었습니다. 제 동생은 친절하지 않은 직원들을 해고한 후 보다 우수한 직원들로 그 자리를 채웠습니다.

> **Note Taking**
>
> **Problem** Professor's brother had some bad servers at his restaurant
> **Solution** Used mystery shoppers to find the good and bad servers

Comparing

Sample Response 🎧 03-56

> The professor tells the class about her brother's restaurant. Her brother thought some of his servers were bad, so he hired some mystery shoppers. These are people who visit businesses and evaluate the staff. They say which workers are good and which ones are bad. This is what her brother's mystery shoppers did. He learned which servers were rude, so he fired them. Then, he hired replacement workers who were much better.

교수는 학생들에게 자신의 남동생의 식당에 대해 이야기한다. 그녀의 동생은 종업원 중 일부가 친절하지 않았기 때문에 미스터리 쇼퍼를 고용했다. 이들은 사업장을 방문해서 직원들을 평가하는 사람들이다. 어떤 직원이 우수하고 어떤 직원이 우수하지 못한지 알려 준다. 교수 동생의 미스터리 쇼퍼들도 바로 그러한 일을 했다. 동생은 어떤 서빙 직원이 친절하지 않은지 알게 되었고, 그들을 해고했다. 그런 다음 보다 우수한 직원들로 그 자리를 채웠다.

Exercise 3 ·· p.110

Reading

신뢰재

사람들이 구입하는 것 중 일부는 그 품질을 판단하는 것이 가능하지 않다. 특히 차량 수리 서비스, 영양제, 그리고 의료 서비스의 경우에 그러하다. 많은 경우, 사람들은 이러한 구매 품목들의 가격이 비쌀 수록 그 품질이 더 우수하다고 믿는다.

> **Note Taking**
>
> **Credence goods** Items whose quality cannot be determined by people purchasing them
> **Examples** Vehicle repairs, supplements, and medical treatments

Organization

Credence goods are purchases such as vehicle repairs, supplements, and medical treatments whose value cannot be determined by people.

Listening

Script 🎧 03-57

> **W Professor**: Last month, I saw an advertisement for some multivitamins. I figured that since I'm getting older, my body could probably use some supplements. So I went and bought a bottle. After a couple of weeks, I started telling everyone about the multivitamins. I couldn't really tell if I was feeling better or not. But I spent a lot of money on them, so I figured that the multivitamins were worth the money I spent.

W Professor: 지난 달에 저는 종합 비타민제 광고를 보았습니다. 저도 나이를 먹고 있기 때문에 아마도 제 몸에 영양제가 필요할 수도 있겠다고 생각했어요. 그래서 한 병을 구입했습니다. 2주 후, 저는 종합 비타민제에 대해 모든 사람들에게 말하기 시작했어요. 사실 몸 상태가 더 좋아졌는지, 그렇지 않은지는 알 수가 없었습니다. 하지만 그에 대해 많은 돈을 썼기 때문에 종합 비타민제가 그만한 가치는 있다고 생각을 했죠.

> **Note Taking**
>
> **Purchase** Bought some multivitamins
> **Reason** Getting older so body needs supplements
> **Result** Told people the multivitamins were good since spent a lot of money

Comparing

Sample Response 🎧 03-58

> The professor says that she bought some multivitamins a month ago. After a couple of weeks, she told people about them and said that they worked. She decided that since she spent a lot of money, the multivitamins must be of good quality. The multivitamins were a credence good. Credence goods are items whose value is hard to determine by people. But they think if they spend a lot of money, the quality must be good.

교수는 자신이 한 달 전에 종합 비타민제를 구입했다고 말한다. 2주 후 그녀는 사람들에게 그에 대해 이야기했고, 그것이 효과가 있었다고 전했다. 그녀는 자신이 많은 돈을 썼기 때문에 종합 비타민제의 품질이 틀림없이 우수할 것이라고 생각했다. 종합 비타민제는 신뢰재였다. 신뢰재는 사람들이 그 가치를 판단하기 힘든 제품이다. 하지만 사람들은 많은 돈을 지출하기 때문에 그 품질이 틀림없이 좋을 것이라고 생각한다.

Exercise 4 ·· p.111

Reading

티저 광고

일부 기업들은 시리즈 광고를 이용하여 자신들의 제품 및 서비스를 홍보한다.

이러한 광고는 종종 신비스럽고 제품을 거의 드러내지 않는다. 이러한 티저 광고의 의도는 긴장감과 흥분을 고조시키는 것이다. 이는 언론의 관심을 불러일으키고 사람들이 해당 제품에 대해 이야기하도록 만든다.

Organization

Teaser campaigns are series of advertisements that reveal little about products in order to increase publicity for them.

Listening

Script 🎧 03-59

M Professor: Did all of you see the big reveal in the advertisement for the fast-food restaurant last night? For three months, there have been mysterious commercials by that restaurant chain. Each ad revealed a bit more information. Finally, last night's ad showed that the restaurant is coming out with a special new burger. I'd say it was a big success. Everyone is talking about it, and I'm going there for lunch today to try it.

해석

M Professor: 여러분 모두 어젯밤 패스트푸드 매장의 광고에서 드디어 밝혀진 것을 보았나요? 3개월 동안 그 식당 체인업체에서 미스터리한 광고들이 나왔습니다. 각각의 광고에서는 약간의 정보들만 드러났죠. 마침내 어젯밤 광고에서 그 식당이 특별한 새로운 버거를 출시할 것이라는 점이 알려졌어요. 저는 이것이 크게 성공한 광고라고 말하고 싶습니다. 모두들 그에 대해 이야기하고 있고, 저도 오늘 점심에 그곳에 가서 하나 먹어보려고 하니까요.

Comparing

Sample Response 🎧 03-60

The professor asks the students if they saw the final ad in a series of advertisements by a fast-food restaurant. He says that each ad revealed more and more about something mysterious. Finally, last night's ad showed that the restaurant is making a new burger. The professor says everyone is talking about the ad. This is an example of a teaser campaign. It is a series of ads that are designed to create suspense and excitement in customers.

해석

교수는 학생들에게 패스푸드 매장의 시리즈 광고 중 마지막 광고를 보았는지 묻

는다. 그는 각각의 광고가 미스터리한 제품을 약간씩 더 드러낸다고 말한다. 마침내 어젯밤 광고에서 그 매장이 새로운 버거를 출시한다는 점이 드러났다. 교수는 모두가 그 광고에 대해 이야기하고 있다고 말한다. 이는 티저 광고의 한 가지 예이다. 이는 소비자들의 긴장감과 흥분을 고조시키기 위해 고안된 시리즈 광고이다.

Exercise 5 .... p.112

Reading

해석

분업

조직은 종종 분업이라고 알려진 작업 과정을 이용한다. 이러한 과정에서는 직원들이 모두 동일한 작업을 하지 않는다. 대신 각자 한 개 혹은 두 개의 작업을 전문적으로 수행한다. 이로써 사람들은 전문가가 될 수 있다. 따라서 보다 뛰어나게, 빠르게, 그리고 효율적으로 자신의 일을 할 수 있다. 이로써 조직이 더 잘 돌아갈 수 있다.

Organization

The division of labor happens when an organization has its workers specialize in tasks. This lets them become better, faster, and more efficient workers.

Listening

Script 🎧 03-61

W Professor: Before I started working here, I had a job at a small tech company. The owner was a brilliant man, but he made a huge mistake. He tried to get everyone to be familiar with all of the other employees' jobs. There were ten of us, and we did some highly specialized tasks. He didn't want us to focus on just one task though. He made us learn everything. It was not a surprise that the company failed. We just couldn't handle all of the assignments he gave us.

해석

W Professor: 저는 이곳에서 일을 하기 전에 작은 기술 개발 회사에서 일을 했습니다. 사장은 명석한 사람이었지만, 커다란 실수를 하나 했어요. 그는 모든 사람들이 다른 직원들의 전체 업무에도 익숙해지도록 만들려 했어요. 총 10명이 있었고, 우리는 매우 전문적인 업무를 다루고 있었습니다. 하지만 사장은 우리가 한 가지 일에만 집중하는 것을 원하지 않았죠. 그는 우리가 모든 것을 익히도록 했어요. 그 회사가 파산한 것은 놀라운 일이 아니었습니다. 그가 부여한 모든 업무를 우리가 처리할 수는 없었으니까요.

Note Taking

Problem Owner made employees learn all other
employees' jobs

Result Company failed

Comparing

Sample Response 🎧 03-62

The professor says that she used to work at a tech
company with ten employees. The owner tried to make
the employees learn everyone's job. He didn't want them
to specialize in just one or two tasks. This was too difficult
for everyone, so the company failed. The problem was that
the owner did not use the division of labor. This happens
when employees become specialists in one or two jobs.
This lets a company become efficient and run better.

해석

교수는 자신이 직원이 10명인 기술 개발 회사에서 일을 한 적이 있었다고 말한
다. 사장은 직원들로 하여금 모든 사람들의 업무를 익히도록 했다. 그는 직원들
이 단지 하나나 두 개의 업무를 전문적으로 하는 것을 원하지 않았다. 이는 모든
사람들에게 너무 어려운 일이었기 때문에 회사는 파산을 했다. 문제는 사장이 분
업을 활용하지 않았다는 점이었다. 분업은 직원들이 하나나 두 개의 작업에서 전
문가가 될 때 이루어진다. 이로써 회사는 효율을 높이고 더 잘 돌아갈 수 있다.

Exercise 6 ·· p.113

Reading

해석

사회적 책임

사회적 책임은 이윤이 아니라 사회에 도움을 주기 위해 이루어지는 기업의 활
동을 가리킨다. 사회적인 책임을 지는 기업들은 자신의 활동이 반드시 사람 및
환경에 도움이 되도록 만든다. 기업들은 최대한의 이윤을 얻지 못할 수도 있다.
하지만 사회적인 책임을 짐으로써 다른 사람들을 도울 수 있다.

Note Taking

Social responsibility Happens when businesses put
society ahead of profits

Result Businesses don't make as much profit but help
others

Organization

Social responsibility is when businesses put people and the
environment ahead of making a profit.

Listening

Script 🎧 03-63

W Professor: Did you hear the announcement made
by the coffee shop in the campus center? It's going to
do two things. First, it will stop using plastic cups and
will instead provide drinks in paper cups that have

been recycled. Second, any customers who bring their
own cups will get a ten-percent discount off their drink
purchase. Now, uh, the coffee shop's profits are likely
to decline. However, what it's doing is good for the
environment.

해석

W Professor: 캠퍼스 센터의 커피숍에서 나온 공지를 들으셨나요? 두 가지
일이 진행될 예정이에요. 첫째, 플라스틱컵의 사용이 중단될 것이며 대신 재활용
된 종이컵으로 음료가 제공될 것입니다. 둘째, 자기 컵을 가지고 오는 고객에게
는 음료 구매 시 10%의 할인이 제공될 것입니다. 자, 어, 커피숍의 이윤은 줄어들
수도 있겠죠. 하지만 그곳에서 하려는 일은 환경에 도움이 되는 것입니다.

Note Taking

Coffee shop's actions Will use recycled paper cups instead
of plastic cups and will give discounts to customers
with their own cups

Results Profits will decline but the environment will
benefit

Comparing

Sample Response 🎧 03-64

The professor says that the university coffee shop will
start doing two new things. First, it will cease its use of
plastic cups and use recycled paper cups. Second, it
will give discounts to customers who bring their own
cups. The professor points out that the store's profits
will decline but that it is helping the environment. This
is an example of social responsibility. It happens when
businesses consider people and the environment to be
more important than profits.

해석

교수는 대학 커피숍이 두 가지 새로운 일을 시작할 것이라고 말한다. 첫째, 플라
스틱컵의 사용이 중단되고 재활용되는 종이컵이 사용될 것이다. 둘째, 자기 컵을
가지고 오는 고객에게 할인이 적용될 것이다. 교수는 이 매장의 이윤이 줄어들
것이지만 이곳이 환경을 돕고 있다고 지적한다. 이는 사회적 책임의 한 예이다.
이는 기업들이 이윤보다 사람과 환경을 더 중요하게 생각할 때 드러난다.

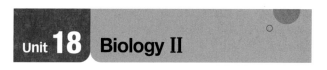

Unit 18 Biology II

Exercise 1 ·· p.114

Reading

해석

침입종

때때로 한 서식지의 토착 동식물들이 다른 곳으로 가는 경우가 있다. 최근에
는 인간의 활동 때문에 새로운 서식지로 이동하고 있다. 새로운 환경에서는 보통

이러한 침입종들에 대한 천적이 존재하지 않는다. 따라서 이러한 동물들이 서식지를 지배함으로써 다른 동물들이 죽을 수도 있다. 그리고 이러한 식물들이 너무 많이 자라면 다른 식물들에게 해를 끼칠 수도 있다.

Invasive species Plants and animals that move to new habitats

Animals May dominate an area because they have no natural predators

Plants May grow too much and cause harm to other plants

Organization

Invasive species are plants and animals that move to new habitats, where they often cause harm.

Listening

Script 🎧 03-65

M Professor: In the 1970s, some people in Florida had Burmese pythons as pets. These animals are native to Southeast Asia. But people released their pets into the wild. Now, Florida has a huge python problem. The pythons have wiped out many native species of animals in Florida. This invasive species is causing an enormous problem.

해석

M Professor: 1970년대 몇몇 플로리다 주민들이 버마왕뱀을 애완용으로 길렀습니다. 이 동물은 동남아시아가 원산지였죠. 하지만 사람들이 자신의 애완 동물을 야생에 풀어 주었습니다. 현재 플로리다는 커다란 뱀 문제를 겪고 있어요. 버마왕뱀이 플로리다의 토착 동물종들을 완전히 없애 버렸습니다. 이 침입종이 커다란 문제를 일으키고 있는 것이죠.

✎ Note Taking

Burmese pythons Released in Florida by pet owners in 1970s

Result Have wiped out many native species of animals in Florida

Comparing

Sample Response 🎧 03-66

The professor says that in the 1970s, people in Florida released pet Burmese pythons in the wild. Now, these snakes are a huge problem. They have wiped out many native animals in Florida. They are a kind of invasive species. Invasive species move to a new habitat and dominate. They can often cause great harm to the animals in their new area.

해석

교수는 1970년대에 플로리다 주민들이 애완용이었던 버마왕뱀을 야생에 풀어 주었다고 말한다. 현재 이 뱀들은 커다란 문제가 되고 있다. 이들이 플로리다의 여러 토착 동물들을 없애 버렸다. 이들은 침입종에 해당된다. 침입종은 새로운

54

서식지에 유입되어 그곳을 지배한다. 이들은 종종 새로운 지역의 동물들에게 막대한 피해를 끼칠 수 있다.

Exercise 2 ·· p.115

Reading

해석

최적 섭식 이론

먹이를 찾기 위해 모든 동물들은 에너지를 소비해야 한다. 때때로 먹이가 가까이 있는 경우에는 에너지를 거의 소비하지 않는다. 하지만 먹이를 구하기가 힘든 경우, 많은 양의 에너지를 소비해야 하는 동물들도 있다. 모든 동물들은 먹이를 찾는 활동을 최적화하려고 노력한다. 이는 동물들이 최소한의 에너지를 소비하여 최대한 많은 먹이를 얻는다는 점을 의미한다. 그렇지 못하는 경우, 동물들은 쇠약해져서 죽을 수도 있다.

✎ Note Taking

Optimal foraging theory Animals try to spend as little energy as possible while getting the most food

Result If cannot do this, may die

Organization

Optimal foraging theory is the idea that animals try to spend the least amount of energy possible while searching for food. But they try to get as much food as possible.

Listening

Script 🎧 03-67

W Professor: I was at the beach the other day and was watching the seals. I noticed that one seal was really good at catching fish. Every time it dived under the water, it came up with a fish. It was a very efficient hunter. Another seal, however, had some problems. It kept diving after fish, but it only caught a fish about every five dives. If that seal doesn't improve its hunting skills, it probably won't live long.

해석

W Professor: 며칠 전 저는 해변에 갔는데, 물개를 볼 수 있었습니다. 물개 한 마리가 정말로 능숙하게 물고기를 잡는 모습을 보았죠. 물속으로 잠수를 할 때마다 물고기 한 마리를 건져 올렸습니다. 매우 효율적인 사냥꾼이었죠. 하지만 다른 물개 하나는 몇 가지 문제를 겪고 있었습니다. 물고기를 따라 계속 잠수를 했지만, 약 5번의 잠수를 할 때마다 물고기 한 마리만 잡더군요. 그 물개는 사냥 기술을 향상시키지 못한다면 아마도 오래 살지 못할 것입니다.

✎ Note Taking

First seal Caught a fish each time it dived

Second seal Caught a fish once every five dives

Comparing

Sample Response 🎧 03-68

The professor talks about watching two seals hunting fish

at the beach. One was very efficient and caught a fish every time it dived. Another seal was inefficient. It only caught a fish about one in every five dives. The first seal was an ideal example of optimal foraging theory. The seal used little energy searching for food and was rewarded with a lot of food. The other seal did not use optimal foraging. It spent too much energy hunting and did not get back much energy from the food it caught.

해석

교수는 해변에서 두 마리의 물개가 사냥하는 모습을 본 일에 대해 이야기한다. 한 마리는 매우 효율적이어서 잠수를 할 때마다 물고기 한 마리씩 잡았다. 다른 물개는 효율적이지 못했다. 다섯 번의 잠수에 한 마리씩만 물고기를 잡았다. 첫 번째 물개는 최적 섭식 이론의 이상적인 예였다. 이 물개는 먹이를 찾는데 거의 에너지를 쓰지 않았고, 많은 물고기를 보상으로 받았다. 다른 물개는 먹이 찾는 행동을 최적화하지 못했다. 사냥에 너무 많은 에너지를 소비했고, 자신이 잡은 먹이로부터 많은 에너지를 되찾아오지 못했다.

Exercise 3 ·· p.116

Reading

해석

동물 체색

많은 동물들이 밝은 색을 띠거나 몸에 정말로 눈에 잘 띠는 한 가지 색을 가지고 있다. 많은 경우, 이러한 색은 다른 동물들에게 경고의 기능을 한다. 색이 화려한 동물들은 몇 가지 측면에서 위험하기 때문에 이들에게 접근하면 안 된다는 점을 포식자들에게 알려 준다. 색이 화려한 동물들은 독을 지니고 있을 수 있고, 혹은 기타 강력한 방어 수단을 지니고 있을 수도 있다.

> ✎ Note Taking
>
> **Animal coloration** Happens when an animal is very colorful or has one color that stands out
> **Result** Is a warning to other animals to stay away

Organization

Animal coloration happens when an animal is brightly colored or has one color that stands out on its body. This often tells predators that the colorful animal is dangerous for some reason.

Listening

Script 🎧 03-69

M Professor: Everyone knows this animal. It's a skunk. How do you know it? The white stripe down its back makes it easily recognizable. Well, animals recognize skunks, too. And they know to stay away. I have a dog that loves to hunt. One time, he got too near a skunk, and the skunk sprayed him. My dog smelled horrible for a week. Now, when my dog sees a skunk, he runs the other way. He has learned to identify skunks based on their coloration.

해석

M Professor: 모두들 이 동물을 아실 거예요. 스컹크입니다. 어떻게 아셨죠? 등 아래에 있는 하얀색 줄무늬 때문에 쉽게 알아볼 수가 있습니다. 음, 동물들 역시 스컹크를 알아봅니다. 그리고 피해야 한다는 점도 알고 있죠. 저에게는 사냥을 좋아하는 개가 한 마리 있습니다. 한 번은 스컹크에게 너무 가까이 다가갔다가 스컹크가 그에게 분사를 했어요. 제 개에서 일주일 동안 끔찍한 냄새가 났습니다. 자, 제 개는 스컹크를 보면 다른 방향으로 달아납니다. 체색에 기반하여 스컹크를 알아보게 된 것이죠.

> ✎ Note Taking
>
> **Skunk** Is recognizable due to the white stripe on its back
> **Action** Professor's dog got sprayed by a skunk and smelled bad for a week
> **Result** The dog avoids skunks now

Comparing

Sample Response 🎧 03-70

The professor tells a story about his dog. He says that it loves to hunt and saw a skunk one day. However, the skunk sprayed the dog, so it smelled terrible for a week. Now, if the dog sees a skunk, it stays away. The skunk is an example of animal coloration. It has a noticeable white stripe on its back. Animals with features like this or bright colors are often dangerous. Their coloration tells other animals to keep away from them.

해석

교수는 자신의 개에 대한 이야기를 한다. 그는 자신의 개가 사냥을 좋아하는데, 어느 날 스컹크를 보았다고 말한다. 하지만 스컹크가 개에게 분사를 했고, 개는 일주일 동안 끔찍한 냄새를 풍겼다. 이제 개는 스컹크를 보면 거리를 둔다. 스컹크는 동물 체색의 한 예이다. 등에 눈에 잘 띄는 하얀색 줄무늬가 있다. 이러한 특성이나 밝은 색을 지닌 동물들은 종종 위험하다. 이들의 체색은 다른 동물들에게 접근하지 말라는 점을 알려 준다.

Exercise 4 ·· p.117

Reading

해석

나무 커뮤니케이션

최근에 과학자들은 같은 종의 나무들이 서로 커뮤니케이션을 할 수 있다는 점을 알게 되었다. 그들은 그러한 커뮤니케이션이 뿌리를 통해 이루어진다고 믿는다. 이러한 커뮤니케이션은 나무들로 하여금 해충 및 가뭄에 대한 정보를 서로 공유하게 해 준다. 또한 뿌리를 통해 영양분을 공유할 수도 있다.

> ✎ Note Taking
>
> **Tree communication** Trees of the same species can communicate
> **Example** Can use their roots to share news regarding pests and droughts

Organization

Tree communication is the using of root systems by trees of

the same species to communicate various information with one another.

Listening
Script 🎧 03-71

> **W Professor**: I live out in the countryside and have a large amount of land. In one area, there are around a dozen willow trees. Interestingly, the other day, some bugs started eating the leaves of one of the trees. However, all of the other willows were unaffected. The injured tree communicated the news to the others. So they pumped out chemicals to ward off the pests. Impressive, isn't it?

해석

W Professor: 저는 시골에서 사는데, 커다란 땅을 가지고 있어요. 한 곳에는 약 12그루의 버드나무가 모여 있죠. 흥미롭게도, 며칠 전 몇몇 벌레들이 한 나무의 나뭇잎을 갉아 먹기 시작했어요. 하지만 다른 버드나무들은 모두 영향을 받지 않습니다. 피해를 입은 나무가 다른 나무들에게 소식을 알려 주었던 것이죠. 그래서 나무들이 해충을 내쫓는 화학 물질을 배출했습니다. 인상적이죠, 그렇지 않나요?

> ✎ Note Taking
>
> **Situation** Pests ate the leaves of a willow tree
> **Action** The tree communicated with the other willows, and they sent out chemicals to get rid of the pests

Comparing
Sample Response 🎧 03-72

> The professor tells the class that she has around twelve willow trees on her land. One day, some pests ate the leaves of one of the willows. However, the tree communicated with the other willows. As a result, they produced chemicals that kept the pests away from their leaves. This was an example of tree communication. Trees use their root systems to let others of the same species know information about pests and droughts.

해석

교수는 자신의 땅에 약 12그루의 버드나무가 있다고 학생들에게 말한다. 어느 날, 몇몇 해충들이 한 버드나무의 잎을 먹었다. 하지만 그 나무는 다른 버드나무들과 커뮤니케이션을 했다. 그 결과 나무들은 잎에서 해충을 떼어놓는 화학 물질을 분비했다. 이는 나무 커뮤니케이션의 한 예이다. 나무들은 뿌리를 이용하여 같은 종의 다른 나무들에게 해충 및 가뭄에 관한 정보를 알려 줄 수 있다.

Exercise 5 ···································· p.118

Reading
해석

수직 이동

이동은 많은 종들에게 있어서 삶의 일부이다. 일부 동물들은 수직 이동을 한다. 특히 수중 동물들이 그렇다. 일부 동물들은 물속에서 하루 중 다양한 시간에

위쪽으로 혹은 아래쪽으로 수영을 할 수 있다. 그렇게 하는 이유는 포식자들을 피하기 위해, 혹은 먹이를 먹기 위해서이다.

> ✎ Note Taking
>
> **Group migration** When animals swim higher or lower in the water at different times
> **Reasons** To stay away from predators and to look for food

Organization
Vertical migration is when creatures such as fish move higher or lower in the water. They normally do this to hunt or to avoid being hunted.

Listening
Script 🎧 03-73

> **M Professor**: If you go to the beach at night, you'll see lots of boats out on the water with their lights on. Those are fishing boats looking for squid. Why do they fish at night? Well, during the day, squid stay deep in the water. They avoid sunlight because that makes it easy for predators to catch them. However, when it gets dark, they rise to the surface, where they can feed.

해석

M Professor: 밤에 해안가로 가면 조명을 켠 채 물에 떠 있는 많은 배들을 볼 수가 있을 거예요. 이들은 오징어를 찾고 있는 낚싯배들입니다. 왜 밤에 낚시를 할까요? 음, 낮에는 오징어가 물속 깊은 곳에 머무릅니다. 햇빛 때문에 포식자가 자신들을 잡아먹을 수 있어서 햇빛을 피하는 것이죠. 하지만 어두워지면 먹이를 먹을 수 있는 수면으로 올라옵니다.

> ✎ Note Taking
>
> **Fishing boats** Fish for squid at night
> **Squid actions** Stay in deep water during the day but go to the surface at night
> **Reason** Avoid light to hide from predators and rise to the surface to feed

Comparing
Sample Response 🎧 03-74

> The professor tells the students that fishermen catch squid at night. The reason is that squid stay in dark, deep water during the day. They do this to hide from predators. At night, they rise to the surface to hunt for food. Their actions are an example of vertical migration. This happens when creatures such as fish move higher or lower in the water at different times of the day.

해석

교수는 학생들에게 어부들이 밤에 오징어를 잡는다고 말한다. 그 이유는 오징어가 낮에는 어둡고 깊은 물속에서 지내기 때문이다. 그렇게 하는 이유는 포식자로부터 몸을 숨기기 위해서이다. 밤에는 먹이를 사냥하기 위해 수면으로 올라온다. 이들의 행동은 수직 이동의 한 가지 예이다. 이는 물고기와 같은 생물들이 하루

중 다양한 시간에 물속에서 위 또는 아래로 이동할 때 나타난다.

Exercise 6 ·· p.119

Reading

해석

개체수의 주기적 변화

서식지 내의 동물종의 수는 거의 항상 변한다. 많은 경우, 먹이가 많아서 피식 동물의 수가 증가할 수 있다. 그러면 포식 동물들이 사냥할 동물들이 늘어나기 때문에 포식 동물의 수도 증가한다. 피식 동물의 수가 감소함에 따라 포식 동물들이 먹을 수 있는 먹이가 줄어들면서 포식 동물도 줄어든다. 이는 항상 반복되는 사이클이다.

Note Taking

Cyclic population change Animal populations undergo constant changes

Example When there are many prey animals, the number of predators increases as well

Organization

Cyclic population change is the constant changing of animal populations in habitats. For example, if there are many prey animals, there will also be many predators since they have more food to eat.

Listening

Script 🎧 03-75

W Professor: As you know, there are coyotes in the national forest near us. Interestingly, their numbers frequently change. A few years ago, there were plenty of coyotes. The reason was that there were lots and lots of rabbits in the forest. The coyotes increased in number since they had so much food. However, as the rabbit population declined, so did the coyote population. They didn't have enough food to eat. Soon, there were few coyotes. This led to the rabbit population increasing again. And guess what . . . The coyote population soon increased.

해석

W Professor: 아시다시피 인근 국유림에는 코요테가 살고 있습니다. 흥미롭게도 이들의 숫자는 종종 바뀌어요. 몇 년 전에는 코요테들이 많았습니다. 그 이유는 숲에 토끼들이 정말로 많았기 때문이었죠. 코요테들의 먹이가 많았기 때문에 코요테의 수가 증가했습니다. 하지만 토끼 개체수가 줄어들면서 코요테의 개체수 역시 줄어들었어요. 먹을 수 있는 먹이가 충분하지 않았던 것이었죠. 곧 코요테가 거의 사라졌습니다. 이는 또 다시 토끼 개체수의 증가로 이어졌죠. 그리고 짐작할 수 있겠지만… 코요테의 개체수가 빠르게 늘어났습니다.

Note Taking

Coyotes Were many coyotes in the forest because they had plenty to eat

Rabbits Numbers became lower because of the coyotes; then, when there were fewer coyotes, their numbers increased again

Comparing

Sample Response 🎧 03-76

The professor says that a nearby forest has coyotes. She says that in the past, there were many rabbits, so there were also a lot of coyotes. The coyotes had a big food supply. But then the number of rabbits declined. So did the number of coyotes. After a while, the rabbit population began to increase. Then, there were more coyotes. This is an example of cyclic population decline. This occurs when animal numbers in a habitat increase and decrease constantly.

해석

교수는 인근의 숲에 코요테가 산다고 말한다. 그녀는 예전에 토끼들이 많았기 때문에 코요테 또한 많았다고 말한다. 코요테가 먹을 수 있는 먹이가 많았던 것이다. 하지만 이후 토끼의 수가 줄어들었다. 코요테의 수 역시 줄어들었다. 얼마 후 토끼의 개체수가 증가하기 시작했다. 그러자 코요테들도 늘어났다. 이는 개체수의 주기적 변화의 예이다. 이는 서식지 내 동물의 수가 끊임없이 증가하고 감소할 때 나타난다.

Unit **19** Economics

Exercise 1 ·· p.126

Listening

Script 🎧 04-05

M Professor: Now, I want to explain the idea of what we call initial price. Initial price is a concept that is applied to new products. The idea of the initial price is to give something a high price so that customers will believe the item is very high in quality or is popular. Well, many people want things that are difficult to obtain. For example, they want to be the first person with a new smartphone or some computer game. Later, the price drops as new products are developed. Initial price usually applies to technological items like computers. Basically, the idea is to set the starting price high and then slowly lower it. The people that can afford the high price will buy it right away, and others will buy it later.

해석

M Professor: 자, 초기 가격이라는 개념에 대해 설명을 드리고자 해요. 초기 가격은 신제품에 적용되는 개념입니다. 초기 가격의 개념은 소비자들로 하여금 어떤 제품의 품질이 상당히 우수하거나 그 제품이 인기 있다고 믿도록 하기 위해 제품에 높은 가격을 책정하는 것입니다. 음, 많은 사람들은 얻기 힘든 것을 원하죠. 예를 들어 새로 출시된 스마트폰이나 다른 컴퓨터 게임을 제일 먼저 갖고 싶어합니다. 이후 새로운 제품들이 개발되면 그 가격은 떨어집니다. 보통 초기 가격은 컴퓨터와 같은 첨단 기술 제품에 적용되어요. 기본적으로 이 아이디어는 시작 가격을 높게 책정한 후 이후에 천천히 낮추는 것입니다. 높은 가격을 감당할 수 있는 사람은 당장 구입할 것이고, 다른 사람들은 나중에 구입을 할 거예요.

> 🖉 Note Taking
>
> **Subject** Initial price
> **Detail** Is high and then gets lower

Organization

1 The term initial price describes the price companies apply to new products.

2 People who can afford the initial price buy the product because they think the high price indicates high quality.

3 Prices drop as newer technology is developed.

Comparing

Sample Response 🎧 04-06

Initial price is the name of a pricing strategy that companies adopt when launching their new products. This strategy is based on two human instincts. First, people want things that are difficult to obtain. Second,

they want to be the first person to obtain these things. Using these human instincts, companies can set high starting prices for their new products.

해석

초기 가격은 기업이 신제품을 출시할 때 책정하는 가격 전략의 명칭이다. 이 전략은 두 가지 인간의 본능에 기초해 있다. 첫째, 사람들은 얻기 힘든 것을 원한다. 둘째, 이러한 것들을 가장 먼저 갖고 싶어한다. 이러한 인간의 본능을 이용해서 기업들은 신제품에 높은 시작 가격을 책정할 수 있다.

Exercise 2 ·· p.127

Listening

Script 🎧 04-07

W Professor: Have you heard about the positive externality effect? The positive externality effect is kind of a difficult theory to explain. Basically, it means that certain actions in society can help society as well as the individual. Let's see . . . A common example is the flu shot. People can help themselves by getting a flu shot and keeping healthy. They might save some money by not missing work, avoiding the doctor, and not having to pay for medicine. They also help society as a whole by not getting others sick. This is the positive externality effect. Of course, sometimes people don't care about society and don't get their shots. This hurts all of society, not just the individual. The government can help by reducing the costs of the shots or by forcing people to get their shots.

해석

W Professor: 긍정적 외부 효과에 대해 들어본 적이 있나요? 긍정적 외부 효과는 설명하기가 어려운 이론이에요. 기본적으로, 이는 사회 내에서의 특정 행동이 개인뿐만 아니라 사회에도 도움을 준다는 의미입니다. 봅시다… 한 가지 일반적인 예는 독감 예방 주사예요. 사람들은 독감 예방 주사를 맞고 건강해짐으로써 이득을 얻을 수 있습니다. 결근을 하지 않고, 진료를 받지 않고, 그리고 약을 구입할 필요도 없기 때문에 돈을 아낄 수가 있습니다. 또한 다른 사람에게 독감을 옮기지도 않으니까 사회 전체에도 도움이 되죠. 이것이 긍정적 외부 효과입니다. 물론 사람들이 종종 사회도 신경 쓰지 않고 예방 주사도 맞지 않는 경우도 있어요. 그러면 해당 개인뿐만 아니라 사회 전체에도 피해가 발생하죠. 정부는 예방 주사의 비용을 내려서, 혹은 예방 접종을 의무화함으로써 도움을 줄 수 있습니다.

> 🖉 Note Taking
>
> **Subject** Positive externality effect
> **Detail** Help self and society at same time

Organization

1 The positive externality effect claims that certain actions help not only an individual but also society as a whole.

2 An example of the positive externality effect is when someone gets a flu shot.

Comparing

Sample Response 🎧 04-08

The positive externality effect is the theory that when one person or a group of people is helped by something, the effect that it has on them will positively affect society as a whole. When a person gets a flu shot, for example, it helps the person, who won't get the flu, and it also helps everyone else that the person might have infected.

해석

긍정적 외부 효과는 어떤 사람이나 그룹이 무언가에 의해 도움을 받을 때 그 효과가 사회 전체에도 긍정적인 영향을 미친다는 이론이다. 예를 들어 어떤 사람이 예방 주사를 맞으면 독감에 걸리지 않아 자신에게도 도움이 되지만, 그 사람이 감염시킬 수도 있었던 모든 사람들도 그로 인해 도움을 받는다.

Exercise 3 .... p.128

Listening

Script 🎧 04-09

M Professor: Now I think we should talk about displaying products. Companies spend a lot of time determining how to organize products in their stores. One basic concept of displaying products is to put the new and expensive products in the front to capture the attention of possible customers. When people walk by, they often stop, and they, um, well, they stop and notice nice, new items. Even if they don't intend to buy them, people notice them. People will then gain interest and look at other items in the store. Many people will notice expensive products and then look through the store for something cheaper. People walking by won't notice cheaper or older products if they are in the front.

해석

M Professor: 이제 제품 진열에 대해 이야기하고자 합니다. 기업들은 많은 시간을 들여 매장에 제품들을 어떻게 진열할지를 결정하죠. 제품 진열의 한 가지 기본 개념은 잠재 고객의 주의를 끌기 위해 값비싼 신제품을 앞쪽에 놓는 것이에요. 사람들은 걸어가다가 종종 멈춰 서서는, 음, 그러니까, 걸음을 멈추고 멋진 신제품에 주목하게 되죠. 구매할 생각이 없는 경우에도 이들을 주목하게 됩니다. 그 후 흥미를 느껴서 점포 내의 다른 제품을 보게 되어요. 많은 사람들이 값비싼 제품을 주목한 후에 보다 싼 제품을 찾기 위해 매장을 둘러보죠. 만약 싸고 오래된 제품들이 앞쪽에 진열되었다면 지나가는 사람들이 이들을 보려고 하지 않았을 것입니다.

> ✏️ **Note Taking**
>
> **Subject** Displaying products
> **Detail** Put expensive items in front

Organization

1 If a store displays expensive merchandise in the front, it will attract customers' attention.

2 This interest will draw customers into other parts of the store, so they will look at other products.

Comparing

Sample Response 🎧 04-10

The way things are displayed in a store is important because merchandise needs to be seen by the customers. Stores try to get customers interested in the more expensive or trendy products by putting them in front. Then, even if people don't want to spend that much money, they'll start looking through other areas of the store to find similar items that might not cost as much but might grab their interest, too.

해석

상품은 소비자의 눈에 띄어야 하기 때문에 매장에서 제품을 진열하는 방식은 중요하다. 매장들은 보다 값비싼 제품이나 최신 유행 상품을 앞쪽에 진열하여 고객들의 관심을 끌려고 한다. 그러면 그렇게 많은 돈을 쓰려고 하지 않은 사람들도 매장 내 다른 구역을 둘러보기 시작하면서, 그만큼 비싸지는 않지만 관심을 끄는, 그와 유사한 제품들을 찾게 된다.

Exercise 4 .... p.129

Listening

Script 🎧 04-11

W Professor: We talked about demand the last time. Now, let's talk about another key element in economics, which is supply. Supply is the amount of a product that exists. Supply is usually directly related to demand. Hmm . . . For example, imagine it takes 250 dollars to build a computer that can be sold for 500 dollars. If the demand for computers goes up and the price rises to 600 dollars, the companies that make computers will find it more profitable to build a new computer factory or to hire more workers to make more computers. The increase in demand and the increase in price cause the supply to increase as well.

해석

W Professor: 지난 시간에는 수요에 대해 논의를 했습니다. 이제 경제학의 또 다른 주요 개념인 공급에 대해 이야기를 해 보죠. 공급은 존재하는 상품의 양입니다. 공급은 보통 수요와 직접적으로 관련되어 있어요. 흠... 예를 들어 500달러에 판매할 수 있는 컴퓨터를 만드는데 250달러가 든다고 가정해 보죠. 컴퓨터에 대한 수요가 증가해서 가격이 600달러까지 오르는 경우, 컴퓨터 제조업체들은 더 많은 컴퓨터를 생산하기 위해 새로운 컴퓨터 공장을 짓거나 노동자를 더 고용하면 이익이 늘어날 것이라는 점을 알게 될 거예요. 수요의 증가와 가격 상승이 또한 공급의 증가를 야기하게 되는 것이죠.

> ✏️ **Note Taking**
>
> **Subject** Supply
> **Detail** Is related to demand

Organization

1 Supply is an economic concept that has to do with the amount of a certain product.

2 Less supply creates more demand. In turn, more demand encourages companies to create more supply in order to increase their profits.

Comparing

Sample Response 🎧 04-12

Technology is always affected by supply and demand. Supply is the amount of a product available, and demand is how much people want it. The professor mentions computers as an example. If a company makes a good profit from building computers and demand for computers is high, then it will expand and hire more employees to make more computers. Because of this, the supply of computers is also increasing. This makes them more available to people.

해석

기술은 항상 공급과 수요의 영향을 받는다. 공급은 구입할 수 있는 제품의 양이며, 수요는 사람들이 제품을 원하는 정도이다. 교수는 컴퓨터를 예로 든다. 만약 기업이 컴퓨터 생산으로 큰 이윤을 내고 컴퓨터에 대한 수요가 높다면 기업은 보다 많은 컴퓨터를 생산하기 위해 확장을 하고 보다 많은 직원을 고용할 것이다. 이로 인해 컴퓨터의 공급 역시 증가할 것이다. 이로써 사람들은 컴퓨터를 보다 저렴하게 구매할 수 있다.

Exercise 5 ·· p.130

Listening

Script 🎧 04-13

M Professor: Most people refer to a recession as an overall slowing of a country's economy. In economics, we have a better definition. A recession occurs when a country's gross domestic product decreases for at least two straight quarters. In other words, the country has six or more months of negative economic growth. One way this can happen is through unemployment. If a specific industry is hurting, companies will begin to employ fewer people. The people that lose their jobs will have less money, and, overall, the country will have less money. Less money spreading throughout a country hurts the economy, thereby causing a recession.

해석

M Professor: 대부분의 사람들이 불황을 국가 경제의 전반적인 침체라고 말합니다. 경제학에서의 정의는 보다 명확해요. 일국의 국내총생산이 최소 연속 2분기 이상 감소할 때 불황이 발생합니다. 다시 말해서 국가가 6개월 동안 혹은 그 이상으로 마이너스 경제 성장을 하는 것입니다. 이런 일이 발생할 수 있는 한 가지 조건은 실업률에 있습니다. 특정 산업이 타격을 입으면 기업들이 고용을 줄이기 시작하죠. 직장을 잃은 사람들의 소득이 감소해서 전반적으로 국가의 돈이

줄어듭니다. 국가 내 화폐 유통량이 줄어들면서 경제가 위축되면 그 결과 불황이 일어납니다.

✏️ **Note Taking**

Subject Recessions

Detail Result from six months of negative economic growth

Organization

1 A recession is a decline in a country's gross domestic product for at least six months.

2 A recession leads to unemployment, which results in a country having less money.

Comparing

Sample Response 🎧 04-14

Recessions affect society because they slow down a country's economy. In addition, they actually cause the country to experience negative economic growth for at least half a year. During or before a recession, a company might lay off its workers if business is bad. These workers will then have less money to spend. Because of this, fewer people in the country buy products. When this happens, recessions start to affect the entire country.

해석

불황은 국가 경제를 위축시키기 때문에 사회에 영향을 미친다. 또한 불황이 일어나면 최소 반 년 동안 해당 국가는 마이너스 경제 성장을 겪는다. 불황이 진행되는 동안이나 그 이전에는 사업이 잘 되지 않기 때문에 기업은 직원들을 해고할 수도 있다. 그러면 이러한 노동자들이 소비할 수 있는 돈이 줄어든다. 이로 인해 그 국가에서 상품을 구입하는 사람이 적어진다. 이러한 일이 벌어지면 불황이 국가 전체에 영향을 미치기 시작한다.

Exercise 6 ·· p.131

Listening

Script 🎧 04-15

W Professor: Last night, you should have read about mentoring. So let's talk about it now. There are two basic kinds of mentoring relationships. They are formal and informal mentoring relationships. In a formal mentoring relationship, the partners are often assigned together by an association. For example, a car maintenance shop gets a new employee. The shop pairs the new employee with an older employee. The older employee teaches the new one about the job. He can learn valuable information, see real examples of how to do the job, ask questions, and learn all the aspects of the job. An informal relationship is usually, um, developed out of proximity or friendship. A younger worker and an older worker can become friends, and the more knowledgeable of the two will help his friend when he is in trouble or has a problem.

해석

W Professor: 어젯밤에 멘토링에 관한 글을 읽어 보셨을 거예요. 그러면 이제 멘토링에 대해 이야기를 해 보죠. 두 가지 기본적인 유형의 멘토링 관계가 존재합니다. 공식적인 멘토링 관계와 비공식적인 멘토링 관계이죠. 공식적인 멘토링 관계에서는 파트너들이 종종 단체에 의해 배정됩니다. 예를 들어 자동차 정비소에서 새로 사람을 뽑는다고 할게요. 정비소는 신입 직원에게 기존 직원과 짝을 맺어 줍니다. 기존 직원은 신입 직원에게 업무를 가르쳐 줘요. 신입 직원은 중요한 정보도 배우고, 업무를 수행하는 실제 사례들도 접하고, 질문을 하고, 그리고 업무에 필요한 모든 것들을 익힐 수가 있습니다. 비공식적인 관계는 보통, 음, 친인척이나 친구 사이에서 만들어져요. 젊은 직원과 나이 많은 직원이 친구가 될 수 있는데, 이 두 사람 중 보다 많이 아는 사람이, 친구에게 문제가 있거나 곤란한 일이 생기면, 친구를 도와 줄 것입니다.

> ✏ **Note Taking**
>
> **Subject** Mentoring relationships
> **Detail** Are both formal and informal mentoring relationships

Organization

1 There are two kinds of mentoring relationships, formal and informal.

2 In formal mentoring relationships, the mentor and the trainee are assigned to work together by the company.

3 In informal mentoring relationships, the relationship is formed naturally by friendship or proximity.

Comparing

Sample Response 🎧 04-16

> One kind of mentoring relationship is the formal one. It is created by an employer when one person needs to be trained to do something by someone who is experienced and can answer all of the trainee's questions. The other kind of mentoring relationship is informal. This one occurs between friends or two people in close proximity because it is convenient and agreeable to the two people who are involved.

해석

멘토링 관계의 한 가지 유형은 공식적인 것이다. 이는 경험도 있고 수련생의 모든 질문에 답을 해 줄 수 있는 누군가에게서 어떤 사람이 교육을 받을 필요가 있을 때 고용주에 의해 만들어진다. 다른 멘토링 관계는 비공식적인 것이다. 이는 친구나 사이가 좋은 두 사람 사이에서 형성되는데, 그 이유는 이러한 관계가 관련된 두 사람에게 편리하고 바람직한 것이기 때문이다.

Exercise 1 .... p.132

Listening

Script 🎧 04-17

> **M Professor**: Let's discuss how to keep food from spoiling. This is important because no one wants a smelly kitchen, and wasting food is bad. The key to stop food from spoiling is to prevent bacteria that spoil food from activating. How do you do that? Bacteria need the proper temperature and moisture to spoil food. If you deny them these conditions, you can prevent food from spoiling. Milk is a liquid that doesn't last very long before it goes bad. If you take the moisture out of milk, it will take longer to spoil. Milk in this form is powdered milk. Powdered milk lasts much longer than liquid milk because it doesn't have any moisture that causes it to go bad.

해석

M Professor: 음식의 부패를 막는 방법에 대해 논의해 보죠. 어느 누구도 냄새가 나는 주방을 원하지 않고 음식을 버리는 일은 바람직하기 않기 때문에 이는 중요한 일입니다. 음식의 부패를 막는 핵심은 음식을 상하게 하는 박테리아가 활동하지 못하게 하는 것이에요. 어떻게 그렇게 할 수 있을까요? 박테리아가 음식을 상하게 하려면 적정한 온도와 습도가 필요합니다. 만약 이러한 상황을 방지한다면 음식의 부패를 막을 수 있죠. 우유는 시간이 조금만 지나도 상하는 액체입니다. 만약 우유에서 수분을 제거한다면 부패하기까지 시간이 더 걸릴 것입니다. 이러한 형태의 우유가 분유예요. 분유에는 이를 상하게 만드는 수분이 전혀 없기 때문에 액상 우유보다 훨씬 오랫동안 보관할 수 있습니다.

> ✏ **Note Taking**
>
> **Subject** Stopping food from spoiling
> **Detail** Keep bacteria from spoiling food

Organization

1 Bacteria need the proper temperature and moisture in order to spoil food.

2 If you remove moisture from food, like with powdered milk, you can prevent it from spoiling.

Comparing

Sample Response 🎧 04-18

> The lecture mentions milk as an example of a food that can be altered to last longer. Milk can be processed to keep it from spoiling. Since moisture is one factor that leads to food spoilage, it is removed from the milk. The milk gets dehydrated into its powdered form. Powdered milk can last for months because it has no moisture that bacteria can use to spoil it.

강의에서는 식품을 보다 오래 보존하기 위해 변화를 줄 수 있는 음식의 예로서 우유를 들고 있다. 우유는 처리를 해서 상하는 것을 막을 수 있다. 수분은 식품을 상하게 만드는 한 가지 요인이므로 우유에서 수분이 제거된다. 수분을 없애면 우유는 분유가 된다. 분유에는 박테리아가 식품을 상하게 만드는데 필요한 수분이 없기 때문에 몇 달 동안 보관이 가능하다.

Exercise 2 ·· p.133

Listening

Script 🎧 04-19

W Professor: Despite being very small, ants have a very advanced society. There are different roles that ants have in their society. And their roles are similar to some of those held by humans. The most common role is the worker. Worker ants collect food and maintain their colonies. Worker ants are always female. They are like people that work in cities because they produce something that benefits society. Another role is that of soldier. Soldier ants are just like soldiers in human societies. Their job is to defend the colony when it is attacked by other ants or predators. The soldiers are always sterile females.

해석

W Professor: 개미는 매우 작지만 고도로 발달된 사회를 갖추고 있어요. 사회에서 개미들은 다양한 역할을 수행합니다. 그리고 이들의 역할은 인간이 담당하는 몇몇 역할들과 비슷해요. 가장 일반적인 역할은 일꾼이에요. 일개미는 식량을 모으고 군락을 관리합니다. 일개미들은 항상 암컷이고요. 이들은 사회에 도움을 주는 무언가를 생산한다는 점에서 도시에서 일하는 사람들과 비슷하죠. 또 다른 역할로는 군인이 있습니다. 병정개미는 인간 사회의 군인과 같아요. 이들의 업무는 다른 개미나 포식자들로부터 공격을 받을 때 군락을 지키는 것입니다. 병정개미는 항상 생식 능력이 없는 암컷이에요.

> 🖉 **Note Taking**
>
> **Subject** Roles of ants
> **Detail** Are many roles that are similar to those of humans

Organization

1 Ants are animals with societies that are advanced like human ones.
2 Worker ants, which are always female, collect food and maintain the colony.
3 Soldier ants, which are always sterile females, defend the colony.

Comparing

Sample Response 🎧 04-20

Ants and humans are alike because they divide the responsibilities in their societies. Ant colonies have workers that produce what the colony needs for its

day-to-day operations and have soldiers that are ready to protect it. Like ants, humans also divide the work. Humans have workers that supply the daily needs of the society as well as soldiers and leaders who protect society.

해석

개미와 인간은 사회 내에서 역할을 분담하기 때문에 서로 비슷하다. 개미 군락에는 매일 군락의 유지에 필요한 것을 생산해 내는 일개미와 군락을 보호할 준비가 된 병정개미가 있다. 개미와 마찬가지로 인간들 또한 역할을 분담한다. 사회에 매일 필요한 것들을 공급하는 노동자와 사회를 보호하는 군인 및 지도자들이 존재한다.

Exercise 3 ·· p.134

Listening

Script 🎧 04-21

M Professor: Here is a sensitive topic. It's climate change. Studying the changes in climate is very difficult. Once a climate changes, it does not leave much evidence of the prior climate. Scientists have some clever ways to learn about climate changes though. One way is by using fossils. Well, you see, fossils can tell us a lot about climate change—for example, thunderbird fossils. Thunderbirds needed to drink water. As a matter of fact, in one situation, scientists found many thunderbird fossils near an ancient water source. They believe the birds went there to drink water during a drought. The drought got worse, and the water dried up. The birds died and left their bones there, and they turned into fossils over time.

해석

M Professor: 민감한 주제를 하나 알려 드리죠. 바로 기후 변화입니다. 기후 변화를 연구하는 일은 상당히 어려워요. 일단 기후가 변화하면 이전 기후에 대한 증거가 그다지 많이 남아 있지 않습니다. 그럼에도 불구하고 과학자들은 몇 가지 영리한 수단을 이용하여 기후 변화에 대해 알아낼 수가 있습니다. 한 가지 수단은 화석을 이용하는 것이에요. 음, 여러분도 아시다시피 화석은 기후 변화와 관련해 많은 것을 알려 줄 수 있는데, 천둥새의 화석을 예로 들어보죠. 천둥새는 물을 마셔야 했습니다. 실제로 한 번은 과학자들이 고대의 수원 근처에서 다수의 천둥새 화석을 발견했어요. 그들은 천둥새들이 가뭄 기간에 물을 마시려고 그곳에 왔다고 생각합니다. 하지만 가뭄이 심해져서 물이 말라 버렸죠. 새들은 죽어서 그곳에 뼈를 남기게 되었고, 이 뼈들이 시간이 지나 화석이 되었습니다.

> 🖉 **Note Taking**
>
> **Subject** Learning about climate change
> **Detail** Can study fossils to learn about it

Organization

1 Climate changes can be identified through studying fossil evidence.
2 Thunderbird fossils indicate where water sources once dried up.

Comparing

Sample Response 🎧 04-22

Scientists look at where and when fossils were made. If large groups of fossilized animal remains are found in the same location, scientists look at possible reasons that the animals might have died. In one case, animals might have lost their water source due to drought. When that happened, the animals died of thirst, and their remains became fossilized within a localized area. That's what scientists believe happened to a group of thunderbirds.

해석

과학자들은 언제 어디에서 화석이 만들어졌는지 조사한다. 다수의 동물 화석들이 동일한 지역에서 발견되면 과학자들은 그 동물들이 죽은 이유를 조사한다. 언젠가 동물들이 가뭄 때문에 자신들이 물을 먹는 장소를 잃었을 수도 있다. 그런 일이 발생하자 동물들은 목이 말라 죽게 되었고 그들의 잔해가 그 지역에서 화석으로 남게 되었다. 과학자들은 천둥새에게 바로 그러한 일이 일어났다고 믿는다.

Exercise 4 ·· p.135

Listening

Script 🎧 04-23

M Professor: One of the biggest questions for scientists is how the dinosaurs died. Well, one theory is the asteroid impact theory. There is evidence that a giant asteroid hit the Earth during the time of the dinosaurs. It was so big that the impact projected a tremendous amount of dust into the atmosphere. The dust actually blocked out much of the sun's light. This caused a chain reaction. Most plant life died when the light was blocked. This caused the plant-eating dinosaurs to die since they had no food. The meat-eating dinosaurs then ran out of food as well, and they died.

해석

M Professor: 과학자들에게 가장 어려운 문제 중의 하나는 공룡이 어떻게 멸종했는지에 관한 것이에요. 음, 한 가지 이론은 소행성 충돌 이론입니다. 공룡이 살던 시대에 거대한 소행성이 지구와 충돌했다는 증거가 있어요. 이 소행성이 너무나 컸기 때문에 그 충격으로 엄청난 양의 먼지가 대기로 유입되었습니다. 이 먼지가 실제로 햇빛의 상당 부분을 차단했어요. 이로 인해 연쇄 작용이 일어났습니다. 햇빛이 차단되자 대부분의 식물이 죽었습니다. 이로써 먹이가 없어진 초식 공룡들이 죽게 되었죠. 그 다음에는 육식 공룡들 또한 먹이가 부족해져 죽게 되었습니다.

🖊 **Note Taking**

Subject How dinosaurs died
Detail May have happened from asteroid strike

Organization

1 A huge asteroid struck the Earth, which set off a chain reaction.

2 First, it caused dust, which blocked sunlight, so most plants died.

3 Then, the plant eaters starved to death, which caused the meat eaters also to starve.

Comparing

Sample Response 🎧 04-24

The asteroid impact theory states that dinosaurs became extinct as the result of an asteroid striking the Earth. When an asteroid hit the Earth, it threw so much dust into the air that the sun was blocked for a very long time. Plants died because they no longer had sunlight and couldn't grow. The plant eaters died because they no longer had plants to eat, and finally, the meat eaters died because their food, the plant eaters and other dinosaurs, had already died. It was a chain reaction that killed all the dinosaurs.

해석

소행성 충돌 이론에 따르면 공룡은 소행성이 지구와 충돌해서 멸종되었다. 소행성이 지구와 충돌했을 때 너무 많은 먼지가 대기에 유입되어 매우 오랜 기간 동안 햇빛이 차단되었다. 식물은 더 이상 햇빛을 받지 못하고 성장을 할 수 없었기 때문에 죽어 버렸다. 더 이상 먹을 식물이 없어지자 초식 동물들이 죽게 되었고, 마지막으로 육식 동물들 역시 자신들의 먹이인 초식 동물과 다른 공룡들이 이미 죽어 버렸기 때문에 죽게 되었다. 연쇄 반응으로 모든 공룡이 멸종된 것이었다.

Exercise 5 ·· p.136

Listening

Script 🎧 04-25

W Professor: Sometimes when humans introduce new species to an environment, the foreign plants and animals dominate their new environment. They might even kill all of the native species. Let me see . . . One example is the acacia tree. Acacia trees spread their roots very far from their trunks. They essentially steal the nutrients in the soil from other plants and take a lot of the space available. Acacias also have large branches and trunks. This makes them grow higher than other plants. Acacias hide other plants and trees with their shadows. These plants, therefore, cannot get any sunlight. Often, native plants die out after acacias are introduced.

해석

W Professor: 때때로 인간이 새로운 종을 어떤 환경에 들여오면 외래 식물종과 동물종이 새로운 환경을 지배하기도 합니다. 토착종을 모두 없애 버릴 수도 있죠. 봅시다… 한 가지 예가 아카시아 나무예요. 아카시아 나무는 몸통으로부터 아주 멀리까지 뿌리를 뻗칩니다. 기본적으로 다른 식물로부터 토양의 양분들을 빼앗고 공간도 많이 차지하죠. 또한 아카시아의 가지와 몸통은 큰 편이에요. 그래서 다른 식물보다 높은 곳까지 자라게 됩니다. 아카시아의 그늘 때문에 다른 식물들과 나무들이 가리게 되어요. 그 결과 그러한 식물들은 햇빛을 전혀 받을 수가 없습니다. 아카시아를 들여온 곳에서는 토착종 식물들이 종종 멸종하는 경우가 있습니다.

> **✎ Note Taking**
>
> **Subject** Introducing new species to environment
> **Detail** Can cause native plants to die

Organization

1 The introduction of a new species to an environment sometimes kills native species.

2 Acacia trees steal nutrients from other plants and grow to be very large.

3 They block the sunlight from reaching other plants, which kills smaller plants.

Comparing

Sample Response 🎧 04-26

When a foreign plant species is introduced to an environment, it sometimes poses a threat to the native species there. Aggressive plants like acacia trees can overrun an area. They use up all of the nutrients in the soil, and as they grow bigger, they even block the sunlight that smaller species need to live. Thus, the native species often die.

해석

외래 식물종을 어떤 환경에 들여오면 때때로 그곳에 있는 토착종이 위협을 받기도 한다. 아카시아 나무와 같은 공격성 짙은 식물은 한 지역을 파괴시킬 수도 있다. 이들은 토양의 양분을 모두 고갈시키고, 자라면서 다른 작은 식물종들에게 필요한 햇빛을 차단시킨다. 그 결과 토착종들이 종종 소멸하게 된다.

Exercise 6 ⋯⋯⋯⋯⋯⋯⋯⋯⋯⋯⋯⋯⋯⋯⋯⋯ p.137

Listening

Script 🎧 04-27

W Professor: Good morning, class. It's hot like a desert in here, so let's talk about desert life. As you know, animal life can be found just about anywhere on the planet. When we think of deserts, we think there is a limited amount of life in them. But, in fact, there is plenty of life in deserts. The animals in them, like the scorpion, must find ways to survive in the hostile environments. A scorpion will bury itself in the ground during the day. This keeps its daytime temperature down. Keeping a lower temperature means an animal needs less water. Um, a scorpion also absorbs the water from the flesh of anything it eats. Lastly, it hunts at night, when the temperature is lower, which again means that it requires less water.

해석

W Professor: 안녕하세요, 여러분. 강의실 안이 사막처럼 더우니 사막의 생물에 대해 논의해 보죠. 아시다시피 지구상 어디에서나 동물을 볼 수가 있습니다. 사막을 떠올리는 경우, 우리는 사막에 한정된 수의 생물만이 존재한다고 생각을 하죠. 하지만 실제로 사막에도 많은 생물들이 살고 있습니다. 사막에 사는 동물

들은, 예컨대 전갈은 혹독한 환경에서 생존할 수 있는 방법을 찾아야 해요. 전갈은 낮 동안 땅속에서 숨어 지낼 것입니다. 그렇게 하면 낮 동안의 체온을 낮출 수가 있죠. 체온을 낮춘다는 것은 동물에게 수분이 덜 필요하다는 것을 의미해요. 음, 전갈은 또한 자신이 잡아 먹는 먹이의 살점에서 수분을 흡수하기도 합니다. 마지막으로 전갈은 기온이 낮은 밤에 사냥을 하는데, 이때도 역시 수분을 덜 필요로 합니다.

> **✎ Note Taking**
>
> **Subject** Surviving in the desert
> **Detail** Are many different methods used to survive

Organization

1 Deserts are hot, but they are still full of animals that have adapted to the heat.

2 The scorpion sleeps in the ground during the day to conserve water and hunts at night.

Comparing

Sample Response 🎧 04-28

Many animals in deserts are nocturnal. They hunt at night and sleep during the day. They do this because it is much cooler at night and they need less water to function. Some animals, like the scorpion, also bury themselves during the day because it is cooler underground. This means that they need less water during the day, too.

해석

사막에 사는 많은 동물들이 야행성이다. 밤에 사냥을 하고 낮에는 잠을 잔다. 그렇게 하는 이유는 밤이 훨씬 더 시원하며 더 적은 수분을 사용해서 활동을 할 수 있기 때문이다. 또한 전갈과 같은 일부 동물들은 낮 동안 땅속에 숨어 있기도 하는데, 그 이유는 지하가 더 시원하기 때문이다. 이 역시 낮 동안 보다 적은 양의 수분만을 필요로 한다는 점을 의미한다.

Unit 21 Psychology

Exercise 1 ⋯⋯⋯⋯⋯⋯⋯⋯⋯⋯⋯⋯⋯⋯⋯⋯ p.138

Listening

Script 🎧 04-29

M Professor: Children are very interesting to study, especially when finding out what influences them. Many things can influence the lives of children. One thing that we often don't think about is the influence of art on children. Art can be a very good, positive influence for kids. Kids often lack several basic skills that adults take for granted. This means they cannot perform the same actions as adults or at least not to the same degree that adults can. This is where art can come in. And, well, if children can accomplish something with art, it can be a good confidence booster. Give kids some clay, and they can build cars or other things. The children will feel very happy about themselves since they have accomplished something.

해석

M Professor: 아이들은 대단히 흥미로운 연구 대상인데, 특히 아동에게 영향을 주는 것을 연구할 때가 그렇습니다. 많은 것들이 아이들의 삶에 영향을 미칠 수 있어요. 우리가 종종 생각하지 못하는 것 중 하나는 아동에게 미치는 미술의 영향입니다. 미술은 아이들에게 매우 바람직하고 긍정적인 영향을 미칠 수 있어요. 종종 성인들에게는 당연한 몇몇 기본적인 능력들이 아이들에게는 부족한 경우가 있습니다. 아이들이 어른과 같은 동작을 할 수 없거나 최소한 성인과 같은 정도로 그렇게 할 수 없다는 의미에요. 바로 이때에 미술이 개입할 수 있습니다. 그래서, 음, 만약 아이들이 미술에서 무엇인가를 이루어낼 수 있다면 이는 자신감을 증진시키는 좋은 계기가 될 수 있어요. 아이들에게 찰흙을 주면 자동차와 같은 것들을 만들어 낼 수도 있습니다. 아이들은 무엇인가를 성취했기 때문에 스스로 뿌듯하게 생각할 것입니다.

> ✎ **Note Taking**
>
> **Subject** Influencing children's lives
> **Detail** Can use art to help influence children

Organization

1 Doing art can have a positive influence on children.

2 Children are competent enough to do artwork.

3 Accomplishing something artistic can boost children's confidence.

Comparing

Sample Response 🎧 04-30

> Children might enjoy doing art as a way of showing that their competence for doing something is equal to an adult's. When children accomplish creative tasks, it gives them a boost in their confidence. They feel empowered. That's why art can be a positive influence and why children often like to do it.

해석

아이들은 어른과 동등하게 무언가를 해낼 수 있는 능력을 보여 주는 수단으로서 미술 활동을 하는 것을 좋아할 수 있다. 아이들이 창의적인 일을 해내는 경우 아이들의 자신감이 증가하게 된다. 아이들은 스스로를 자랑스럽게 생각한다. 미술이 긍정적인 영향을 미칠 수 있고 아이들이 종종 미술을 좋아하는 이유가 바로 그러한 점 때문이다.

Exercise 2 p.139

Listening

Script 🎧 04-31

M Professor: Kids are incredibly fast learners. I often

like to describe their brains as sponges in water. They simply absorb everything. Sometimes this can be good, but sometimes it is bad. For example, children can learn languages a lot faster than adults. They do this by remembering almost everything. This is called the mapping process. That is a child's ability to place a word with a sight or action to remember its meaning. Sometimes this can be bad though. For example, if a child sees a horse and his father tells him it is a horse, the child might later see a cow or another four-legged animal and think it is also a horse.

해석

M Professor: 아이들은 믿을 수 없을 정도로 학습 속도가 빠릅니다. 저는 종종 아이들의 뇌를 물속에 있는 스펀지로 묘사해요. 모든 것을 흡수해 버리죠. 이러한 점은 때때로 장점일 수 있지만 때때로 단점일 수도 있습니다. 예를 들어 아이들은 어른들보다 훨씬 빨리 언어를 익힐 수가 있어요. 거의 모든 것을 기억함으로써 언어를 익히죠. 이를 맵핑 프로세스라고 부릅니다. 이는 단어의 뜻을 기억하기 위해 단어를 어떤 장면이나 행동과 연관시키는 아이의 능력이에요. 하지만 이러한 점은 때때로 단점이 될 수도 있어요. 예를 들어 한 아이가 말을 보고 아이의 아빠가 아이에게 그것이 말이라고 말해 주는 경우, 아이는 나중에 소나 네 발 동물을 보고서 그것 역시 말이라고 생각할 수 있습니다.

> ✎ **Note Taking**
>
> **Subject** Children's learning processes
> **Detail** Can often learn much faster than adults

Organization

1 Kids learn languages faster than adults because their memories are like sponges.

2 Kids use an ability to connect a word to a sight or action.

3 They may misunderstand that "horse" means any four-legged animal.

Comparing

Sample Response 🎧 04-32

> It might be easier for children to learn a language than adults because children are faster learners. When they hear a word, they connect the word with something they see or do—an object or an action—and that connection helps them remember the word. Making these connections is called the mapping process, and children are very good at it.

해석

아동들은 학습 속도가 빠르기 때문에 성인보다 언어를 더 쉽게 배울 수 있다. 아이들은 한 단어를 듣고 자신이 보거나 행하는 것, 즉 물체나 행동을 연결시키는데, 그러한 연상 작용이 단어 기억에 도움을 준다. 이러한 연상 작용은 맵핑 프로세스라고 불리며, 아이들은 이를 매우 능숙하게 해낸다.

Answers, Scripts, and Translations **65**

Listening

Script 🎧 04-33

W Professor: Moving on, let's get to framing. Framing is a very useful skill. Framing is how you set up information. Like, you can present information in different ways to influence how people see it. For example, if you turn on the weather channel and the weather forecaster says, "Today it's going to be cloudy with a fifty-percent chance of rain," most people will dress for rain and bring their umbrellas. Um, on the other hand, if the forecast is, "Today, it's going to be sunny with a fifty-percent chance of rain," many people will wear shorts, and only some will carry umbrellas. The people were given the same information, but it was framed differently.

해석

W Professor: 그럼 계속해서 프레이밍으로 넘어가 봅시다. 프레이밍은 매우 유용한 기술이에요. 프레이밍은 정보를 구성하는 방식입니다. 가령 다양한 방식으로 정보를 제시하여 사람들이 정보를 바라보는 방식에 영향을 끼칠 수가 있죠. 예를 들어 일기 예보 채널을 틀었는데 기상 캐스터가 "오늘은 흐리겠고 비가 올 확률은 50%입니다"라고 말한다면 대부분의 사람들은 비를 대비해 옷을 입고 우산을 챙길 거예요. 음, 반대로 캐스터가 "오늘은 맑겠고 비가 올 확률은 50%입니다"라고 말한다면 많은 사람들이 반바지를 입을 것이며 소수의 사람들만이 우산을 챙길 것입니다. 사람들에게 동일한 정보가 주어졌지만 각기 다르게 프레이밍이 이루어졌던 것이죠.

✎ Note Taking

Subject Framing
Detail Reactions of people are different depending upon how something is presented

Organization

1 Framing is presenting information in a certain way in order to influence people.

2 Weather can have different meanings according to the frame used.

Comparing

Sample Response 🎧 04-34

Framing is used to present information in a way that the speaker wants to. One example the professor uses is how the weatherman frames the weather. If he says that the weather will be partly cloudy with a fifty-percent chance of rain, people will prepare for rain. However, if he instead says that it will be sunny with a fifty-percent chance of rain, people will dress like they would for a sunny day.

해석

프레이밍은 화자가 원하는 방식으로 정보를 제시하기 위해 사용된다. 교수가 든 한 가지 예는 기상 캐스터가 날씨를 프레이밍하는 경우이다. 만약 그가 날씨가

부분적으로 흐리고 비가 올 확률이 50%라고 말한다면 사람들은 비에 대비할 것이다. 하지만 그가 날씨가 맑을 것이며 비가 올 확률은 50%라고 말한다면 사람들은 맑은 날에 입는 옷을 입을 것이다.

Listening

Script 🎧 04-35

W Professor: All humans are subject to the fundamental character judgment flaw. This flaw is very simple to explain. When we see other people doing something that we consider bad or wrong, we assume those people are bad. Well, for example, if we see someone that is driving too quickly, we assume that person is a jerk. On the other hand, we often excuse our own actions as being subject to our circumstances. When we are driving too quickly, we excuse it because we are in a hurry for what we consider to be an important reason. Even though we did the same thing, we know we are not jerks. We know the situation we are in, but we fail to consider other people's situations.

해석

W Professor: 인간은 누구나 기본적인 성격 판단 결함을 가지고 있습니다. 이 결함은 설명하기 아주 쉬워요. 우리가 나쁘거나 잘못되었다고 생각하는 것을 다른 사람들이 하는 모습을 볼 때 우리는 그 사람들이 나쁘다고 생각합니다. 음, 예를 들어 과속으로 운전하는 사람을 보면 우리는 그 사람을 나쁜 사람이라고 생각을 하죠. 반면에 우리 자신의 행동에 대해서는 상황 때문에 어쩔 수 없는 것이었다고 종종 변명을 합니다. 만약 우리가 과속으로 운전을 한다면 중요하다고 생각되는 이유로 상황이 급하다고 변명을 합니다. 비록 똑같은 행동을 했지만 우리는 우리 자신이 나쁜 사람이 아니라는 점을 알고 있어요. 우리는 우리 자신이 처해 있는 상황은 알지만 다른 사람들이 처해 있는 상황은 고려하지 못하는 것이죠.

✎ Note Taking

Subject Fundamental character judgment flaw
Detail Opinion of person's actions depends upon who the person is

Organization

1 People justify their own bad behavior, but they don't justify others' bad behavior.

2 People assume that if someone does a good thing, that person has a good character, and vice-versa.

Comparing

Sample Response 🎧 04-36

The fundamental character judgment flaw states that people associate bad behavior with bad people and good behavior with good people. More than that, people are quick to justify their own wrong actions, but they have a very difficult time understanding that other people might have good reasons for doing what they are doing, too.

해석

기본적인 성격 판단 결함은 사람들이 나쁜 행동은 나쁜 사람과, 그리고 좋은 행동은 좋은 사람과 연관시킨다는 점을 알려 준다. 게다가 사람들은 자신의 잘못된 행동은 빨리 정당화시키지만, 다른 사람에게 그러한 행동을 할 수 밖에 없는 충분한 이유가 있을 수도 있다는 점은 좀처럼 이해하지 못한다.

Exercise 5 ·· p.142

Listening

Script 🎧 04-37

M Professor: One important thing that we often overlook in our lives is that our points of view affect how we see the world. Uh, our experiences, beliefs, situations, and even our simple positions in life can change how we see something. For example, everyone, take a look at me. To the students in the front of the class, I look very big. You can see many details, like how I spilled some food on my tie. So you may think I look a little messy. The students in the back see me as very small and can't notice the stain on my tie. You are looking at the same person at the same time, but you are seeing different things.

해석

M Professor: 인생에서 우리가 종종 간과하는 한 가지 중요한 점은 우리의 관점이 우리가 세상을 보는 방식에 영향을 끼친다는 것입니다. 어, 우리의 경험, 신념, 상황, 그리고 삶에서의 단순한 위치조차 우리의 시각을 변화시킬 수 있습니다. 예를 들면, 모두들 저를 봐 주세요. 앞쪽에 있는 학생들에게 저는 매우 크게 보일 것입니다. 넥타이에 묻은 음식 얼룩과 같은 세부적인 것들을 많이 볼 수가 있죠. 따라서 제가 약간 지저분하게 보인다고 생각할 수도 있을 거예요. 뒤쪽에 앉아 있는 학생들에게 저는 아주 작게 보이고 넥타이의 얼룩은 보이지 않을 것입니다. 여러분들은 동시에 같은 사람을 보고 있지만 각기 다른 것들을 보고 있는 것이죠.

✏ Note Taking

Subject Points of view
Detail Is different depending upon where person is

Organization

1 Our point of view depends on who and where we are.

2 One thing can be seen in many different ways depending upon the point of view.

Comparing

Sample Response 🎧 04-38

A person's point of view clearly affects the way that individual looks at something. The professor uses himself as an example. He mentions that the students in the front of the class probably see him as being very big. They also probably notice the stain on his tie, which

may cause them to think that he is not very clean. To the students in the back, he appears smaller, and they cannot see his stained tie, so they have no opinion of him not being clean.

해석

한 사람의 시점은 개인이 무언가를 바라보는 방식에 분명한 영향을 끼친다. 교수는 자기 자신을 예로 든다. 그는 강의실 앞에 앉은 사람에게 아마도 자신이 크게 보일 것이라고 말한다. 그들은 또한 교수의 넥타이에 묻은 얼룩을 볼 수도 있을 것이며, 그로 인해 그가 그다지 깔끔하지 않은 사람이라고 생각할 수도 있다. 뒤쪽에 앉은 학생들에게는 교수가 더 작아 보이고, 그들은 넥타이의 얼룩을 볼 수 없기 때문에 그가 깔끔하지 않다고 생각을 하지 않는다.

Exercise 6 ·· p.143

Listening

Script 🎧 04-39

M Professor: Our memories are very fascinating. We have both short-term and long-term memories. Our long-term memory can be broken down into procedural memory and declarative memory. Declarative memory is remembering the process of how things work. For example, if you want to ride a bike, you would know that your feet must go on the pedals and that you have to balance yourself. That is declarative memory. You remember what the process of riding a bike is. But when you get on the bike and ride it, you are using procedural memory. That is the actual physical action you are doing, which is something you no longer have to give as much attention to as when you were first learning. You just do it. Declarative memory is more of a description of knowledge whereas procedural memory is performing an action almost automatically.

해석

M Professor: 우리의 기억은 대단히 훌륭합니다. 단기 기억과 장기 기억이 모두 존재하죠. 장기 기억은 절차 기억과 서술적 기억으로 구분될 수 있어요. 서술적 기억은 어떤 일이 진행되는 과정을 기억하는 것입니다. 예를 들어 여러분이 자전거를 타고 싶어한다면 발을 페달에 올려야 하고 균형을 잡아야 한다는 점을 알고 있을 것입니다. 그것이 서술적 기억에요. 자전거를 타는 과정이 어떤 것인지 기억하는 것입니다. 하지만 자전거에 올라타게 되면 절차 기억을 사용하게 됩니다. 이는 여러분이 하는 실제 신체 활동으로, 더 이상 처음에 배울 때만큼 주의를 기울일 필요가 없는 것입니다. 그냥 하게 됩니다. 절차 기억은 거의 자동적으로 어떤 행동을 하는 것인데 비해 서술적 기억은 보다 지식을 설명하는 것에 가까운 편이죠.

✏ Note Taking

Subject Two types of long-term memory
Detail Declarative memory and procedural memory

Organization

1 There are two types of memory, short term and long term.

2 Long-term memory is both declarative and procedural.

Comparing

There are two kinds of memory, short term and long term, and there are two kinds of long-term memory, declarative and procedural. Declarative memory is the memory about how to do something. For example, it covers knowing about something such as the steps one must take to ride a bicycle. Procedural memory is different. It's the memory that your brain and body have from doing something so many times that you can do it without thinking about it anymore, like actually riding a bicycle without having to think about how to do it.

해석

기억에는 단기 기억과 장기 기억 두 가지가 있으며, 장기 기억에는 두 가지 유형의 기억, 즉 서술적 기억과 절차 기억이 있다. 서술적 기억은 어떤 일을 하는 방법에 대한 기억이다. 예를 들어 자전거를 타기 위해 밟아야 하는 단계와 같은 것을 아는 것이다. 절차 기억은 다르다. 이는, 어떻게 타는지에 대해 생각할 필요 없이 자전거를 타는 경우처럼, 더 이상 그에 대해 생각을 하지 않고서도 할 수 있을 정도로 어떤 일을 여러 차례 반복하면 뇌와 신체가 갖게 되는 기억이다.

Unit 22 Others

Exercise 1 ·········· p.144

Listening

M Professor: When we watch TV, we see many advertisements. Advertisements are very tricky. You see, advertisers use many strategies. One strategy is to exaggerate something. Advertisers can exaggerate an idea so much that the audience actually begins to believe it. Why else would it be in the commercial if it weren't true? Cars are in lots of commercials. One problem that small cars have is that people want more space. So an example of an exaggerated commercial is to have a lot of people getting out of a car. Obviously, a little car cannot hold twenty people. But by using exaggeration, the audience will think that the little car really does have a lot of room.

해석

M Professor: TV를 보면 많은 광고를 보게 됩니다. 광고는 대단히 교묘해요. 아시다시피 광고는 많은 전략을 사용합니다. 한 가지 전략은 과장을 하는 것이에요. 광고 제작자들은 어떤 아이디어를 심하게 과장해서 실제로 시청자들이 그것을 믿도록 만들 수가 있죠. 만약 그게 사실이 아니라면 왜 광고에 나왔겠어요? 많

은 광고에서 자동차가 등장합니다. 소형차가 가진 문제점 중 하나는 사람들이 더 넓은 공간을 원한다는 점이에요. 그래서 과장 광고의 한 가지 사례에서는 많은 사람들이 자동차에서 내리게 됩니다. 분명 소형차에는 20명이 탈 수가 없어요. 하지만 과장을 함으로써 시청자들은 그 소형차에 실제로 넓은 공간이 있다고 생각할 것입니다.

✎ Note Taking

Subject Exaggeration in advertisements
Detail Exaggeration used by advertisers to make audience believe something

Organization

1 One effective advertising strategy employs the use of exaggeration.

2 Exaggeration implies information that is not true, but advertisers using exaggeration can lead audiences to believe it could be true.

Comparing

Advertisers use strategies like exaggeration to make people associate different things with their products. In a car commercial, you might see twenty people getting out of a small car. Everyone knows that it's impossible for that many people actually to fit in a car, but advertisers show it anyway. That gives the impression that the small car is much roomier than it looks.

해석

광고 제작자들은 사람들이 제품과 다양한 것들을 연관시키도록 만들기 위해 과장과 같은 전략을 사용한다. 자동차 광고에서 20명의 사람들이 소형차에서 내리는 모습을 볼 수도 있다. 그렇게 많은 사람들이 실제로 차 안에 타는 일은 불가능하다는 점은 모두가 알고 있지만, 광고 제작자들은 어쨌든 그런 장면을 보여 준다. 그럼으로써 소형차가 보기 보다 훨씬 넓은 공간을 갖추고 있다는 인상을 남기게 된다.

Exercise 2 ·········· p.145

Listening

M Professor: We all remember how fun it was to play when we were kids, right? So why is playing so much fun for children? When children play, they gain a sense of control that they cannot have with their parents. Parents do everything and tell them everything to do. That's not fun, right? Um, when kids play, they get to make the rules. Let me see . . . Playing, for example, allows children to be destructive. They can entertain their imagination by destroying things. They can do this since they are in charge. So their curiosity can be satisfied through playing.

M Professor: 우리는 모두 어렸을 때 노는 것이 얼마나 재미있었는지 기억하고 있습니다, 그렇죠? 왜 아이들은 노는 것이 그렇게 재미있을까요? 아이들은 부모와 같이 있을 때 가질 수 없는 통제감을 갖게 됩니다. 부모들이 모든 것을 다 하고 아이들이 해야 할 일들을 다 말해 줍니다. 그건 즐거운 일이 아니에요, 그렇죠? 음, 아이들은 놀 때 규칙을 정합니다. 봅시다… 예를 들어 놀이를 통해 아이들은 파괴적이 될 수도 있어요. 무언가를 파괴함으로써 상상력을 자극할 수 있습니다. 자신이 책임을 지기 때문에 그럴 수 있는 것이죠. 그래서 놀이를 통해 호기심을 충족시킬 수 있습니다.

> **✎ Note Taking**
>
> **Subject** Why children enjoy playing
> **Detail** Like to play because they can be in charge

Organization

1 Playing is fun for kids because it gives them a sense of control.

2 It also entertains them.

3 And it can satisfy their curiosity.

Comparing

Sample Response 🎧 04-44

> Playing gives kids a break from being told what to do all of the time by their parents and teachers. It gives them a chance to make the rules and to exert some control over what they do and how they do it. Even if some games seem a little destructive, they are merely creative ways in which kids can entertain themselves and relieve their stress.

놀이를 통해 아이들은 항상 무언가를 해야 한다는 부모 및 교사의 말로부터 잠시 벗어날 수 있다. 놀이에서는 아이들이 규칙을 정하고 자신들이 무엇을, 그리고 어떻게 해야 하는지에 관한 통제력을 가질 수 있다. 비록 일부 게임이 약간 파괴적으로 보일 수도 있지만, 이는 아이들이 재미있어 하고 스트레스를 해소할 수 있는 창의적인 방법이다.

Exercise 3 .... p.146

Listening

Script 🎧 04-45

> **W Professor**: Teachers are important, but not anyone can be a teacher. An effective teacher must not only be able to communicate ideas to students but must also be supportive and able to respond to difficult situations immediately. Um, this supportive attitude is very important. Let me see . . . For example, a good teacher will always emphasize the positive part of any failure by a student. Students learn better when they feel good about the subject they are learning. So if a student struggles, she needs to see and hear positive things. For example,

if a student learning a language mispronounces a word, a teacher could say something like, "You used the word correctly, but let me correct your pronunciation." The student will then realize she did something well instead of just having done something incorrectly.

W Professor: 교사는 중요하지만 아무나 교사가 될 수 있는 것은 아니에요. 효과적인 교사는 학생들에게 아이디어를 전달해 줄 수 있을 뿐만 아니라 지지적이어야 하며 힘든 상황에서도 즉각적으로 대처할 수 있어야만 하죠. 음, 이러한 지지적인 태도는 매우 중요합니다. 봅시다… 예를 들어 좋은 교사라면 어떤 학생이 한 실수에 대해 항상 긍정적인 부분을 강조할 거예요. 학생들은 자신이 배우는 과목에 대해 좋은 느낌을 가질 때 더 잘 배웁니다. 그래서 학생이 힘들어할 경우 학생은 긍정적인 것을 보고 들어야 해요. 예를 들어 언어를 배우는 학생이 어떤 단어를 잘못 발음한다면 교사가 다음과 같이, "단어는 제대로 사용했지만 발음을 고쳐볼게요."라고 말할 수 있을 거예요. 그러면 학생은 자신이 잘못을 했다고 생각하는 대신 무엇인가 잘 해냈다는 점을 깨닫게 될 것입니다.

> **✎ Note Taking**
>
> **Subject** The art of teaching
> **Detail** Need to be supportive to be good teacher

Organization

1 Effective teachers are supportive and responsive to their students.

2 They also emphasize the positives in their students' performances.

Comparing

Sample Response 🎧 04-46

> To be an effective teacher, the teacher has to look for positive things to say to his students. The teacher shouldn't make his students feel like failures if they don't learn everything the first time that he teaches it. The important things are to recognize what they have learned and to help them feel good about themselves. That way, they'll want to learn more.

효과적인 교사가 되기 위해서는 교사가 학생들에게 해 줄 긍정적인 말을 찾아야 한다. 교사가 처음 가르치는 것을 학생이 모두 배우지 못한다고 해서 학생으로 하여금 실패했다고 느끼게 해서는 안 된다. 중요한 것은 학생들이 배운 것을 인식하는 것과 학생들이 자기 자신에 대해 뿌듯함을 느끼는 것이다. 그러면 학생들이 더 많이 배우고 싶어할 것이다.

Exercise 4 .... p.147

Listening

Script 🎧 04-47

> **W Professor**: One of the most important parts about designing a good house interior is the color. Colors can

be used in several ways. One common use of color is contrast. By using two different and even clashing colors, they can be emphasized in a room. For example, if someone has a green sofa that he thinks looks good, he can put brown cushions on it. The clash of colors will draw people's attention to the green sofa and make it stand out. Of course, if too many colors are contrasted, this will make a room look like a crayon box. Too much contrast looks very bad. It can even make visitors feel sick or confused.

해석

W Professor: 훌륭한 주택 인테리어 디자인에서 가장 중요한 것 중 하나가 색상입니다. 색상은 여러 가지 방법으로 사용될 수 있어요. 색상을 사용하는 한 가지 일반적인 방법은 대비입니다. 서로 다른 두 가지 색상과 심지어 전혀 어울리지 않는 색상들을 사용함으로써 실내를 강조할 수가 있죠. 예를 들어 멋지다고 생각하는 초록색 소파가 있는 경우, 그 위에 갈색 쿠션을 둘 수 있어요. 색상들이 충돌함으로써 사람들이 초록색 소파에 주목하게 될 것이고 소파가 두드러져 보일 거예요. 물론 너무 많은 색상이 대비된다면 실내가 마치 크레용 상자처럼 보이겠죠. 너무 지나친 대비는 정말 끔찍하게 보입니다. 방문객을 어지럽게 만들거나 혼란스럽게 만들 수도 있어요.

✎ Note Taking

Subject Interior design
Detail Can use contrast of colors to make something stand out

Organization

1 Color is important in interior design.

2 Color contrast can add emphasis to certain elements, but it can be easily overdone.

Comparing

Sample Response 🎧 04-48

In interior design, a person has to consider how different colors look together. Sometimes contrasting colors work very well together and add emphasis to certain pieces of furniture, like the professor's example of the green sofa with brown cushions. But a person has to be careful not to have too many colors or too much contrast because it can make a room look pretty ugly, too.

해석

인테리어 디자인에서는 서로 다른 색상들이 함께 있으면 어떻게 보일지 고려해야 한다. 때때로 색상을 대비시키면 잘 어울려 보일 수 있으며, 교수가 예로 든 갈색 쿠션이 있는 초록색 소파의 경우처럼 특정 가구가 강조될 수 있다. 하지만 색상이 너무 많거나 지나친 대비가 이루어지지 않도록 주의를 해야 하는데, 그 이유는 그렇게 될 경우 실내가 상당히 좋지 않게 보일 수 있기 때문이다.

Exercise 5 ·· p.148

Listening

Script 🎧 04-49

M Professor: Some scientists study animal behavior to determine if some things animals do have less to do with instinct and more to do with what the animals have learned or know. One study was done with a goose. Now, geese are good protectors of their young. If they see an egg near their nest, they'll usually take it and care for it. Anyway, the scientists took this goose and watched what it would do if they put objects that looked like eggs near its nest. They put all kinds of things, like black and white marbles, around it. What happened was the goose pulled all of the objects into its nest. So the scientists figured that the goose's behavior was purely instinctive. I mean, it obviously wasn't using its intelligence to notice that the marbles weren't like its eggs.

해석

M Professor: 일부 과학자들은 동물들이 하는 행동이 본능보다 학습한 것이나 인지하고 있는 것과 더 관련이 있는지 알아내기 위해 동물 행동을 연구합니다. 한 가지 연구는 거위를 대상으로 한 것이었어요. 자, 거위는 새끼를 잘 돌봅니다. 만약 보금자리 가까이에 있는 알을 본다면 보통 알을 가지고 와서 보살피죠. 어쨌든, 과학자들은 이러한 거위를 선택해서 보금자리 근처에 알처럼 보이는 물체를 놓고 거위의 행동을 관찰했습니다. 그들은, 예컨대 검정 구슬이나 흰 구슬과 같이, 온갖 종류의 물건들을 보금자리 주변에 두었습니다. 그러자 거위는 모든 물건들을 둥지 안으로 끌고 갔어요. 그래서 과학자들은 거위의 행동이 순전히 본능적이라는 점을 알아냈습니다. 제 말은, 거위가 지능을 이용해서 구슬이 알과는 다르다는 점을 알아채지 못했다는 것이에요.

✎ Note Taking

Subject Animal behavior
Detail Can be connected to instinct or learned behavior

Organization

1 Animal behavior falls under two types, instinctive and learned.

2 A goose showed protective behavior by gathering all the egg-like objects near its nest.

3 This behavior of the goose appeared to be instinctive.

Comparing

Sample Response 🎧 04-50

For scientists to study animal intelligence, they have to observe the behavior of animals. They set up different situations to see how animals react to them and then try to explain why the animals do what they do. In the talk, the example of the goose was given to show that scientists wanted to know just how much of what animals do is instinctive and how much they do with real thought.

해석

동물의 지능을 연구하는 학자들은 동물의 행동을 관찰해야 한다. 그들은 동물이 어떻게 반응하는지를 관찰하기 위해 서로 다른 상황을 설정하고 왜 동물들이 그런 행동을 하는지 설명하고자 한다. 강의에서는 과학자들이 동물 행동 중 얼마나 많은 부분이 본능적인 것이고 얼마나 많은 부분이 실제 사고와 관련된 것인지 알아내고 싶어한다는 점을 보여 주기 위해 거위의 사례를 들고 있다.

Exercise 6 ······································· p.149

Listening

Script 🎧 04-51

M Professor: Do you ever wonder why so many people get lost on road trips? Basically, uh, they can't read maps. When reading maps, it is very important to notice the scale. The scale tells how the distance on the map correlates to the distance in real life. See, uh, a map will usually have a key that tells you how to figure out the distance. For example, a city map might read on the bottom, "One centimeter equals 100 meters." This means that if two buildings are three centimeters away on the map, they are 300 meters away in real life. Or it might have a little box with symbols and an explanation of what the symbols represent. For instance, if it's a tourist map, there might be little buildings to show where historical places are or tents to show the locations of campgrounds.

해석

M Professor: 왜 그렇게 많은 사람들이 여행을 하다 길을 잃는지 궁금했던 적이 있나요? 기본적으로, 어, 지도 읽는 법을 모르기 때문이죠. 지도를 읽을 때에는 척도를 아는 것이 매우 중요합니다. 척도는 지도상의 거리와 실제 거리가 어떤 관계에 있는지 알려 주죠. 가령, 어, 지도에는 보통 거리를 알아 내는 방법을 알려 주는 기호 해설이 있을 거예요. 예를 들어 시내 지도 밑에 "1인치=100미터"라고 쓰여 있다고 할게요. 이는 지도상에서 두 건물이 3인치 떨어져 있다면 실제로는 300미터 떨어져 있다는 것을 의미합니다. 또는 기호와 기호가 의미하는 바를 설명하는 작은 상자가 있을 수도 있어요. 예컨대 관광 지도라면 역사 유적지가 있는 곳을 나타내는 작은 건물이나 캠핑 장소를 나타내는 텐트 그림이 있을 수 있죠.

> ✎ Note Taking
>
> **Subject** Reading maps
> **Detail** Have scales and keys that tell people how to read maps

Organization

1 Maps use both a scale and a key.

2 The scale on a map indicates sizes and distances in the real world.

3 A key is used to translate symbols on the map to objects in the real world.

Comparing

Sample Response 🎧 04-52

To read a map, you have to know what scale is and know how to read a key. The scale is the proportional measurement of distance that lets you know how much area the map and its parts represent. The key is a code of symbols that pinpoint natural or manmade landmarks found in the mapped area.

해석

지도를 읽기 위해서는 척도의 의미와 기호 해설 읽는 법을 알아야 한다. 척도는 거리의 비례 측정값으로 지도 및 지도의 일부가 나타내는 지역의 크기를 알려 준다. 기호 해설은 지도에 표시된 지역에서 찾아볼 수 있는 자연적인 랜드마크나 인공적인 랜드마크를 가리키는 기호를 설명해 준다.

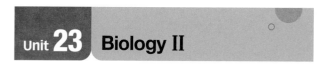

Unit 23 Biology II

Exercise 1 ······································· p.150

Listening

Script 🎧 04-53

W Professor: The vast majority of birds build nests. They may build nests on the ground or in bushes or trees. Others may build nests on cliffs or high on mountains. There are two primary reasons birds make nests. The first is that nests provide birds with places to lay their eggs and then to hatch them. Female birds first lay their eggs in their nests. Then, they spend varying amounts of time sitting on the eggs to keep them warm and safe. This enables their babies to hatch. Another reason birds make nests is to provide protection from the elements. This includes rain and snow. It also includes wind and cold temperatures. By staying in their nests, birds can avoid freezing to death, getting blown away by the wind, and getting wet from rain or snow.

해석

W Professor: 대다수의 새들이 둥지를 짓습니다. 땅 위에 지을 수도 있고 수풀이나 나무에 지을 수도 있죠. 절벽이나 높은 산 속에 둥지를 짓는 새들도 있습니다. 새들이 둥지를 짓는 두 가지 중요한 이유가 있어요. 첫 번째는 둥지가 새들에게 알을 낳고 부화시킬 수 있는 장소를 제공해 주기 때문이죠. 먼저 암컷 새들이 둥지에 알을 낳습니다. 그런 다음에는 다양한 기간에 걸쳐 알이 따뜻하고 안전할 수 있도록 알을 품어요. 이로써 새끼들이 부화할 수 있게 됩니다. 새들이 둥지를 짓는 또 다른 이유는 비바람으로부터 보호를 받기 위해서예요. 여기에는 비와 눈이 포함됩니다. 또한 바람과 추운 날씨도 포함되고요. 둥지 안에 있으면 새들은 얼어 죽지 않고, 바람에 날려가지 않으며, 비나 눈으로부터 젖지 않을 수 있습니다.

Organization

1 Most birds make nests in different places.

2 Birds make nests in order to lay their eggs and to sit on them so that they hatch.

3 Birds also make nests to protect themselves from the elements.

Comparing

Sample Response 🎧 04-54

The professor lectures to the students about birds and their nests. She says that birds make nests for two main reasons. The first reason is that they need a place to lay their eggs. Then, they can sit on the eggs to keep them safe. After a certain amount of time, the eggs will hatch. The second reason is that nests help protect birds from bad weather. This can include rain, snow, wind, and cold temperatures. Thanks to their nests, birds can stay alive and be dry.

해석

교수는 새와 새의 둥지에 관해 학생들에게 강의를 하고 있다. 교수는 새들이 두 가지 주된 이유로 둥지를 짓는다고 말한다. 첫 번째 이유는 새들에게 알을 낳을 수 있는 장소가 필요하기 때문이다. 그러면 알을 품어서 알을 지킬 수 있다. 일정 기간이 지나면 알이 부화하게 될 것이다. 두 번째 이유는 둥지가 악천후로부터 새들을 보호해 주기 때문이다. 악천후에는 비, 눈, 바람, 그리고 추위가 포함될 수 있다. 둥지 덕분에 새들은 생존할 수 있고 젖지 않을 수 있다.

Exercise 2 ·· p.151

Listening

Script 🎧 04-55

M Professor: This is a picture of a rhesus monkey. Now, uh, when babies are born, their mothers take care of them carefully. Babies may drink their mother's milk for up to a year. But when they become infants and are not totally reliant on their mothers, something interesting happens. You see, uh, the mothers often stop caring for their infants all the time. Instead, young female monkeys look after the infants. This accomplishes a couple of things. First of all, it allows the mothers the opportunity to do other activities. These include searching for food, grooming, and spending time with other adult monkeys. Another benefit is that it gives young females experience taking care of infants. This helps prepare these females for when they become mothers themselves.

해석

M Professor: 이것은 붉은털원숭이의 사진입니다. 자, 어, 새끼가 태어나면 어미들이 새끼들을 정성껏 보살피죠. 새끼들은 최대 1년 동안 어미의 젖을 먹을 수도 있어요. 하지만 더 자라면 어미에게 전적으로 의지를 하지 않게 되는데, 이 때 흥미로운 일이 일어납니다. 아시다시피, 어, 더 이상 어미들이 어린 원숭이들을 항상 돌보지는 않게 됩니다. 대신 젊은 암컷 원숭이들이 어린 원숭이들을 돌보죠. 이로써 두 가지 목적이 달성됩니다. 먼저 그로 인해 어미들이 다른 활동을 할 수 있는 기회를 얻게 되어요. 여기에는 먹이 찾기, 그루밍, 그리고 다른 성체 원숭이들과의 시간 보내기가 포함되죠. 또 다른 이점은 그렇게 함으로써 젊은 암컷들이 새끼를 돌보는 경험을 하게 된다는 것이에요. 이로써 젊은 암컷들이 스스로가 어미가 되는 것에 대한 준비를 할 수가 있습니다.

Organization

1 Mother rhesus monkeys often stop taking care of their infants all the time and let young females help.

2 The mothers have time to do other activities.

3 The young females gain child-raising experience.

Comparing

Sample Response 🎧 04-56

The professor points out that when baby rhesus monkeys get older and become infants, something interesting happens. The mothers stop caring for them all the time. What happens is that young female monkeys watch the infants. Because they help, the mothers can look for food, hang out with other adults, and groom themselves. At the same time, the young females learn how to care for the infants. This helps them prepare for motherhood in the future.

해석

교수는 새끼 붉은털원숭이가 시간이 지나 자란 후에 흥미로운 일이 일어난다는 점을 지적한다. 어미가 더 이상 이들을 항상 돌보지는 않게 된다. 그러면 젊은 암컷 원숭이들이 어린 원숭이들을 돌본다. 이들이 도움을 줌으로써 어미들은 음식을 구하고, 다른 성체 원숭이들과 어울리고, 그리고 그루밍을 할 수 있다. 이와 동시에 젊은 암컷들은 새끼들을 돌보는 법을 배우게 된다. 이로써 미래에 자신이 어미가 되기 위한 준비를 할 수 있다.

Exercise 3 ·· p.152

Listening

Script 🎧 04-57

M Professor: Animals have numerous ways to protect themselves from predators. You all know about sharp teeth and claws, great speed, and camouflage. Let me tell you about a couple of other types of defense mechanisms. The porcupine is a large rodent with a unique form of defense. It has long, sharp quills on its back. Porcupines can't shoot them, but they can detach the quills from their bodies. So when a predator attempts to bite a porcupine, it often gets a mouthful of extremely painful quills. On the other hand, the horned lizard does have a defense mechanism that it can shoot at predators. It's capable of shooting a stream of blood from its eyes. This blood doesn't cause harm; however, it usually manages to frighten away predators. This lets the horned lizard escape.

해석

M Professor: 동물들은 포식자로부터 스스로를 보호할 수 있는 여러가지 방법을 가지고 있습니다. 여러분 모두 날카로운 이빨과 발톱, 빠른 속도, 그리고 위장에 대해 아실 거예요. 저는 두어 가지 다른 방어 기제에 대해 말씀을 드리고자 합니다. 호저는 독특한 방어 수단을 가지고 있는 커다란 설치류입니다. 등에 길고 날카로운 가시를 가지고 있죠. 호저는 가시를 쏠 수는 없지만 대신 신체로부터 가시를 떼어낼 수 있습니다. 그래서 포식자가 호저를 물려고 시도하면 포식자는 종종 극도의 고통을 가져다 주는 가시를 먹게 되죠. 반면에 뿔도마뱀은 포식자를 향해 쏠 수 있는 방어 기제를 가지고 있습니다. 눈에서 한 줄기 피를 뿜어낼 수 있어요. 이 피는 해를 끼치지는 않습니다. 하지만 보통 포식자들에게 겁을 줘서 달아나게 만들죠. 이로써 뿔도마뱀은 위기를 모면할 수 있습니다.

> **Note Taking**
>
> **Subject** Unique animal defense methods
> **Detail** Quills of porcupines and blood from eyes of horned lizards

Organization

1 Porcupines have quills on their backs that they can use for defense.

2 Horned lizards can protect themselves by shooting blood from their eyes.

Comparing

Sample Response 🎧 04-58

The professor states that some animals have unique defense methods. One animal like this is the porcupine. It has very long, sharp quills on its back. If a predator attacks it, it can use the quills to protect itself. The quills can detach when animals attack, and they can cause pain. Another animal with a unique defense method is the horned lizard. It is capable of shooting blood from its eyes. It does this to frighten off predators attacking it.

해석

교수는 일부 동물들이 독특한 방어 수단을 가지고 있다고 말한다. 그러한 한 가지 동물이 호저이다. 호저는 등에 매우 길고 날카로운 가시를 가지고 있다. 포식자가 호저를 공격하는 경우 호저는 가시를 이용해 스스로를 보호할 수 있다. 독특한 방어 수단을 지닌 또 다른 동물은 뿔도마뱀이다. 뿔도마뱀은 눈에서 피를 뿜어낼 수 있다. 자신을 공격하려는 포식자에게 겁을 줘서 달아나도록 만들기 위

해 그렇게 하는 것이다.

Exercise 4 .... p.153

Listening

Script 🎧 04-59

W Professor: There are many different species of whales in the world's oceans. We can divide whales into two separate groups. The first is baleen whales while the second is toothed whales. Baleen whales include both blue whales and humpback whales. They are filter feeders. What they do is open their mouths and take in water. In the process, they also suck in krill and small fish. The water is then filtered out of their mouths, and they consume the creatures that remain. Toothed whales are hunters like sperm whales, killer whales, and dolphins. These animals have sharp teeth they use when they hunt. They typically catch big fish such as tuna, squid, and even aquatic mammals such as seals and sea lions.

해석

W Professor: 전 세계의 바다에는 여러 다양한 고래종들이 살고 있어요. 우리는 고래를 두 가지 서로 다른 그룹으로 나눌 수 있습니다. 첫 번째는 수염고래이고 두 번째는 이빨고래예요. 수염고래에는 흰긴수염고래와 혹등고래가 모두 포함됩니다. 이들은 여과 섭식 동물이에요. 이들이 하는 일은 입을 벌리고 물을 들이 마시는 것이죠. 그러한 과정에서 크릴새우 및 작은 물고기들도 따라 들어옵니다. 그런 다음 이들은 입에서 물을 내보내고 남아 있는 생물들을 먹습니다. 이빨고래는 향유고래, 범고래, 그리고 돌고래와 같이 사냥을 하는 고래입니다. 이러한 고래들은 사냥할 때 사용되는 날카로운 이빨을 가지고 있죠. 보통은 다랑어, 오징어, 그리고 물개 및 바다사자와 같은 해양 포유류를 잡아먹습니다.

> **Note Taking**
>
> **Subject** Two kinds of whales
> **Detail** Are baleen and toothed whales

Organization

1 Baleen whales like blue whales and humpback whales are filter feeders.

2 Toothed whales are hunters that eat big fish, squid, and aquatic mammals.

Comparing

Sample Response 🎧 04-60

The professor states that there are baleen whales and toothed whales. Blue whales and humpback whales are both baleen whales. To eat, these whales open their mouths and bring large amounts of water into them. They filter the water out of their mouths, but they eat the krill and small fish that remain. Toothed whales are hunters like killer whales, sperm whales, and dolphins. They use their teeth to catch big fish, squid, and aquatic mammals.

해석

교수는 수염고래와 이빨고래가 존재한다고 말한다. 흰긴수염고래와 혹등고래 모두 수염고래이다. 이러한 고래들은 먹이를 먹기 위해 입을 벌리고 다량의 물을 입안에 들인다. 이들은 입에서 물을 내보내고 남아 있는 크릴새우와 작은 물고기들을 먹는다. 이빨고래는 범고래, 향유고래, 그리고 돌고래와 같이 사냥을 하는 고래이다. 이들은 이빨을 이용해서 커다란 물고기, 오징어, 그리고 수생 포유류를 잡아먹는다.

Exercise 5 ·· p.154

Listening

Script 🎧 04-61

M Professor: Venom is a type of toxin some animals utilize. Some venom may just cause minor irritation, but other venom is so powerful that it can kill even the biggest animals. Snakes are the best-known animals that use venom. But others utilize it as well. You might be surprised to learn that venom has both offensive and defensive purposes. Snakes commonly use venom for offensive purposes. Rattlesnakes, cobras, and kraits use venom when hunting. They bite their prey, wait for it to succumb to their venom, and then consume it. Many species of bees produce venom, but they don't use it to hunt. Instead, they sting enemies and inject venom when they are protecting their hives. In this way, bees use venom for defensive purposes.

해석

M Professor: 독은 일부 동물들이 사용하는 독성 물질입니다. 몇몇 독은 미미한 염증 정도 일으킬 수 있지만 너무나 강력해서 몸집이 가장 큰 동물들조차 죽일 수 있는 독도 있어요. 뱀은 독을 사용하는 것으로 가장 잘 알려져 있는 동물입니다. 하지만 다른 동물들도 사용합니다. 독에는 공격적인 목적과 방어적인 목적 모두 존재한다는 점을 알게 되면 놀라실 수도 있을 것 같군요. 뱀은 보통 공격적인 목적으로 독을 사용합니다. 방울뱀, 코브라, 그리고 크레이트는 사냥을 할 때 독을 사용하죠. 먹이를 물어서 먹이가 독으로 쓰러질 때까지 기다렸다가 잡아먹습니다. 여러 종의 꿀벌도 독을 만들어 내지만 이들은 사냥을 하기 위해 독을 사용하지는 않습니다. 대신 벌집을 지키려고 할 때 적에게 침을 쏘고 독을 주입하죠. 이러한 방식으로 꿀벌은 방어적인 목적을 위해 독을 사용합니다.

> 🖊 Note Taking
>
> **Subject** Venom
> **Detail** Can be used for offensive and defensive purposes

Organization

1 Some snakes use venom in order to kill prey and to eat it.

2 Bees use venom in order to protect their hives from attackers.

Comparing

Sample Response 🎧 04-62

The professor tells the class that venom can be used

both offensively and defensively. First, he mentions snakes such as cobras, rattlesnakes, and kraits. These animals have offensive venom. They bite their prey and use venom to kill it. Then, they eat the animal. On the other hand, bees use venom defensively. When other animals attack their hive, bees sting the animals and use venom. In this way, they use venom to protect themselves and their homes.

해석

교수는 수업에서 독이 공격적으로도 사용될 수 있고 방어적으로도 사용될 수 있다고 말한다. 먼저 교수는 코브라, 방울뱀, 그리고 크레이트와 같은 뱀을 언급한다. 이 동물들은 공격 목적의 독을 가지고 있다. 이들은 먹이를 문 후 독을 이용해 먹이를 죽인다. 그런 다음 동물을 잡아먹는다. 반면에 꿀벌들은 독을 방어적으로 사용한다. 다른 동물들이 자신의 벌집을 공격하면 꿀벌들은 그 동물에게 침을 쏘고 독을 사용한다. 이러한 방식으로 꿀벌들은 자신과 자신의 거처를 지키기 위해 독을 사용한다.

Exercise 6 ·· p.155

Listening

Script 🎧 04-63

W Professor: It's well known that plants need sunlight to grow. In fact, many plants lean toward the sun as they grow. Not all plants do this though. As a matter of fact, some plants can survive with very little sunlight. There are typically a couple of reasons for this. Look here . . . This is the arrowhead plant. Notice that it's a vine. It grows very well in shaded conditions. In addition, like most vines, it attaches itself to other structures, including trees and walls. For this reason, the arrowhead plant doesn't lean toward the sun. Another plant that avoids the sun is the fuchsia. This plant can actually survive in full shade, mainly because it is not resistant to heat. However, it needs to be in soil that retains moisture well.

해석

W Professor: 식물들이 자라기 위해서는 햇빛이 필요하다는 점은 잘 알려져 있어요. 실제로 많은 식물들이 자라는 동안 태양 쪽으로 몸을 기울이죠. 하지만 모든 식물이 다 그런 것은 아닙니다. 사실 일부 식물들은 햇빛이 거의 없어야 생존할 수 있어요. 보통 두 가지 이유에서 그렇습니다. 여기를 보시면… 이것은 싱고니움이에요. 덩굴 식물이라는 점에 주목해 주시고요. 그늘이 있는 환경에서 매우 잘 자랍니다. 게다가 대부분의 덩굴 식물과 마찬가지로 몸을, 나무와 벽을 포함하여, 다른 구조물에 붙입니다. 이러한 이유에서 싱고니움은 태양 쪽으로 몸을 기울이지 않습니다. 태양을 피하는 또 다른 식물은 푸크시아예요. 이 식물은 실제로 완전히 그늘진 곳에서 생존할 수 있는데, 그 이유는 주로 이들이 열기를 견디지 못하기 때문입니다. 대신 수분을 많이 포함하고 있는 토양을 필요로 하죠.

> 🖊 Note Taking
>
> **Subject** Plants that need little sunlight
> **Detail** Include the arrowhead plant and fuchsia

Organization

1 Most plants lean toward the sun when they grow, but some need little sunlight.

2 The arrowhead plant grows well in shade and is a vine that attaches itself to structures.

3 Fuchsia is not resistant to heat, so it grows well in full shade.

Comparing

Sample Response 🎧 04-64

The professor talks about the arrowhead plant and fuchsia. Both plants don't lean toward the sun when they grow. The arrowhead plant is a vine that attaches itself to walls and other structures. It also needs little sunlight, so it doesn't lean toward the sun. In addition, fuchsia grows in full shade because it cannot resist heat well. It does, however, require soil with lots of water in it.

해석

교수는 싱고니움과 푸크시아에 대해 이야기한다. 두 식물 모두 자라는 동안 태양 쪽으로 몸을 기울이지 않는다. 싱고니움은 덩굴 식물로 벽이나 기타 구조물에 몸을 부착시킨다. 또한 햇빛을 거의 필요로 하지 않기 때문에 태양 쪽으로 몸을 기울이지 않는다. 푸크시아 역시 완전히 그늘진 곳에서 자라는데, 그 이유는 푸크시아가 열기를 잘 견디지 못하기 때문이다. 대신 푸크시아는 수분이 많이 포함되어 있는 토양을 필요로 한다.

Unit 24 Business

Exercise 1 .... p.156

Listening

Script 🎧 04-65

W Professor: When businesses want to expand, they require financing. There are two ways to obtain the money they need. They can rely on internal financing or external financing. Internal financing is money that comes from the company itself. Companies typically use this type of financing when they want a limited amount of money. Internal financing also prevents companies from expanding too much. External financing is money that comes from sources outside the company. It can be bank loans, investments by outsiders, or other similar means. Companies use this financing when they need large sums of money. They typically do this when they are trying to expand to become either national or global companies.

해석

W Professor: 사업체가 확장하고자 하면 자금이 필요하죠. 필요한 자금을 마련할 수 있는 두 가지 방법이 있습니다. 내부 자금이나 외부 자금을 이용할 수 있어요. 내부 자금은 기업 자체에서 조달하는 자금입니다. 기업들은 보통 한정된 양의 돈이 필요한 경우에 이러한 자금을 이용하죠. 내부 자금 조달 방식은 또한 기업이 지나치게 확장하는 것을 예방해 줍니다. 외부 자금은 기업 외부의 출처로부터 조달되는 자금이에요. 은행 대출, 외부의 투자, 혹은 기타 그와 유사한 수단에 의한 자금일 수 있습니다. 기업들은 다량의 자금이 필요한 경우에 이러한 자금 조달 방식을 이용해요. 보통은 전국적인 혹은 세계적인 기업으로 확장하고자 할 때 그렇게 하죠.

✎ Note Taking

Subject Financing
Detail Can be internal or external financing

Organization

1 Companies use internal financing when they need a small amount of money.

2 Companies use external financing to acquire large amounts of money.

Comparing

Sample Response 🎧 04-66

The professor says that businesses can raise money that they need through internal or external financing. Internal financing comes from the company itself. It is used for a limited amount of money and doesn't allow a company to expand much. When companies need much more money, they use external financing. This can be money from banks or investors. This financing can be used to increase the size of a company to a national or global level.

해석

교수는 사업체가 내부 자금 조달 혹은 외부 자금 조달을 통해 자금을 마련할 수 있다고 말한다. 내부 자금은 해당 기업 자체로부터 조달되는 자금이다. 이는 한정된 양의 자금이 필요할 때 사용되며 기업의 지나친 확장을 방지한다. 훨씬 더 많은 자금이 필요한 경우에는 기업들이 외부 자금을 이용한다. 이는 은행이나 투자자로부터 조달되는 자금일 수 있다. 이러한 자금 조달 방식은 기업이 전국적인 혹은 세계적인 수준으로 그 크기를 확대시키려고 할 때 사용될 수 있다.

Exercise 2 .... p.157

Listening

Script 🎧 04-67

W Professor: Companies advertise to make their goods and services better known. There are many advantages to advertising. There are also disadvantages though. Here are a couple . . . Print advertisements are still popular. Businesses may print flyers, posters, brochures, and other similar advertisements. Unfortunately, these ads are printed on paper. This means companies using this form of advertisement are responsible for cutting down trees, which is bad for the environment. In addition, drive on a highway or interstate, and you will see numerous billboards alongside these roads. These advertisements are often eyesores. Sure, they promote products. But they are basically a form of pollution since they make the environment look bad.

해석

W Professor: 기업들은 자사의 제품 및 서비스를 더 잘 알리기 위해 광고를 합니다. 광고에는 많은 이점이 존재해요. 하지만 단점도 존재합니다. 두어 가지 말씀을 드리면… 인쇄물 광고는 여전히 인기가 높습니다. 기업체들은 전단, 포스터, 브로셔, 그리고 기타 그와 유사한 광고물들을 인쇄할 수 있죠. 안타깝게도 이러한 광고는 종이에 인쇄가 됩니다. 이는 이러한 형태의 광고를 이용하는 기업이 벌목에 책임이 있다는 점을 의미하는데, 이는 환경에 좋지 않은 일이에요. 게다가 고속도로 및 주간 고속도로에서 운전을 하면 도로를 따라 수많은 옥외 광고판들을 보게 됩니다. 그래요, 이들은 제품을 홍보하죠. 하지만 경관을 망치기 때문에 기본적으로 이들도 일종의 공해입니다.

Note Taking

Subject Disadvantages of advertising
Detail Bad for the environment and cause pollution

Organization

1 Print advertisements use paper, so trees must be cut down. This harms the environment.

2 Billboards by roads are a form of pollution since they are eyesores.

Comparing

Sample Response 🎧 04-68

Advertising has advantages, but according to the professor, it also has disadvantages. For example, print advertisements include posters and brochures. These are printed on paper, which comes from trees. So they cause trees to be cut down, which is harmful to the environment. Next, billboards can be signs by roads. These are eyesores that are essentially a kind of pollution.

해석

광고에는 장점이 있지만 교수에 따르면 단점도 존재한다. 예를 들어 인쇄 광고물에는 포스터와 브로셔가 포함된다. 이들은 종이에 인쇄되는데, 종이는 나무로부터 나오는 것이다. 따라서 이 때문에 나무가 베어지며, 그로써 환경에 해를 끼치게 된다. 다음으로 옥외 광고판이 도로변에 세워져 있을 수 있다. 이는 눈에 거슬리는 것으로서 본질적으로 일종의 공해이다.

Exercise 3 .... p.158

Listening

Script 🎧 04-69

M Professor: Businesses are always trying to get new customers. When they acquire these customers, they want to keep the customers and get these individuals to make more purchases in the future. Let me tell you a couple of ways that businesses can create regular customers. One is to provide outstanding customer service. This comes in many forms. For instance, uh, the staff at the physical store should be helpful and polite. They should recommend the items that customers ask for and need. The people whom customers talk to online and on the phone must be helpful as well. A second effective way to keep customers is to provide discounts. I'm not talking about sales for the entire store. I'm referring to special discounts just for regular customers. Those are always appreciated and keep regular customers coming back for more.

해석

M Professor: 기업들은 항상 신규 고객을 모집하려고 노력합니다. 그러한 신규 고객들을 유치하면 고객을 확보해서 고객 개개인들이 추후에 더 많이 구입하도록 만들고 싶어하죠. 기업들이 단골 고객을 만들 수 있는 두 가지 방법을 알려 드리겠습니다. 한 가지는 뛰어난 고객 서비스를 제공하는 것이에요. 이는 다양한 형태로 이루어질 수 있습니다. 예를 들어, 어, 오프라인 매장의 직원들은 도움이 되고 공손해야 해요. 고객들이 요구하거나 필요로 하는 제품을 추천해 주어야 합니다. 온라인이나 전화로 고객들과 대화를 나누는 사람들 또한 반드시 도움이 되어야 하죠. 고객을 확보할 수 있는 효과적인 두 번째 방법은 할인을 제공하는 것이에요. 매장 전체에 적용되는 세일을 말씀드리는 것이 아닙니다. 단골 고객에게만 적용되는 특별 할인을 말씀드리는 거예요. 이는 항상 고마운 것으로 생각되며 단골 고객들이 다시 찾아와 더 많이 살 수 있도록 만들어 주죠.

Note Taking

Subject How to keep customers
Detail Outstanding customer service and special discounts

Organization

1 Stores can keep customers by providing them with excellent customer service.

2 Stores can also keep these customers by giving them special discounts.

Comparing

Sample Response 🎧 04-70

The professor mentions that businesses want customers to keep returning so that they can buy more products. He states that one way is to provide excellent customer service. This includes the sales staff at stores, who should be helpful and kind. It also includes employees that customers talk to on the phone and online. Another way to keep customers is to provide special discounts only for regular customers.

해석

교수는 고객들이 재방문하여 더 많은 제품을 구입하는 것을 기업들이 바란다고 말한다. 그는 한 가지 방법이 뛰어난 고객 서비스를 제공하는 것이라고 언급한다. 여기에는 매장 내의 판매 직원이 포함되는데, 이들은 도움이 되어야 하고 친절해야 한다. 또한 전화나 온라인으로 고객과 대화를 나누는 직원들도 여기에 포함된다. 고객을 확보할 수 있는 또 다른 방법은 단골 고객들에게만 특별 할인을 제공하는 것이다.

Exercise 4 ·· p.159

Listening
Script 🎧 04-71

W Professor: When advertising agencies create commercials and ads for companies, they typically focus on two different strategies to appeal to customers. One strategy is to employ visual clues. By this, I mean images. For instance, let's say a restaurant is creating print ads. It would likely want close-up images of its food. These images must be as attractive as possible to entice customers to visit the restaurant. A second strategy is to focus on verbal clues, uh, you know, words. In these advertisements, providing as much information as possible is crucial. A car company making a TV commercial would have a narrator describing all of the benefits of the car on sale. These would include the price, the safety features, and the type of engine.

해석

W Professor: 기업을 위한 TV 광고 및 일반 광고를 제작하는 경우, 광고 회사들은 보통 고객들에게 어필할 수 있는 서로 다른 두 가지 전략에 초점을 맞춥니다. 한 가지 전략은 시각적인 단서를 이용하는 것이에요. 이는 이미지를 의미합니다. 예를 들어 한 식당이 인쇄물 광고를 제작하고 있다고 해 보죠. 아마도 식당은 음식이 클로즈업된 사진을 원할 것입니다. 이러한 이미지는 고객들의 식당 방문을 유도할 수 있을 정도로 매력적이어야 하죠. 두 번째 전략은 언어적인 단서, 어, 아시다시피 말에 초점을 맞추는 것이에요. 이러한 광고에서는 가능한 많은 양의 정보를 제공해 주는 것이 중요합니다. TV 광고를 제작 중인 자동차 회사는 판매되고 있는 자동차의 모든 이점을 설명해 주는 내레이터를 이용할 수 있어요. 여기에는 가격, 안전 사양, 그리고 엔진의 종류 등이 포함될 수 있죠.

✏ Note Taking

Subject Making appealing advertisements to customers
Detail Can use visual clues and verbal clues

Organization

1 Visual clues in advertisements can include close-up images of food.

2 Verbal clues in advertisements are words that provide a lot of information.

Comparing
Sample Response 🎧 04-72

The professor discusses two different strategies that advertising agencies use when making ads for businesses. First, they may rely on visual clues, which are images. The professor gives an example of a restaurant. It might have attractive close-up images of its food on print advertisements. Second, companies might use verbal clues, which are words. The professor talks about a car company as an example. She says that an advertisement for a car would use verbal clues to explain all of its benefits. The ad might discuss the car's price, safety features, and engine.

해석

교수는 광고 회사가 기업용 광고를 제작할 때 사용하는 서로 다른 두 가지 전략에 대해 논의한다. 첫째, 그들은 시각적인 단서인 이미지에 의존할 수 있다. 교수는 식당의 사례를 든다. 식당은 인쇄물 광고에 클로즈업된 매력적인 음식 사진을 넣을 수 있다. 둘째, 기업들은 언어적인 단서, 즉 말을 이용할 수도 있다. 교수는 한 가지 예로서 자동차 회사를 언급한다. 교수는 자동차 광고가 언어적인 단서를 이용해서 자동차의 모든 장점을 설명할 수 있다고 말한다. 이러한 광고에서는 자동차의 가격, 안전 사양, 그리고 엔진에 대한 언급이 이루어질 수 있다.

Exercise 5 ·· p.160

Listening
Script 🎧 04-73

M Professor: Virtually all products purchased at stores come in some type of packaging. They may be wrapped in plastic or boxes, for instance. I wonder if you have ever noticed something interesting about product packaging. In many cases, cheap items come in cheap packaging. Let me use candy bars as an example. If you buy a chocolate bar at a store, you'll notice it's packaged in a cheap, thin plastic wrapper. You immediately discard it after eating the chocolate because the wrapper is worthless. However, the opposite is true for expensive items. If you purchase an expensive watch, it will almost surely come in a good-looking, expensive box. It's so nice that people often keep the box rather than throwing it out. In this way, product packaging can tell you about the value of an item.

해석

M Professor: 매장에서 구입할 수 있는 사실상 모든 제품이 일정한 형태로 포장되어 있습니다. 예컨대 비닐이나 상자에 들어있을 수 있어요. 여러분이 제품 포장에 관한 흥미로운 점에 주목해 본 적이 있는지 궁금하군요. 많은 경우, 저렴한 제품들은 저렴한 포장지로 포장되어 있습니다. 한 가지 예로 초코바를 들어보죠. 매장에서 초코바를 구입하면 초코바가 저렴하고 얇은 포장지에 포장되어 있다는 점을 알게 될 거예요. 포장지는 가치가 없기 때문에 초콜릿을 먹은 후에는 포장지를 바로 버리게 되죠. 하지만 값비싼 제품의 경우에는 사실 그 반대입니다. 값비싼 시계를 구입하는 경우, 그 시계는 거의 틀림없이 보기 좋고 값비싼 상

자에 들어 있을 거예요. 너무나 멋지게 보이기 때문에 사람들은 종종 상자를 버리지 않고 보관해 두죠. 이러한 방식으로 제품 포장은 제품의 가치에 대해 알려 줄 수가 있습니다.

> ✏ Note Taking
>
> Subject   Product packaging
> Detail   Can determine the value of an item from its packaging

Organization

1 Cheap products often come in cheap packaging that people throw away.

2 Expensive products often come in nice packaging that people want to keep.

Comparing

Sample Response 🎧 04-74

The professor talks to the students about product packaging. He points out that it's frequently possible to tell the value of an item based on the packaging it comes in. For example, he mentions a cheap chocolate bar. He states that it comes in a cheap wrapper that people just throw away. However, he then talks about an expensive watch. It almost always comes in a very nice box. As a matter of fact, most people keep the box because it has value to them.

해석

교수는 학생들에게 제품 포장에 대해 이야기한다. 그는 제품이 포장된 포장 상태를 근거로 제품의 가치를 파악하는 것이 종종 가능하다고 지적한다. 교수는 저렴한 초코바를 예로 든다. 그는 초코바가 저렴한 포장지로 포장되어 있으며 사람들은 포장지를 버린다고 말한다. 하지만 그 후 교수는 값비싼 시계에 대해 이야기한다. 시계는 거의 항상 매우 멋진 상자에 포장되어 있다. 실제로 사람들은 상자에 가치가 있기 때문에 상자를 보관해 둔다.

Exercise 6 .... p.161

Listening

Script 🎧 04-75

W Professor: Advertisements are everywhere these days. They are in newspapers and magazines and on television and the Internet. Now, think about their content. In many cases, ads emphasize the quality of items. For instance, there's a popular ad for sneakers these days. I'm sure everyone has seen it. The ad focuses on the material the shoes are made of. It also stresses that the shoes will last for a long time. That ad focuses on the shoes' quality. Meanwhile, other ads emphasize special characteristics of products. I saw an ad for some potato chips on TV last night. The ad stressed that they are the hottest—uh, you know, the spiciest—potato chips on the

market. That's about all the ad mentioned. In that case, the ad focuses on a unique feature of the item.

해석

W Professor: 요즘은 사방에 광고가 존재합니다. 뉴스와 잡지에서, 그리고 텔레비전과 인터넷에서도 존재하죠. 자, 광고의 내용에 대해 생각해 보세요. 많은 경우, 광고는 제품의 품질을 강조합니다. 예를 들어 최근에 인기를 끌고 있는 신발 광고가 있습니다. 틀림없이 모두들 보셨을 거예요. 이 광고는 신발의 재료에 초점을 맞추고 있어요. 또한 신발이 오래 간다는 점을 강조하죠. 이 광고는 신발의 품질에 초점을 맞추고 있습니다. 반면에 제품의 특성을 강조하는 광고들도 있어요. 저는 어젯밤에 TV에서 감자칩 광고를 보았습니다. 광고에서는 그 감자칩이 시중에 나와 있는 것 중에서 가장 맵다는 점을, 어, 아시다시피 가장 맛이 강하다는 점을 강조했어요. 광고에서 언급된 것은 그게 다였죠. 이 경우, 광고는 제품의 독특한 특징에 초점을 맞추고 있습니다.

> ✏ Note Taking
>
> Subject   The content of ads
> Detail   May focus on quality or a unique feature

Organization

1 An ad for sneakers focuses on the quality of the shoes by stressing their materials and how long they last.

2 An ad for potato chips stresses how hot it is, which focuses on the item's unique feature.

Comparing

Sample Response 🎧 04-76

The professor tells the students that ads may focus on two different features. They are quality and a unique characteristic. First, she covers an ad for some sneakers. It stresses the quality of the shoes by focusing on the materials they are made of. The ad also mentions that the shoes will last a long time. A different ad she mentions is for potato chips. It stresses a unique feature of the chips, which is how spicy they are.

해석

교수는 학생들에게 광고가 각기 다른 두 가지 특성에 초점을 맞출 수 있다고 말한다. 바로 품질과 독특한 특성이다. 먼저 교수는 한 신발 광고에 대해 이야기한다. 광고는 신발의 재료에 초점을 맞춤으로써 신발의 품질을 강조한다. 이 광고는 또한 신발이 오래 간다고 말한다. 그녀가 언급한 다른 광고는 감자칩에 관한 것이다. 이 광고는 감자칩의 독특한 특성, 즉 그것이 얼마나 매운지를 강조한다.

Actual Test

Actual Test 01

p.164

Task 1

Sample Response 🎧 05-03

I prefer using a desktop primarily because the keyboard is bigger. I have trouble typing on notebooks because the keys are smaller and closer together, so I make a lot of mistakes. A desktop also has a bigger screen, making it better for watching movies. While laptops are portable, this actually causes me some problems. First, notebooks are easily stolen. In fact, several notebooks have been stolen from my school's library recently. However, with a desktop, I don't have to worry about anyone stealing it. In addition, with a notebook, printing isn't easy since I always have to connect it to the printer. My desktop, meanwhile, is always connected. Finally, I know my desktop will never run out of batteries since it's plugged into the wall. I don't have that luxury with a laptop.

해석

나는 키보드가 크기 때문에 데스크톱 컴퓨터 사용을 선호한다. 자판이 작고 가까워서 노트북 컴퓨터로는 타이핑하기가 어려우며 그로 인해 오타가 많이 난다. 또한 데스크톱은 화면이 커서 영화를 보기가 더 좋다. 노트북은 휴대가 가능하지만 실제로는 이러한 점 때문에 문제가 생기기도 한다. 우선 노트북은 도난당하기가 쉽다. 실제로 최근에 학교 도서관에서 몇 대의 노트북이 도난을 당했다. 하지만 데스크톱의 경우 다른 사람이 훔쳐갈 걱정은 하지 않아도 된다. 또한 노트북의 경우에는 항상 프린터와 연결을 해야 하기 때문에 인쇄가 쉽지 않다. 반면에 데스크톱은 항상 연결되어 있다. 마지막으로 데스크톱은 벽에 플러그가 꽂혀 있어서 배터리가 방전되는 일이 없는 것으로 알고 있다. 노트북에서는 그러한 호사를 누릴 수 없다.

Task 2

Reading

해석

잔디밭에서의 스포츠 활동 금지

도서관 앞 잔디밭은 학교의 상징으로 잘 알려져 있습니다. 많은 방문객들이 잔디밭 옆을 지나 다니며 학생들은 잔디밭에서 휴식을 취하는 것을 좋아합니다. 학교측은 잔디밭을 관리하고 단장하기 위해 예산을 편성합니다. 하지만 학생들이 잔디밭에서 경기를 하고 스포츠 행사를 개최하면서 잔디가 손상되고 있으며 학생들이 가고 난 자리는 종종 쓰레기로 더럽혀집니다. 그래서 학교측은 학생들이 잔디밭을 경기 장소로 사용하지 못하도록 결정했습니다. 이러한 학교의 상징을 훌륭하게 잘 관리해서 우리 모두가 자부심을 가질 수 있는 공간으로 만듭시다. 이번 규정은 즉시 효력을 갖습니다.

Listening

Script 🎧 05-04

W Student: Can you believe that new rule? This messes up our dorm's volleyball league. It seems like every time we find something fun to do, they make a rule against it.

M Student: I know. We love throwing the Frisbee out there between classes.

W: Yeah, after a boring lecture, we need to let off some steam. And the nearest playing fields are too far away from the classroom buildings.

M: Good point.

W: My friends and I never leave trash there. Do yours?

M: To be honest, a few do leave some stuff, but I never thought it was enough to ruin the lawn as a so-called symbol of the whole school.

W: And the people who just sit on the lawn to study or eat lunch leave stuff, too. Why not ban them?

M: Right. It's not fair to pick on sports teams.

W: Yeah, I think the administration is overreacting again. Somebody should have asked the student government before doing anything.

M: Yeah, I totally agree with you.

해석

W Student: 새로운 규정이 말이 되니? 이로 인해 기숙사 배구 대회가 엉망이 됐어. 우리가 뭔가 즐거운 일을 찾을 때마다 그것을 금지하는 규정을 만들어지는 것 같아.

M Student: 나도 알아. 공강 시간에 잔디밭에서 프리스비를 하는 것도 재미있는데.

W: 그래, 지겨운 수업이 끝나면 스트레스를 해소해야 하지. 그리고 가장 가까운 운동장도 강의실에서 너무 멀리 떨어져 있잖아.

M: 좋은 지적이군.

W: 내 친구들과 나는 절대로 잔디밭에 쓰레기를 버리지 않아. 너희들은 그러니?

M: 솔직히 말하면 쓰레기를 버리는 애들이 소수 있긴 하지만, 그렇다고 해서 소위 학교 전체의 상징인 잔디밭을 망칠 정도는 아니라고 생각해.

W: 그리고 공부하거나 점심을 먹기 위해 잔디밭에 앉아 있는 사람들도 쓰레기를 버리지. 왜 그 사람들은 안 막아?

M: 맞는 말이야. 스포츠를 하는 팀만 괴롭히는 건 불공평하지.

W: 그래, 나는 학교 당국이 또 과민 반응을 하고 있다고 생각해. 무언가를 하기 전에 누군가 학생회에 물어 봤어야 했어.

M: 그래, 나도 전적으로 동감이야.

Sample Response 🎧 05-05

The woman doesn't think the rule is fair because her volleyball league plays games on the lawn. She complains that the rule takes away a place for the students to let off some steam between classes. She claims that there is no other place near the classrooms where they can play sports since every playing field is far away. She also says that other people use the lawn. She claims that other students study, rest, and eat lunch on the lawn, where they also make a mess, so the new rule should apply to them, too. She feels it is unfair of the school to single out only people playing sports. She accuses the administration of overreacting to a minor problem and trying to protect its image. She also thinks that the administration should have asked the student government for its opinion first.

여자는 배구 대회가 잔디밭에서 열리기 때문에 그러한 규정이 불공평하다고 생각한다. 그녀는 규정으로 인해 학생들이 공강 시간에 스트레스를 해소할 장소가 사라질 것이라고 불평한다. 그녀는 운동장이 전부 멀리 떨어져 있기 때문에 강의실 근처에는 스포츠 활동을 할 수 있는 장소가 없다고 주장한다. 또한 그녀는 다른 사람들도 잔디밭을 사용한다고 말한다. 다른 학생들도 잔디밭에서 공부를 하고 휴식을 취하고 점심을 먹는데, 그들 또한 더럽히기는 마찬가지여서 새로운 규정이 그 사람들에게도 적용되어야 한다고 주장한다. 그녀는 학교측이 운동을 하는 사람들만 꼬집어서 얘기하는 것은 불공평하다고 생각한다. 또한 학교측이 사소한 문제에 과민 반응을 하고 학교 이미지를 지키기에 급급하다고 비난한다. 그녀는 또한 학교 당국이 먼저 학생회의 의견을 물어 보았어야 한다고 생각한다.

Task 3

Reading

아동 교육

아동을 교육시키는 방법에 대한 이론은 두 가지 범주, 즉 정적 강화 또는 부적 강화 중 하나에 속한다. 정적 강화는 착한 행동에 대해 보상을 하는 것이다. 착한 행동이 칭찬, 애정, 혹은 유형의 보상을 이끌어 낸다는 점을 아동이 알게 되면 아동은 보상을 더 받기 위해 그러한 행동을 계속할 것이다. 그와 반대로 부적 강화는 나쁜 행동을 한 아동에게 벌을 주는 것이다. 그러한 벌에는 체벌, 자기 방으로 가기, 또는 친구들과의 놀이 금지가 포함될 수 있다.

Listening
Script 🎧 05-06

M Professor: Well, now, did you know that corporal punishment—physically striking a child—was accepted in American schools for much of our history? But in the mid-1900s, states started to pass laws banning corporal punishment. Sociologists found that smacking a kid might work in the short term but that it had no long-term effects. And, uh, I'm embarrassed to say this. Okay, I, uh, spanked my daughter maybe twice when she was very little. I felt terrible, she felt terrible, and it didn't work. So, uh, the experts began to stress the better results obtained from positive reinforcement, such as praise for good behavior or a monetary allowance for doing chores. The theory is that, um, when they are given positive feedback, kids will act in their own self-interest and

repeat that good conduct. Still, there are limits to how well this works. For example, when my daughter, um, refused to dive into the water at her first swim meet, my wife's offer of ice cream had no effect on her. Well, sometimes human nature is just too strong to be overcome by a tangible reward. I think, uh, that nonviolent negative reinforcement still has a place today. This includes things like taking timeouts, sending the kid to his room, or taking away privileges.

M Professor: 음, 자, 여러분은 역사의 상당 기간 동안 미국 학교에서 체벌, 즉 아동을 때리는 벌이 허용되었다는 점을 아셨나요? 하지만 1900년대 중반에 주들은 체벌을 금지하는 법을 통과시키기 시작했어요. 사회학자들은 아동을 때리는 것이 단기적으로 효과를 나타낼 수 있지만 장기적으로는 효과가 없다는 점을 알게 되었습니다. 그리고, 어, 이런 말을 하기가 당황스럽네요. 그래요, 저도, 어, 제 딸이 아주 어렸을 때 아마 두 번 정도 딸을 때린 적이 있었어요. 저도 기분이 몹시 좋지 않았고, 제 딸도 기분이 몹시 좋지 않았으며, 효과도 없었어요. 그래서, 어, 전문가들은 착한 행동에 칭찬을 하거나 집안일을 하면 용돈을 주는 것과 같은 정적 강화가 보다 나은 결과를 낳는다는 점을 강조하기 시작했죠. 이 이론에 따르면, 음, 아이들은 긍정적인 피드백을 받는 경우, 사리사욕에 따라 행동을 해서 그러한 착한 행동을 반복할 것입니다. 하지만 이것이 내는 효과에는 한계가 있습니다. 예를 들어 제 딸이, 음, 처음 수영을 할 때 물속에 들어가지 않으려고 했는데 제 아내가 아이스크림을 사주겠다고 해도 아무런 소용이 없었죠. 음, 때로는 인간의 본성이 너무나 강해서 유형의 보상으로도 이를 극복할 수 없는 경우가 있습니다. 저는, 어, 오늘날에도 부적 강화가 설 자리가 있다고 생각해요. 여기에는 타임아웃, 아이를 방으로 보내기, 혹은 특권을 빼앗는 것 등이 포함됩니다.

Sample Response 🎧 05-07

The professor mentions that sociologists have determined that positive reinforcement of children is more effective than negative reinforcement. So instead of spanking children, the professor believes parents should try something more positive. First, he suggests giving children positive feedback. He says that parents could praise their children or give them money for doing their chores or acting properly. These are examples of tangible rewards, which are discipline methods using positive reinforcement. Since the children want more rewards, they will continue acting properly. The professor adds that positive reinforcement doesn't always work. He cites his wife's offer of ice cream to their daughter when encouraging her to dive into the swimming pool. Their daughter wouldn't, thereby showing that positive reinforcement doesn't always work. That's why the professor supports some nonviolent means of discipline, such as sending children to their rooms and not permitting them to do something.

교수는 사회학자들이 부적 강화보다 정적 강화가 더 효과적이라는 점을 알아냈다고 언급한다. 따라서 아동에게 체벌을 가하는 대신 부모들이 보다 긍정적인 수단을 사용해야 한다고 교수는 생각한다. 우선 그는 아동에게 긍정적 피드백을 줄 것을 제안한다. 그는 아이들이 집안일을 하거나 착한 행동을 하면 부모가 칭찬을 하거나 용돈을 줄 수 있다고 말한다. 이러한 점은 유형 보상의 예인데, 이는 정적 강화를 이용하는 교육 방법이다. 아동들은 더 많은 보상을 원하기 때문에 계속해서 착하게 행동할 것이다. 교수는 또한 정적 강화가 항상 효과를 나타내는 것은 아니라고 말한다. 그는 자신의 아내가 딸을 수영장에 들어가도록 만들기 위해 딸에게 아이스크림을 사 주려고 했던 일을 예로 든다. 딸은 그러지 않았는데, 이는 정적 강화가 항상 효과적인 것은 아니라는 점을 보여 준다. 바로 이러한 점 때문에 교수는 아이를 자기 방으로 보내는 것과 어떤 일을 허락하지 않는 것과 같은 비폭력적인 훈육 수단을 지지한다.

Task 4

Listening

Script 🎧 05-08

W Professor: Listen up. I want to talk about two different concepts in advertising, direct and indirect advertising. Direct advertising focuses on a specific, indisputable fact about a product. Okay, let's use the example of a car commercial. Cars can be described with a bunch of statistics, such as engine size, horsepower, and fuel efficiency. These are all things that can be converted into numbers. Well, if you are trying to sell a small car, one good point could be its fuel efficiency. In your commercial, you can say, "This car gets fifty miles per gallon of gas." People cannot dispute this since it was determined in testing under federal standards.

Indirect advertising is the opposite. It focuses on something that cannot be proven or quantified. Okay? Instead of talking about something concrete, like, uh, fuel efficiency or cost, a car company might talk about the car's image, design, or coolness. Many car commercials try to link their cars to a fun image, and, um, they emphasize how popular you will be for having bought their car.

So why is it important to know both of these strategies? Well, the reason is that each targets a different audience. Direct advertisements focus more on, uh, knowledgeable buyers, like a father buying a car for his daughter. He wants a car that is safe and gets good mileage. But a twenty-three-year-old college student wants to look, uh, cool to his friends. Maybe his dad will give him gas money, so he doesn't care about mileage. He just wants to make sure he will look good in his car.

해석

W Professor: 잘 들으세요. 광고의 서로 다른 두 가지 개념인 직접 광고와 간접 광고에 대해 논의하고자 합니다. 직접 광고는 제품에 관한 구체적이고 명백한 사실에 초점을 맞추어요. 좋아요, 자동차 광고를 예로 들어보죠. 자동차는 엔진 크기, 마력, 그리고 연비와 같은 다수의 통계 자료들로 설명될 수 있습니다. 이들은 모두 숫자로 환산이 가능한 것이죠. 음, 만약 소형차를 판매하려고 하는 경우 연비가 좋은 포인트가 될 수 있을 거예요. 광고에서 "이 차는 1갤런당 50마일을 운행합니다."라고 말할 수 있죠. 이는 연방 기준에 따른 테스트에서 얻은 수치이기 때문에 이를 반박을 할 수는 없습니다.

간접 광고는 그 반대예요. 입증이나 수량화가 불가능한 것에 초점을 맞추죠. 구체적인 사항, 그러니까, 어, 연비나 가격에 대해 말을 하는 대신 자동차 회사는 차의 이미지, 디자인, 혹은 세련미 같은 점을 이야기할 수 있어요. 많은 자동차 광고들은 자동차를 재미있는 이미지와 연결시키려 하며, 음, 자동차를 구입하면 구매자의 인기가 올라갈 것이라는 점을 강조합니다.

그러면 왜 두 가지 전략을 다 아는 것이 중요할까요? 음, 그 이유는 각 전략의 타깃이 다르기 때문이에요. 직접 광고는, 딸에게 차를 사 주려는 아버지와 같이, 어, 보다 지적인 구매자에게 초점을 맞춥니다. 그는 안전하면서도 연비가 좋은 차를 원하죠. 하지만 23살의 대학생은, 어, 친구들에게 멋지게 보이고 싶어합니다. 어쩌면 자신의 아버지가 기름값을 내 줄 것이기 때문에 연비는 신경을 쓰지 않을 거예요. 그저 자신이 차에 탔을 때 멋지게 보였으면 하죠.

Sample Response 🎧 05-09

Direct advertising means that an ad tells some facts about the product. For example, a car commercial might stress a vehicle's price, size, gas mileage, or horsepower, which are all factors that the company can describe with statistics. The information in direct advertising is not an opinion. Instead, the information is entirely factual and can be proven. A buyer interested in saving money might be attracted to this kind of ad. In contrast, indirect advertising focuses on a product's image, such as how cool it is, how good it looks when being used by the purchaser, and how popular the product makes people seem. So a commercial for a different car might ignore the car's statistics and instead stress its cool design and the fact that it's a symbol of high status. This kind of ad might appeal to a young person who wants to look cool to others.

해석

직접 광고는 제품에 대한 사실을 말해 주는 광고를 말한다. 예를 들어 자동차 광고는 차량의 가격, 크기, 연비, 혹은 마력을 강조할 수 있는데, 이는 모두 해당 기업이 수치로 설명할 수 있는 요소들이다. 직접 광고의 정보들은 의견이 아니다. 대신 그러한 정보들은 전적으로 사실에 근거한 것으로서 입증이 가능하다. 돈을 아끼는데 관심이 있는 구매자라면 이러한 종류의 광고에 이끌릴 것이다. 이와 반대로 간접 광고는 제품이 얼마나 멋진지, 구매자가 이를 사용할 때 얼마나 좋아 보이는지, 그리고 제품이 구매자를 얼마나 인기 있게 보이도록 만드는지와 같은 제품의 이미지에 초점을 맞춘다. 그래서 또 다른 자동차의 광고에서는 자동차의 수치들을 무시하고 그 대신 차의 멋진 디자인과 이 차가 상류층의 상징이라는 점을 강조할 수도 있다. 이런 종류의 광고는 다른 사람에게 멋지게 보이고 싶어하는 젊은 층에게 호소력을 가질 수 있다.

Actual Test 02   p.172

Task 1

Sample Response 🎧 05-12

Writing is always my choice of means of contacting people. Phone calls often interrupt the other person, or the person might not be home. But letters and email are read only when the other person is ready to read it, so they will not bother anyone. In addition, email is free and can be sent anytime. A great example of this is a recent experience I had. I wanted to ask my friend for some help on a homework assignment. But it was too late to call him on the phone. I didn't want to awaken his parents, and I was not sure if he was still awake. So I sent him an email. Within a few minutes, he returned my email with the answer to my question.

해석

나는 사람들에게 연락을 취할 때 항상 글을 쓰는 편이다. 전화 통화는 종종 상대방을 방해하며, 상대방이 집에 없을 수도 있다. 하지만 편지나 이메일은 상대방이 읽을 준비가 되었을 때에만 읽히기 때문에 누구에게도 방해가 되지 않는다. 게다가 이메일은 무료이며 언제라도 보낼 수 있다. 이에 대한 좋은 사례는 내가 최근에 겪었던 일이다. 나는 친구에게 과제물에 대한 도움을 요청하고 싶었다. 하지만 전화를 걸기에는 너무 늦은 시간이었다. 나는 친구의 부모님을 깨우고 싶지도 않았고 그가 깨어있는지도 알 수 없었다. 그래서 나는 친구에게 이메일을 보냈다. 몇 분 지나지 않아서 친구가 이메일로 내 질문에 대한 답을 보내 주었다.

Task 2

Reading

해석

교환 학생 프로그램

가을 학기가 시작하는 대로 학생들은 교환 학생으로서 외국에서 공부할 기회를 갖게 될 것입니다. 등록금 및 기타 경비는 현재 학교에서 생활하는 것과 비슷한 수준이며 학생들은 한 학기 유학이나 두 학기 유학 중 하나를 선택할 수 있습니다. 숙소는 주로 주최 학교의 기숙사 형태로 제공될 것입니다. 이번 프로그램은 새로운 언어를 배우고 학문적 지평을 넓힐 수 있는 절호의 기회입니다. 또한 세계적인 일류 석학들과 연구할 수 있는 기회를 누릴 수도 있습니다. 참가 대학 리스트 및 기타 세부 사항에 관한 정보는 취업 지도실에서 얻을 수 있습니다.

Listening

Script 🎧 05-13

M Student: Did you see that notice about the study-abroad program?

W Student: Yes, I think it's great. I'm going to sign up for it next year.

M: Really? I don't think I can afford it. The school claims the expenses are the same, but I don't believe that. Everything is more expensive in Europe.

W: Well, I think it's worth the money. I know that my sister had a great experience in Paris.

M: Sure, but I just don't have that kind of money.

W: I understand.

M: And here's another thing. I've heard that you sometimes lose credits. I have a friend who took a lot of business courses in London as an exchange student, but

when he got back, he found out that many of his credits would not count toward his business degree here. He ended up having to take a couple of classes again.

W: Well, he should've checked into that before he took the classes. I don't see that as being much of a problem.

해석

M Student: 저 유학 프로그램에 대한 공지 봤어?

W Student: 응, 정말 좋다고 생각해. 나는 내년에 신청할 예정이야.

M: 정말? 나는 감당이 안 될 것 같은데. 학교측은 경비가 동일하다고 주장하지만 나는 그 말을 믿지 않아. 유럽에서는 모든 게 다 비싸지.

W: 음, 나는 그럴 만한 가치가 있다고 생각해. 우리 언니도 파리에서 멋진 경험을 했던 것으로 알고 있어.

M: 물론 그랬겠지만 나에게는 그럴만한 돈이 없어.

W: 이해해.

M: 그리고 또 한 가지가 있어. 때때로 학점을 인정받지 못하는 경우가 있다고 들었거든. 내 친구 한 명이 교환 학생으로 런던에서 경영학 수업을 많이 들었는데, 돌아오고 나서는 자기가 받은 학점 중에 상당수가 이곳에서 경영학 학점으로 인정이 되지 않는다는 점을 알게 되었지.

W: 음, 그가 수업을 듣기 전에 그 점은 먼저 확인을 했어야 해. 나는 그게 큰 문제라고 생각하지는 않아.

Sample Response 🎧 05-14

The man responds negatively to the university's announcement that students can spend one or two semesters abroad at foreign institutes as exchange students. First, he remarks that the program is going to cost too much money, so he can't participate in it. Even though the school claims that tuition and expenses are roughly the same as they are on campus, he states that he knows that the prices of everything in Europe are much more expensive than in his area. He says that he just doesn't have enough money. He also makes a comment about one of his friends who studied abroad. Apparently, his friend could not transfer the credits he took while abroad in London, so he had to repeat a couple of classes. He feels that this could happen to him, so he doesn't want to take the risk of wasting his time.

해석

남자는 학생들이 교환 학생으로 외국 학교에서 한 학기나 두 학기를 보낼 수 있다는 대학의 공지에 부정적인 반응을 보인다. 우선 그는 비용이 너무 많이 들 것이기 때문에 자신이 프로그램에 참가할 수가 없다고 말한다. 학교측은 학비 및 기타 경비가 이곳에서 대학을 다니는 경우와 비슷하다고 안내하지만, 그는 유럽에서 모든 것의 가격은 이곳보다 비싸다는 점을 자신이 알고 있다고 말한다. 또한 그는 유학 생활을 했던 자신의 친구에 대해 언급한다. 그에 따르면 자신의 친구는 런던에 있을 때 이수했던 학점을 인정받을 수 없었기 때문에 두어 과목을 다시 들어야만 했다. 그는 자신에게도 그러한 일이 발생할 수 있다고 생각하기 때문에 시간 낭비가 될 수 있는 모험을 하고 싶어하지 않는다.

Reading

해석

역할 갈등

역할 갈등은 한 사람의 삶에서의 두 가지 측면이 양립 불가능한 경우에 발생한다. 예를 들어 어떤 어머니는 부모로서의 역할과 직장에서의 역할이 경합하여 발생하는 압박감을 느낄 수 있다. 자녀를 돌보는데 필요한 시간적 요구로 인해 업무에 필요한 시간적 요구를 충족시키는 것이 불가능할 수 있다. 그러한 갈등은 한 가지 역할을 포기함으로써, 혹은 두 가지 다에서 성공하기 위해 희생을 함으로써 해결될 수 있다. 따라서 어머니는 보육비를 지불해야 할 수도 있고 혹은 덜 힘든 직장을 구해야 할 수도 있다.

Listening

Script 🎧 05-15

M Professor: You can't perform your role as a worker without some, um, juggling of the demands of your other roles. I'll give an example that happened in my class last semester. A student—I'll call him Mark—had to give an oral presentation in my class at, uh, 3:00. Well, Mark was on a scholarship that required him to, uh, work in the genetics lab from 3:00 to 7:00. His roles as a student and worker were in conflict. His lab boss wouldn't excuse him. I resolved the conflict by letting Mark do his presentation in my office before class.

And, uh, another time, I had a friend who took a job teaching astronomy at a college close to his home and family. But another university across the country offered him a job working with, uh, the best equipment. That job would've given him the chance to advance his career. But, you know, he didn't want to move his children out of their school. Plus, his wife had a successful career at the first school. Unfortunately for his family, he took the job offer and moved to the new school. He was planning to come home, uh, on weekends and during the summer. But, eventually, his marriage failed. This shows, um, that sometimes one role might have to win out over the other.

해석

M Professor: 다른 역할에서 요구되는 것과 어느 정도의, 음, 갈등 없이 노동자의 역할을 수행할 수는 없어요. 지난 학기에 제 수업에서 일어났던 일을 예로 들어보겠습니다. 한 학생이, Mark라고 부르죠, 어, 3시 수업에서 발표를 해야 했어요. Mark는 근로 장학생이어서 3시부터 7시까지는 유전공학 실험실에서 근무를 해야만 했습니다. 학생으로서의 역할과 노동자로서의 역할에서 갈등이 생긴 것이었죠. 실험실 관리자는 그를 봐 주지 않으려 했어요. 저는 Mark가 수업 전에 제 사무실에서 발표를 하도록 함으로써 그러한 갈등을 해소시켰습니다.

그리고, 어, 또 한 번은 제 친구가 저희 집과 가족들 가까이에 있는 대학에서 천문학을 가르치고 있었어요. 하지만 우리나라 반대편에 있는 다른 대학에서 그에게, 어, 최고의 시설에서 일할 수 있는 일자리를 제안했습니다. 그 일자리는 그의 경력을 돋보이게 할 수 있는 기회가 될 수 있었죠. 하지만 아시다시피 그는 아이들이 전학하는 것을 원하지 않았습니다. 게다가 그의 아내도 첫 번째 학교에서 성공적으로 경력을 쌓고 있었죠. 그의 가족에게는 안타까운 일이지만 그는 이직 제안을 받아들였고 새로운 학교에 가게 되었습니다. 주말과 여름 방학에는, 어,

집에 올 계획이었죠. 하지만 결국 그의 결혼은 실패로 끝났어요. 이는, 음, 때때로 하나의 역할이 나머지 역할을 눌러야 할 수도 있다는 점을 보여 줍니다.

Sample Response 🎧 05-16

Role conflict occurs when one part of a person's life interferes with another part. For example, the professor's student Mark had to be two places at the same time. His role as a student conflicted with his role as an employee. Luckily, one role gave him some flexibility. The professor let him give his presentation at a different time in the professor's office. But if the professor had insisted that Mark appear at 3:00, Mark would've had to choose, and he would have failed in one of his two roles. That's what happened when the professor's friend chose his career role over his family role. He thought he could succeed at both, but the circumstances made them incompatible. His job was simply too far away for him to be able to tend to his family role as well. The only way out would've been for his wife to compromise her own career role and to disrupt her children's school roles.

해석

역할 갈등은 어떤 사람의 삶의 한 부분이 또 다른 부분과 충돌할 때 발생한다. 예를 들어 교수가 가르치던 Mark라는 학생은 동시에 두 장소에 있어야 했다. 학생으로서의 역할과 직원으로서의 역할 사이에 갈등이 생겼다. 다행히도 하나의 역할이 그에게 유연성을 부여했다. 교수는 그에게 교수의 사무실에서 다른 시간에 발표를 하도록 시켰다. 하지만 교수가 3시에 오라고 Mark에게 고집을 부렸다면 Mark는 선택을 해야 했을 것이고, 자신의 두 가지 역할 중 하나에 있어서는 실패를 겪었을 것이다. 그러한 일은 교수의 친구가 가족의 역할보다 직장인으로서의 역할을 선택했을 때 일어났다. 그는 두 가지 모두에 있어서 성공을 거둘 수 있을 것으로 생각했지만 상황으로 인해 역할들은 양립이 불가능한 것이었다. 그의 직장이 너무 멀리 떨어져 있어서 그가 가족의 역할을 수행하는 것은 불가능했다. 유일한 해결책은 그의 아내가 자신의 직장을 포기하고 아이들의 학업에도 차질을 주는 것이었다.

Task **4**

Listening

Script 🎧 05-17

W Professor: Okay, two main theories have been proposed to explain dinosaur extinction. Um, first, it was the impact of an asteroid, and second, there were extensive volcanic eruptions. Researchers have found an abnormally high amount of iridium in the layer that was, uh, at the Earth's surface at the time of the dinosaur extinctions. Asteroids and meteorites contain a high concentration of iridium, suggesting, you know, that the Earth was bombarded by impacts from those space objects. Such impacts would have stirred up huge dust clouds, which would have blocked sunlight and prevented photosynthesis in plants. Without plants to eat, the dinosaurs would have died off.

Well, the other leading theory is that the mass extinctions were caused by the eruptions of a string of volcanoes. Volcanic eruptions release greenhouse gases, which trap carbon dioxide near the Earth's surface. Excessive carbon dioxide reduced photosynthesis, taking away the dinosaurs' main source of food. And the hotter air temperatures resulted in too many male dinosaurs and too few females to give birth to new dinosaurs. By the way, I bet you all didn't know that as the air temperature increases, the number of male births from certain animals' eggs increases.

Some have suggested, you know, that an asteroid impact might have been the event that triggered the volcanic activity. The sun-blocking effects of an asteroid impact, um, would have lasted only about ten years, after which the atmosphere would, uh, be clear again. It is doubtful that the dinosaurs would have gone extinct in such a short time. But the effects of volcanic eruptions would have remained for thousands of years, long enough to see a species die out.

해석

W Professor: 좋아요, 공룡의 멸종을 설명하는 두 가지 이론이 제시되어 있습니다. 음, 첫 번째는 소행성 충돌이고 두 번째는 광범위한 화산 폭발이 있었다는 것이에요. 연구자들은 공룡이 멸종했던 시기의 지표면에 있던 층에서 비정상적으로 많은 양의 이리듐을 발견했어요. 소행성과 운석에는 많은 양의 이리듐이 포함되어 있는데, 이는, 아시다시피, 지구가 그러한 천체로부터 충격을 받았다는 것을 암시합니다. 그러한 충격으로 인해 거대한 먼지 구름이 일어났고, 이로써 햇빛이 차단되어 식물이 광합성을 할 수 없게 되었어요. 먹을 수 있는 식물이 없어지자 공룡도 멸종해 버렸습니다.

음, 또 다른 중요한 이론에 따르면 일련의 화산 폭발에 의해 대량 멸종이 일어났어요. 화산 폭발로 온실 가스가 배출되었고, 그로 인해 지표면 근처에 이산화탄소가 갇히게 되었죠. 과도한 양의 이산화탄소는 광합성을 방해했고, 그 결과 공룡들의 주요 먹이가 사라지게 되었습니다. 그리고 기온이 오름으로써 수컷의 수는 너무 많아지고 새끼 공룡을 낳을 수 있는 암컷의 수는 너무 적어졌어요. 그건 그렇고, 기온이 올라가면 특정 동물의 난자에서 생기는 수컷의 수가 증가한다는 점은 분명 여러분 모두가 잘 모르실 것 같네요.

몇몇 사람들은, 아시다시피, 소행성 충돌이 화산 폭발을 촉진시킨 사건일 수도 있다고 생각합니다. 소행성 충돌로 인한 햇빛 차단의 효과는, 음, 단 10년 정도 지속되었을 것이며, 그 후에 대기는, 어, 다시 깨끗해졌을 거예요. 공룡이 그처럼 짧은 기간에 멸종했다는 점은 의심스럽습니다. 하지만 화산 폭발의 효과는 수천 년이나 지속되었는데, 이는 어떤 종이 자취를 감추기에 충분히 긴 시간이죠.

Sample Response 🎧 05-18

The professor discusses two theories about why dinosaurs disappeared from the Earth. The first theory is that their extinction was caused by asteroid impacts on the Earth. The evidence for this is that asteroids contain iridium, which is also found at the layer that was at the Earth's surface at the time of the extinctions. The impacts of the asteroids created huge clouds of dust that blocked sunlight and interfered with plant growth.

As a result, the dinosaurs died out because their food sources disappeared. The second theory is there were volcanic eruptions, which released greenhouse gases that trapped carbon dioxide near the Earth's surface. The increased carbon dioxide hindered plant growth, thereby decreasing the amount of available food for the dinosaurs. In addition, the rise in temperature caused more males than females to be born. With fewer females, fewer baby dinosaurs were born.

해석

교수는 지구상에서 공룡이 자취를 감춘 이유에 관한 두 가지 이론을 설명한다. 첫 번째 이론은 소행성과 지구의 충돌로 인해 공룡이 멸종했다는 것이다. 이에 대한 증거는 소행성에 이리듐이 포함되어 있다는 점으로, 멸종 당시 지표면에 있던 지층에서도 이리듐이 발견되고 있다. 소행성 충돌로 거대한 먼지 구름이 만들어지면서 먼지 구름이 햇빛이 차단하고 식물의 성장을 방해했다. 그 결과 공룡의 먹이가 사라졌기 때문에 공룡도 멸종했다. 두 번째 이론은 화산 폭발이 일어났다는 이론인데, 화산 폭발로 온실 가스가 배출되어 지표면 근처에 이산화탄소가 갇히게 되었다. 이산화탄소의 증가는 식물의 성장에 방해가 되었고, 그 결과 공룡이 먹을 수 있는 먹이의 양이 줄어들었다. 또한 기온 상승으로 암컷보다 수컷이 더 많이 태어났다. 암컷의 수가 줄어들자 태어나는 새끼 공룡의 수도 줄어들었다.

How to
Master Skills for the

TOEFL® iBT

SPEAKING   Basic